KNOWING THE NATURAL LAW

KNOWING THE NATURAL LAW

From Precepts and Inclinations to Deriving Oughts

STEVEN J. JENSEN

THE CATHOLIC UNIVERSITY
OF AMERICA PRESS

Washington, D.C.

Copyright © 2015
The Catholic University of America Press
All rights reserved
The paper used in this publication meets the minimum requirements of
American National Standards for Information Science — Permanence
of Paper for Printed Library Materials, ANSI Z39.48-1984.
∞

Design and typesetting by Kachergis Book Design

Library of Congress Cataloging-in-Publication Data
Jensen, Steven J., 1964–
Knowing the natural law : from precepts and inclinations to
deriving oughts / Steven J. Jensen.
pages cm
Includes bibliographical references and index.
ISBN 978-0-8132-2733-7 (pbk. : alk. paper)
1. Christian ethics.   2. Christian ethics — Catholic authors.
3. Thomas, Aquinas, Saint, 1225?–1274.   4. Aristotle.   I. Title.
BJ1251.J374 2015
171'.2 — dc23   2014039020

FOR CHRISTINE,
ever faithful,
loving guide,
true companion

CONTENTS

Acknowledgments	ix

1. The Problem	1
2. The Text	26
3. Inclinations	44
4. Good	61
5. Nature	85
6. The Will	108
7. Ought	126
8. Obligation	150
9. Principles	175
10. Action	201

Bibliography	231
Index	237

ACKNOWLEDGMENTS

I would like to thank all those who have helped with this book. For the very idea of the book, and for the ideas in it, I am most indebted to James Stromberg, who first set me on the path of understanding the truth of the natural law. He also generously read the entire manuscript and provided helpful insights. Others who supplied needed comments include Peter Koritansky, Stephen Brock, and an anonymous reviewer. Still others have helped through careful reading and correction, most especially my wife, Christine, whose loving support has sustained me through all of my endeavors. The beautiful cover I owe to Barbara Stirling, who first suggested the artwork, and to Rebecca Schreiber at Kachergis Book Design, whose keen artistic sense provided the balance and harmony for the striking design. Finally, I would like to thank all those at the Catholic University of America Press who have brought this project to realization, especially Jim Kruggel, Trevor Lipscombe, Theresa Walker, and Brian Roach.

I

THE PROBLEM

In the 1960s a long-standing secular philosophical dispute entered Thomistic circles. For centuries the use of nature as the basis and foundation of ethical judgments was presumed for interpretations of Thomas Aquinas. In contrast, modern philosophy, as characterized by G. E. M. Anscombe, utilized a "moral ought" divorced from human nature.[1]

In 1965 some Thomists began to wonder whether in fact the modern doctrine was found within Aquinas, who had, they said, anticipated the divide between nature and ethics; unfortunately, this insight of Aquinas had been buried and distorted by subsequent commentators. We might well wonder what precipitated this new approach to the thought of Aquinas.

1.1

THE NATURALISTIC FALLACY

1.1.1: Some Historical Development

In 1903 G. E. Moore published his *Principia Ethica* in which he condemned "naturalistic" ethics, which seeks to define the good in terms of natural attributes.[2] His target was not Thomistic philosophy, although his censure would have encompassed it; rather, his target was utilitarianism, which defined the good in terms of the natural attribute of pleasure. All such views, claimed Moore, committed what he called the "naturalistic fallacy." The credit for first identifying this fallacious reasoning, in which a move is made from is-statements to ought-

---

1. See G. E. M. Anscombe, "Modern Moral Philosophy," in *Ethics, Religion, and Politics* (Minneapolis: University of Minnesota Press, 1981).

2. G. E. Moore, *Principia Ethica* (New York: Barnes and Noble Books, 2005), 38–39.

THE PROBLEM

statements, is usually attributed to David Hume.[3] He suggested that it is illegitimate to begin with a statement of fact about the way the world is and to conclude with a statement of value, of what is good or of what should be.

In sound deductive reasoning the conclusion never contains anything not already present in the premises. Consider the following reasoning: "All mammals have hair; whales are mammals; therefore, whales have hair." The conclusion contains the subject "whales" and the predicate "have hair." Both of these elements are already present in the premises. Similarly, if we conclude, "we ought to help the needy," then whatever is found in the conclusion must have first been in the premises, including the "ought." We cannot begin, in our premises, with only is-statements and derive a conclusion with a new kind of predicate, containing an "ought."

One of our premises can be an is-statement, for the conclusion can be reached validly just so long as at least one premise contains an ought-term. Indeed, practical reasoning invariably contains a major premise with an ought-term and a minor premise that is simply a statement of fact. One might reason, for instance, "Dry foods should be eaten (by me); this bread is dry food; therefore, I ought to eat this bread." The minor premise is simply a statement of the way things are, that this bread is dry food. Nevertheless, the ought in the conclusion does not indicate invalidity, since the major premise already contains an ought.

G. E. Moore claimed that statements about value are nonnatural, that is, they do not pick out any natural attributes of an object, such as its color or shape; rather, they refer to nonnatural attributes, which are essentially evaluative. We know nonnatural attributes immediately, not by way of natural attributes. To suppose that we grasp nonnatural value attributes by way of natural attributes, such as color or shape, is precisely to commit the naturalistic fallacy.

Subsequent thinkers accepted Moore's criticism of naturalistic ethics but rejected his positive offer of a substitute.[4] They were uncon-

---

3. David Hume, *Treatise on Human Nature,* book 3, part 1, section 1.
4. For a brief summary of this development of thought, see Anthony J. Lisska, *Aquinas's Theory of Natural Law: An Analytic Reconstruction* (Oxford: Clarendon Press, 1996), 56–71.

THE PROBLEM

vinced of the existence of these shadowy nonnatural attributes. They agreed, then, that values are not anything natural; but neither, they claimed, are they anything nonnatural. What was left? Value statements must say nothing at all about the thing itself; rather, values express something about the person making the statement. To say that friendship is good is not to designate any attribute, natural or otherwise, concerning friendship itself; rather, it is to say that I like friendship, or that I recommend friendship. This view came to be called "emotivism" or "prescriptivism."

Predictably, a reaction set in.[5] In 1956 Peter Geach published "Good and Evil," defending what came to be called "descriptivism" or "naturalism," which claims that value judgments describe the thing itself; they are factual statements along the lines of "Murder ends a life." Value statements are simply descriptions of the way the world is. They are not mere expressions of the speaker's desires, nor do they designate shadowy nonnatural attributes.

1.1.2: Germain Grisez

Descriptivism did not win the day in the secular debate, at least not for many years. The error of the naturalistic fallacy was largely considered incontestable. All the while, however, those following the thought of Thomas Aquinas were committing the naturalistic fallacy with abandon. They regularly derived moral truths from truths about human nature. Such reasoning was deemed part of the "natural law," that is, those moral truths, available to everyone, that follow upon our human nature.

Secular philosophers attacked the natural law precisely on the grounds of the naturalistic fallacy. Kai Nielsen, for instance, claimed that Aquinas's natural law must be rejected. It depends upon a teleological worldview (that is, the view that nature moves toward ends), disproven by modern science; it commits the naturalistic fallacy; and it makes no sense without God.[6]

---

5. See, for instance, P. T. Geach, "Good and Evil," *Analysis* 17 (1956): 33–42; Philippa Foot, "Goodness and Choice" and "Moral Beliefs," in *The Is-Ought Question: A Collection of Papers on the Central Problem in Moral Philosophy*, ed. W. D. Hudson (London: McMillan, 1969).

6. See Kai Nielsen, "An Examination of the Thomistic Theory of Natural Law," *Natu-*

THE PROBLEM

Someone wishing to defend Aquinas, it seems, would have to defend his teleology (not a pleasant thought), dismiss the naturalistic fallacy (at the time, almost universally accepted in English-speaking philosophy), and argue (to largely nonreligious philosophers) that God legitimately enters into our discussions of nature and ethics. It looked to be an uphill battle. Might there be any easier way?

Enter Germain Grisez. With a single blow, he dismisses all of the objections against Aquinas. Aquinas, it turns out, has been misunderstood. His ethics depends neither upon teleology nor upon God; furthermore, he did not commit the naturalistic fallacy. The villain — the one who makes all of these mistakes — is Suárez, not Aquinas.[7] Unfortunately, most Thomists, claims Grisez, have followed Suárez rather than Aquinas.

Grisez attempted to achieve his goal by emphasizing one single truth about Aquinas's natural law, namely, that the first principles of the natural law are *per se nota*, that is, they are known immediately from an understanding of the terms, with no need for deductive reasoning. These first principles, which seem to be something like ought-statements, cannot possibly be derived from is-statements. After all, they are not derived from anything else whatsoever. They are their own starting points, depending upon nothing prior. Practical reason has its starting points, just as does speculative reason. The one does not depend upon the other.

With this move, teleology has also been swept away. In order to know the truths about morality, we do not need to know anything about the end or purpose of activity. Indeed, we cannot possibly start with speculative truths concerning human beings and their actions and then reach the ought-statements of practical truth. That would be to commit the naturalistic fallacy. That would be to ignore the *per se nota* character of the first principles of practical reason. These principles are

---

ral Law Forum 4 (1959): 63–71; see also Kai Nielsen, "The Myth of Natural Law," in *Law and Philosophy: A Symposium*, ed. Sydney Hook (New York: New York University Press, 1964). John Finnis (in *Natural Law and Natural Rights* [Oxford: Clarendon Press, 1980], 22–49, esp. 48) attempts to dismiss Nielsen as having an incorrect perception of the natural law.

7. Germain Grisez, "The First Principle of Practical Reason: A Commentary on the Summa Theologiae, 1-2, Question 94, Article 2," *Natural Law Forum* 10 (1965): 168–201, at 192–93; Finnis, *Natural Law,* 45–48.

THE PROBLEM

known without knowing anything about teleology. From these first principles, which are themselves ought-statements, we reach other ought-statements concerning ethics. No fallacy is committed; no teleology is needed.

In the same manner, God is no longer necessary for moral reasoning. We can understand ethical truths without understanding God. The truths are known in themselves, independently of our knowledge of God. We have no need to derive ethics from God's will.

Grisez's account included other features that impinge less directly upon our concern. The first principles of the natural law, he claimed, and especially the very first principle of practical reasoning, are premoral, that is, they direct us to pursue various goods but not necessarily in a moral manner.[8] The sinner, as well as the virtuous person, uses the first principles. The very first principle, for instance, says that we should pursue what is good and avoid what is evil. Even the sinner, however, pursues some good, for instance, the adulterer pursues pleasure as if it were good.

Grisez also claimed that the basic goods of human beings, which correspond with the first precepts of the natural law, are incommensurable, that is, they cannot be measured one against another.[9] They are all equally important. We cannot say, for instance, that the good of knowledge is more important than the good of play or that the good of friendship is more important than the good of life. This incommensurability follows, thought Grisez, upon the underived character of the first precepts. If the basic goods were derived from some higher good, then they could all be compared in relation to this highest good. As it is, each good is independent.

Incommensurability has further implications. No single good serves as the ultimate end of human life; since no good is greater than another, all are equally ends. Our reasoning concerning one good being for the sake of another good, which in turn is for the sake of another good, and so on, must stop at some basic good. All the basic goods, however, are

---

8. Grisez, "First Principle," 181–86.

9. Germain Grisez et al., "Practical Principles, Moral Truth, and Ultimate Ends," *American Journal of Jurisprudence* 32 (1987): 99–151, at 110. See also Finnis, *Natural Law*, 92–95; and John Finnis et al., "The Basic Principles of Natural Law: A Reply to Ralph McInerny," *American Journal of Jurisprudence* 26 (1981): 21–31, at 28–31.

THE PROBLEM

good in and of themselves, without reference to something further. Our reasoning, then, can stop at any of the basic goods and need not work its way back to one single end.

Grisez has had his detractors. Figures such as Ralph McInerny and Henry Veatch have attacked Grisez's nonnaturalism, arguing instead for a naturalism or descriptivism grounded in Aquinas.[10] No aspects of Grisez's thought, as expressed above, has gone untouched.Within the Thomistic discussion, the dispute concerning is-statements and ought-statements took on a slightly different hue, coming to be phrased in terms of speculative knowledge as opposed to practical knowledge.[11] Grisez claimed that our knowledge of the natural law, which is practical knowledge, has its own practical starting points, with no dependence upon speculative knowledge. Others claimed that practical knowledge always arises from speculative knowledge.

1.1.3: A Return to an Older Approach

The shift in approach within Thomistic ethics, then, was part of a greater shift. It was part of a worldview in which value statements, including ought-statements, are sui generis. They do not belong to the ordinary descriptions of the world around us, which might be called facts. They belong to another realm entirely. Perhaps they are nonnatural, or perhaps they express nothing at all about the world, expressing rather something about the speaker. In any event, they have nothing to do with the world of nature.[12]

Alasdair MacIntyre has famously traced the history leading up to

---

10. See, for instance, Ralph McInerny, "Grisez and Thomism," in *The Revival of Natural Law: Philosophical, Theological and Ethical Responses to the Finnis-Grisez School*, ed. Nigel Biggar et al. (Sydney: Ashgate, 2000); Ralph McInerny, "The Principles of Natural Law," *American Journal of Jurisprudence* 25 (1980): 1–15; Henry B. Veatch, "Natural Law and the 'Is'-'Ought' Question: Queries to Finnis and Grisez," in *Swimming against the Current in Contemporary Philosophy: Occasional Essays and Papers* (Washington, D.C.: The Catholic University of America Press, 1990); Henry Veatch et al., "Does the Grisez-Finnis-Boyle Moral Philosophy Rest on a Mistake?" *Review of Metaphysics* 44 (1991): 807–30; Steven A. Long, "Natural Law or Autonomous Practical Reason: Problems for the New Natural Law Theory," in *St. Thomas Aquinas and the Natural Law Tradition: Contemporary Perspectives*, ed. John Goyette et al. (Washington, D.C.: The Catholic University of America Press, 2004).

11. See, for instance, Steven A. Long, "St. Thomas Aquinas through the Analytic Looking-glass," *Thomist* 65 (2001): 259–300; and Long, "Autonomous Practical Reason."

12. Leading Finnis (*Natural Law*, 374) to lament the "rather unhappy term 'natural law.'"

THE PROBLEM

this shift. It finds its roots, he argues, in the rejection of teleology in nature. Once teleology is lost, then value also is lost.[13] If we want to make sense of ethics, then we must either restore Aristotle's natural teleology or find teleology elsewhere, perhaps in human practices. In contrast to MacIntyre, Grisez thinks that we can make sense of ethics without teleology. Who is correct?

The journey from "is" to "ought" will be our focus, and Aquinas will be our guide. He does not explicitly lay out every step of the way, but he does provide the tools by which we can find a way. Contrary to the claims of Grisez, Aquinas does think that practical truth is founded upon speculative truth. Even the very first principles of practical reasoning, the first precepts of the natural law, find their basis in speculative truths about nature.

In this study, we will attempt to understand the thought of Thomas Aquinas. In particular, we wish to determine how, according to Aquinas, we come to know ethical truths. How does the thought of Aquinas relate to the naturalistic fallacy? Does he think that our knowledge of nature leads us to knowledge of ethics? Or does he think that moral knowledge is independent of our knowledge of nature?

In order to answer these questions we will often need to address the view of Grisez and his collaborators, a view that has come to be dubbed "the new natural law theory,"[14] a term that I will use for convenience. I have no desire to expound a full account of the new natural law theory. I am concerned only with one point: moving from is-statements to ought-statements, in particular as this move is found in Aquinas. Other points, such as the role of God within ethics or the incommensurability of goods, will come into play only insofar as they impinge upon the is-ought question.

As the dispute has developed, the new natural law theory has come to be associated less with Aquinas. It began as an account of the correct interpretation of Aquinas. With time, however, it became clear that in some respects it was irreconcilable with Aquinas. Eventually his thought came to be seen simply as the point of departure, and, one

---

13. Alasdair MacIntyre, *After Virtue: A Study in Moral Theory* (Notre Dame, Ind.: University of Notre Dame Press, 1984), 1–62.

14. For an excellent summary of the highlights of this view, see Christopher Tollefsen, "The New Natural Law Theory," *Lyceum* 10 (2009): 1–17.

might add, a departure on a very distant journey.[15] Most glaringly, for instance, Aquinas unquestionably asserts a single final end for human beings, while the new natural law theory claims that there are several incommensurable ends.[16] Nevertheless, the arguments of the new natural law theory will often bear upon our topic.

Likewise, the arguments in the secular literature will also raise questions for interpretations of Aquinas. As we proceed, then, we will sometimes address the views of prescriptivism and descriptivism.

I.2
LEVELS OF PRACTICAL KNOWLEDGE

The dispute among Thomists has centered around the relative roles of speculative and practical knowledge. Is practical knowledge independent or does it depend upon speculative knowledge? Unfortunately, the terms "speculative" and "practical" are often used without precision. What exactly does practical knowledge mean? The danger is that "practical reason" — or speculative reason, for that matter — might become a mantra, repeated for its salutary effect, with no clear thought as to what it means.

The secular debate is not saddled with the vague terminology of practical and speculative reason, but it, too, has lacked clarity.[17] What exactly is an ought-statement? Does it refer to some special "moral" ought, a Kantian imperative?

The first order of business, then, is a clarification of terms. What is meant by practical knowledge as opposed to theoretical knowledge?[18] In some manner, theoretical knowledge grasps the way things are in the world. In contrast, practical knowledge takes what is known and

---

15. John Finnis, *Aquinas: Moral, Political, and Legal Theory* (Oxford: Oxford University Press, 1998), viii–ix.

16. See especially Germain Grisez, "The True Ultimate End of Human Beings: The Kingdom, Not God Alone," *Theological Studies* 69 (2008): 38–61; see also Germain Grisez et al., "Practical Principles," 99; McInerny, "Grisez and Thomism."

17. Christopher Martin ("The Fact/Value Distinction," in *Human Values: New Essays on Ethics and Natural Law*, ed. David Oderberg et al. [New York: Palgrave Macmillan, 2004]) argues that the "fact/value distinction" has never been explained by its many defenders.

18. I will use *speculative reason* and *theoretical reason* interchangeably. Neither term is ideal, but nothing better is available.

THE PROBLEM

applies it to action. Knowing that the sun rises is theoretical knowledge; knowing that I ought to get up and begin my day is practical knowledge.

This division, however, is much too simplistic. Aquinas distinguishes four different levels of speculative and practical knowledge, based upon three criteria: object, mode, and end. The text is worth quoting at length.

> Some knowledge is purely speculative, some is purely practical, and some is speculative in some manner and practical in another manner. This can be made evident by recognizing that knowledge can be called speculative in three ways. First, knowledge is speculative on the part of the things known, which are speculative insofar as they are unable to be brought about through the activity of the one knowing, as is the case in human knowledge concerning natural or divine things.
>
> Second, knowledge is speculative with respect to the mode of knowing, for example, a builder might consider a house by defining and dividing and by considering what can be said of it in general. This manner of knowing considers — in a speculative mode — what can be brought about through human activity, but not precisely insofar as it can be brought about, for to bring something about through activity is achieved by applying form to matter, not by resolving a composite into formal universal principles.
>
> Third, knowledge is speculative with regard to its end, for the practical intellect differs from the speculative in its end, as is said in book 3 of the *De anima*. The practical intellect is ordered to the end of activity, while the speculative intellect is ordered to the consideration of the truth. Therefore, if a builder who considers how he might be able to construct a house does not order his knowledge to the end of activity but only to the end of knowing, his knowledge will be, with respect to the end, a speculative consideration, even though it concerns the matter of how to bring something about.
>
> Therefore, knowledge that is speculative on account of the very thing that is known is purely speculative; that which is not speculative with regard to the object known but is speculative either according to its mode or according to its end is in some manner speculative and in some manner practical; finally, that which is ordered to the end of operation is purely practical.[19]

19. I, 14, 16. "Aliqua scientia est speculativa tantum, aliqua practica tantum, aliqua vero secundum aliquid speculativa et secundum aliquid practica. Ad cuius evidentiam, sciendum est quod aliqua scientia potest dici speculativa tripliciter. Primo, ex parte rerum scitarum, quae non sunt operabiles a sciente, sicut est scientia hominis de rebus naturalibus vel divinis. Secundo, quantum ad modum sciendi, ut puta si aedificator consideret domum

THE PROBLEM

Some objects are theoretical by nature, that is, they are not the sorts of things that we can bring about through our actions, such as the sun or the moon. Knowledge of these things is purely speculative. In contrast, some objects are practical by nature, that is, they are the sorts of things that can be brought about through our actions, such as a house or a car.

Aquinas has a good word for these things: *operabilia*. No comparable word can be found in English. Aquinas's word covers not only the products of our actions, such as a house, but also actions themselves, so that moves in a game of chess would belong to *operabilia*. These are objects (taken broadly) that we in some manner bring about.

It is possible to think of these objects, however, simply in a speculative manner, with no concern about how to bring them into existence. Someone might be very interested in the workings of a car engine, in its parts and their interactions with one another. He has no interest, however, in how he might make an engine, fix an engine, or in any other way act upon an engine. Since practical knowledge is ordered to action, he does not have practical knowledge. Nevertheless, it is practical at least in this way: the object is something that he could bring about; the object is *able to be* ordered within human actions.

His curiosity might go further. He might become interested in how engines are made; at this point, ought-statements might be introduced. His knowledge is now practical not only in object but also in the mode of his knowing. He knows how to bring something about; he now has how-to knowledge. Still, he has no interest in making an engine himself. He simply wants to know; it is interesting to see how others make engines. His knowledge, therefore, is not practical according

---

definiendo et dividendo et considerando universalia praedicata ipsius. Hoc siquidem est operabilia modo speculativo considerare, et non secundum quod operabilia sunt, operabile enim est aliquid per applicationem formae ad materiam, non per resolutionem compositi in principia universalia formalia. Tertio, quantum ad finem, nam intellectus practicus differt fine a speculativo, sicut dicitur in III de anima. Intellectus enim practicus ordinatur ad finem operationis, finis autem intellectus speculativi est consideratio veritatis. Unde, si quis aedificator consideret qualiter posset fieri aliqua domus, non ordinans ad finem operationis, sed ad cognoscendum tantum, erit, quantum ad finem, speculativa consideratio, tamen de re operabili. Scientia igitur quae est speculativa ratione ipsius rei scitae, est speculativa tantum. Quae vero speculativa est vel secundum modum vel secundum finem, est secundum quid speculativa et secundum quid practica. Cum vero ordinatur ad finem operationis, est simpliciter practica."

THE PROBLEM

TABLE 1-1. Types of Speculative and Practical Knowledge

Knowledge	Object	Mode	End
purely speculative	nonoperable	resolving	knowing
materially practical	operable	resolving	knowing
virtually practical	operable	composing	knowing
fully practical	operable	composing	doing

to end. Only if he actually applies his knowledge, and begins building an engine for himself, does he have purely practical knowledge.

We have, then, four levels. (1) The object known might be speculative; it is not the sort of thing that human beings order in their actions. (2) The object known might be practical, such as an engine, but all that is known of it is speculative: what it is, how it functions, and so on. (3) The object and mode might be practical, as when someone knows how to make an engine. (4) The end of the agent himself might be practical, that is, he applies his knowledge to the activity; he actually builds the engine.

Level (1) can be called purely speculative and level (4) can be called purely practical (see table 1-1). Are there good names for the other two levels? Elsewhere, Aquinas calls level (3) virtually practical, which seems appropriate.[20] I do not know that he has a name for level (2), but "materially practical" seems fitting. In his commentary on Boethius's *De Trinitate,* Aquinas says, "The *material* of a practical science must be those things that can be done by us" (emphasis added).[21]

What Aquinas calls precepts of the natural law have the form of ought-statements, such as "The good (or some particular good, such as knowledge) ought to be pursued." These precepts, then, seem to be either virtually practical or purely practical. They provide some very general how-to knowledge concerning fundamental goods. How do we bring about these goods? By pursuing them.

If these precepts depend upon some prior speculative knowledge, then it would seem that they depend upon purely speculative knowl-

---

20. *De veritate,* 3, 3.
21. *Super De Trinitate,* 5, 1 (Leonine ed., v. 50, 137, 103–5). "Oportet practicarum scientiarum materiam esse res illas que a nostro opere fieri possunt."

THE PROBLEM

edge, materially practical knowledge, or perhaps both. Indeed, if there is some derivation, then it seems plausible that it might be gradual, step-by-step. Beginning with purely speculative knowledge, we might then move to materially practical knowledge. From there, we might arrive at virtually practical knowledge, and then finally to purely practical knowledge.[22]

1.3
FOUR ARGUMENTS

One encounters four primary arguments purporting to show that, for Aquinas, practical knowledge is independent of speculative knowledge. A brief consideration of each will better clarify our problem.

1.3.1: Derivation

By far the most common argument is that with which Grisez began the whole debate.[23] Aquinas states that the first precepts of the natural law are *per se nota*; they are known immediately, without deduction. In no way, then, can these first practical propositions be deduced from speculative knowledge.

This manner of stating the case sidesteps the naturalistic fallacy. Suppose that the naturalistic fallacy is no fallacy at all, that it is possible to derive an ought-statement from an is-statement. Nevertheless, this first argument suggests, Aquinas did not make this legitimate move. At least for the very first and most basic ought-statements, Aquinas used

---

22. As our discussion proceeds, then, we must always be clear at which level of knowledge we are. Some authors recognize Aquinas's fourfold distinction, but then they do not use it; they do not make clear at what level they are arguing. Worse yet, they end up collapsing different levels together. Mark Murphy, for instance, distinguishes the levels ("Self-Evidence, Human Nature, and Natural Law," *American Catholic Philosophical Quarterly* 69 [1995]: 471–84, at 483) but then explicitly says that virtually practical knowledge is just the same thing as materially practical knowledge, except that it is held in practical reason rather than speculative reason.

23. Grisez, "First Principle," 195. See also Grisez, "Practical Principles," 110. Finnis, *Natural Law*, 33–36; Alfonso Gomez-Lobo, "Natural Law and Naturalism," *Proceedings of the American Catholic Philosophical Association* 59 (1985): 232–49, at 244–46; and Patrick Lee, "Is Thomas's Natural Law Theory Naturalist?" *American Catholic Philosophical Quarterly* 71 (1997): 567–87, at 568–69, who also adds the argument from silence, that Aquinas does not provide the argument moving from the theoretical knowledge to practical knowledge.

THE PROBLEM

no derivation from anything. Consequently, he used no derivation from speculative reason.

As stated, the argument seems incontestable. By a *per se nota* proposition, Aquinas means a proposition whose truth is known immediately, simply by knowing the content of the subject and predicate terms. No middle term is needed. Consequently, no deductive syllogism is needed; indeed, no deductive syllogism is possible.[24]

Unfortunately, the force of the argument depends upon ambiguity surrounding the term "derivation," which can have a broad meaning and a narrow meaning; the argument under consideration uses the narrow meaning. As Henry Veatch puts it, this argument takes "the terms 'deduction' and 'inference' in a somewhat straightened and overly technical sense."[25]

Broadly speaking, "derivation" might refer to any epistemological dependence, in which case an ought-statement is derived from an is-statement just so long as the former depends in any way upon knowledge of the latter. More narrowly, "derivation" refers to deduction in a syllogistic argument, in which two terms (the terms of the conclusion) are related by some third term, called the middle term.

Derivation in this narrower sense seems to underlie a common understanding of the naturalistic fallacy. If the conclusion contains an ought-statement, then one of the premises must also contain an ought-term. Therefore, no argument that uses only is-statements in the premises will ever validly generate an ought-statement for a conclusion.

Whatever else Aquinas is doing, Grisez makes it clear that he is not making this fallacy. Aquinas never claims to deduce an ought-statement from an is-statement. To the contrary, he argues for immediate knowledge of certain basic ought-statements. By definition, what is *per se nota* cannot be known by way of any middle term. Rather, the connection between the subject term and the predicate term is known immediately. In the narrow sense of derivation, then, Aquinas agrees that the

---

24. Craig Paterson ("Finnis, Non-Naturalism, and Aquinas," in *Analytical Thomism: Traditions in Dialogue*, ed. Craig Paterson et al. [Aldershot, England: Ashgate, 2006], 179) tries to get around the difficulty by claiming that Aquinas uses "*per se nota*" analogically for the first precepts of the natural law.

25. Veatch, "Is-Ought Question," 298; see also Lawrence Dewan, "St. Thomas, Our Natural Lights, and the Moral Order," *Angelicum* 67 (1990): 285–307, at 291.

THE PROBLEM

very first precepts of the natural law cannot be derived from speculative knowledge.

Nothing Aquinas says, however, excludes derivation in the broader sense.[26] The first precepts might depend — in some manner or other — upon prior knowledge, perhaps even speculative knowledge. The difficulty will be spelling out the "in some manner or other." At this point, however, it suffices to note that the *per se nota* character of the first precepts does not make them independent from speculative knowledge. It only makes them independent from deductive syllogistic reasoning. It leaves open the possibility of other sorts of epistemological dependence.

Grisez's argument could be used as the beginning of a disjunctive argument. The first step lists possible manners of derivation: If an ought-statement is derived from an is-statement, then it must be either (1) by syllogistic deduction, (2) by induction, (3) by material contribution to the terms.... The second step eliminates each of the possibilities: syllogistic deduction is not possible because the first precepts are not deduced; induction is not possible.... Finally, after eliminating every possibility, the argument concludes that practical reason depends in no way upon speculative reason.

This disjunctive argument has not in fact been used. To the contrary, when the misleading character of the argument has been pointed out, a typical response has been to protest, with wounded dignity, any intention to separate practical knowledge from speculative.[27] Of course (comes the reply) practical knowledge arises from speculative knowledge; after all, our knowledge of natural inclinations helps us to arrive at knowledge of basic human goods.

But if there was never any intention to assert the independence of practical knowledge against speculative, then why was the argument raised within this context?[28] To show that practical principles are not

26. Finnis ("Natural Law and the 'Is'-'Ought' Question: An Invitation to Professor Veatch," *The Catholic Lawyer* 26 [1981]: 266–77) concedes that the first principles might depend epistemologically upon some prior (speculative?) knowledge; he does not seem to recognize that he thereby allows knowledge of nature as a requirement (by epistemological dependence) for knowledge of the good, which seems to be contrary to the spirit of his whole theory. Then again, perhaps he does recognize it, since the gist of the article is to deny that he explicitly maintains that which he seems to hold in spirit.

27. See Finnis, "Is-Ought Question."

28. See Ralph McInerny, *Aquinas on Human Action: A Theory of Practice* (Washington, D.C.: The Catholic University of America Press, 1992), 198.

THE PROBLEM

deduced syllogistically from theoretical principles? But what is the significance of this point? By itself, this limited observation has no implications for the overall relationship between speculative and practical knowledge. Yet even after the protests are made, the argument is retained as if it still said something significant about the relationship between theoretical and practical knowledge.

What is going on here? The disjunctive argument is probably in the background. Suppose a distinction is made between two different ways in which theoretical knowledge might underlie practical knowledge. On the one hand, speculative knowledge might be what could be called an occasion for the operation of practical knowledge; speculative knowledge provides the material with which practical reason will work, but it does nothing more. On the other hand, speculative knowledge might provide the very formal structure, or part of it, found within practical reason. No doubt, the distinction is not very precise, but then no one has made it explicitly. I am merely surmising what seems to be going on in the exchange concerning the significance of *per se nota* propositions.

Suppose someone denies the latter sort of role — formal dependence — for speculative knowledge. It seems plausible that he has made a significant assertion regarding the relationship between speculative and practical knowledge. The only sort of relationship he allows is minimal; speculative knowledge provides only a material contribution.

Within this context the disjunctive argument begins to make sense. One further assumption is needed, namely, that formal dependence arises only through syllogistic deductive reasoning. If the content of practical knowledge depends upon theoretical knowledge for more than its occasion, or for more than the stuff out of which it is made, then it must come — so the argument goes — from deductive reasoning.

The complete disjunctive argument, then, runs as follows: (1) Either practical knowledge depends upon speculative knowledge for its formal content and structure or it does not (in which case it still might depend upon speculative knowledge as an occasion). (2) Formal dependence must arise through syllogistic deduction. (3) Practical knowledge does not depend upon speculative knowledge by way of syllogistic reasoning (this step is Grisez's explicit argument). (4) Therefore, practical knowledge does not depend upon speculative knowledge for its formal content.

THE PROBLEM

The second premise is the key. Premise #1 is an indisputable binary disjunction, although the exact meaning of the terms is not clear. Premise #3 will readily be granted by those following Aquinas. Premise #2, however, might well be disputed. Resolving such a dispute will not be easy, given that the key term — formal dependence — is unclear. Stipulating that formal dependence *just is* syllogistic dependence trivializes the argument, stripping the disjunctive argument of all its force. The greatest difficulty in resolving the dispute is that it has never been made explicit. Nevertheless, I think it is the best account of the discussion.

The argument as it has been stated explicitly simply does not work. It is a fallacy of associating the lack of syllogistic dependence with a lack of all significant dependence. The argument works only when restructured into a disjunctive argument. Then its weakness arises simply from the many unstated assumptions.

At times the new natural law theorists concede some kind of dependence of practical reason upon speculative reason.[29] All the while, they seem to think that they are saying something significant when they assert that an ought-statement cannot be derived from an is-statement. Why? Perhaps because the sort of dependence they discuss is minimal.

Unfortunately, the exact nature of this purported dependence has consistently remained obscure. Somehow our knowledge of natural inclinations, which is not practical knowledge, assists us in coming to know the very first precepts of practical knowledge. John Finnis tells us that the inclinations (with other experiences) are conditions of our knowledge.[30] Presumably, a condition is something short of a cause, but what exactly it is remains obscure. Elsewhere, the inclinations are described as "data."[31] It seems that the inclinations point to the particular instances from which we abstract some knowledge of the good.[32]

---

29. Robert Matava ("'Is,' 'Ought' and Moral Realism: The Roles of Nature and Experience in Practical Understanding," *Studies in Christian Ethics* 24 [2011]: 311–28, at 324–26) wants to say that the knowledge upon which practical reason depends is not speculative but rather factual. The precise words used, however, seem irrelevant, as long as the knowledge concerns what is the case, a conformity of the mind with what is actual.

30. Finnis, *Natural Law*, 73.

31. Grisez, "Practical Principles," 108–9. Matava ("Moral Realism," 320–24) is helpful in understanding the position of the new natural law theory. It seems that the natural inclinations operate more at the sensible level than at the intellectual level; they simply direct the attention of the intellect.

32. See John Finnis, "Natural Inclinations and Natural Rights: Deriving 'Ought' from

THE PROBLEM

They are the singular in which we grasp the universal good.[33] At other times, the inclinations seem to be a kind of material in which reason impresses its knowledge of the good.[34] We can then subsequently come to recognize this act of reason within these inclinations. They do help us to come to know the good, but only insofar as they help us to see what practical reason is doing.

All of these suggested explanations seem to fall into the category of a weak dependence.[35] The formal structure of practical reason does not depend upon any theoretical knowledge. Rather, practical reason is presented with some stuff upon which it operates; the presentation comes from speculative reason, but the very nature of the practical knowledge arises solely from practical reason. In short, the hidden disjunctive argument seems to be operative.

1.3.2: The Order of Knowing and the Order of Being

The second argument for the independence of practical knowledge is the strongest. Indeed, it will prove to be largely correct. The argument actually arose as a kind of defensive countermeasure. The new natural law theory could not deny the connection between nature and the good. The connection is evident not only in Aquinas but in our daily speech as well. Knowledge is good for human beings, for instance, *because* we have minds by which we can know, that is, *because* we have a nature that includes a mind. The good, it seems, depends upon nature, the practical upon the speculative.

John Finnis, however, managed to minimize the damage. He distinguished between the ontological order and the epistemological order, or the order of causality in things and the order of causality in our knowl-

---

'Is' according to Aquinas," in *Lex et Libertas: Freedom and Law according to St. Thomas Aquinas*, v. 30, ed. Leo Elders et al. (Rome: Studi Tomistici, 1987), 47–48.

33. Finnis, *Natural Law*, 34.

34. Grisez ("First Principle," 180) speaks in this manner; Finnis indicates that they provide the possibilities of what might be pursued; see Finnis, *Aquinas*, 94.

35. On this reading, Ralph McInerny's observation (*Human Action*, 191–92, 204–6) that the knowledge of the good presupposes the knowledge of being does not touch the argument. This dependence can be acknowledged, while claiming that it is not an instance of formal dependence; our knowledge of being provides the material subject which is grasped as good.

THE PROBLEM

edge.[36] Ontologically, our good depends upon our nature. Because we are beings with minds, knowledge is good for us; because a tree has no mind, knowledge is not good for it. Epistemologically, however, our awareness of what is good for us does not depend — according to Finnis — upon any awareness of our nature. Knowledge of the good is a fundamental given, derived from no other knowledge.

Kai Nielsen might well pounce upon this distinction; it has not saved the natural law from an outdated teleology. Perhaps — he might argue — our knowledge of the natural law does not depend upon our knowledge of teleology; nevertheless, the very existence of the natural law — the goods upon which it is based — depends ontologically upon teleology. If there is no teleology, then there is no natural law. Since modern science has dispelled teleology, natural law cannot stand on the ontological plane; neither, then, can it stand epistemologically.

Finnis, however, is ready with a response. Rather than base our ethics upon nature, we must base our view of nature upon ethics.[37] We immediately perceive that some things are good for us as human beings, such as life and knowledge. This ethical perception in no way depends upon our knowledge of nature. Given this awareness, however, we recognize that these things could not be good unless we had a certain nature. Knowledge would not be good for us, if we did not have minds to know. We move back, then, from our knowledge of the good to a knowledge of nature.

Finnis brings Aquinas to his defense. Aquinas considers how we come to know four things: a nature, its powers, its activities, and the objects of activities. A bird, for instance, has a living nature, such that it has the power to reproduce, and it sometimes actually does reproduce.

---

36. Finnis, "Deriving Ought"; Finnis, *Aquinas*, 90–94. Others have also picked up this argument. See Robert P. George, "Natural Law and Human Nature," in *Natural Law Theory: Contemporary Essays*, ed. Robert P. George (Oxford: Clarendon Press, 1992), 35; Lee, "Naturalist," 573–74; Martin Rhonheimer, *Natural Law and Practical Reason: A Thomist View of Moral Autonomy* (New York: Fordham University Press, 2000), 15–16; Martin Rhonheimer, "The Moral Significance of Pre-Rational Nature in Aquinas: A Reply to Jean Porter (and Stanley Hauerwas)," in *The Perspective of the Acting Person: Essays in the Renewal of Thomistic Moral Philosophy* (Washington, D.C.: The Catholic University of America Press, 2008), 133–34; Martin Rhonheimer, *The Perspective of Morality: Philosophical Foundations of Thomistic Virtue Ethics* (Washington, D.C.: The Catholic University of America Press, 2011), 268.

37. Finnis, "Deriving Ought." See also Rhonheimer, "Pre-Rational Nature," 136.

THE PROBLEM

Finally, the object of reproduction is a new life of the same species.

These four have a certain priority among them. Interestingly, however, the ontological priority is the exact reverse of the epistemological priority. Ontologically, a bird has a certain nature, on account of which it has the power to reproduce; because it has the power to reproduce, it can actually reproduce; and when it actually reproduces, it brings about offspring. Epistemologically, however, Aquinas says that we know things in the reverse order. "The acts of all potencies of the soul are known by their objects, and the potencies are known by their acts, and the soul is known by its potencies."[38] Only by knowing offspring do we understand what it means to reproduce; by knowing the act of reproducing, we know that birds have the power to reproduce; finally, by understanding the power of reproduction, we know that a bird is a living being.

The object of action, then, is the beginning of it all, that is, it is the beginning of our knowledge; in contrast, nature is the final stage of our knowledge. Now knowledge of nature seems, unquestionably, to be speculative knowledge. What of the knowledge of the objects of actions? Is it speculative or practical? If Finnis can show that it is practical, then it seems he has made his case. We begin with practical knowledge — of the objects of actions — and we move backwards to speculative knowledge — of natures and their powers.

But why should we suppose that the knowledge of the objects of activities is practical knowledge? Because, says Finnis, the objects of activities are their ends. As Aquinas states,

> Objects are compared to the acts of active powers, however, as terms and ends, just as the object of the power of growth is the completed size, which is the end of growth.[39]

Aquinas repeatedly says, however, that the good has the character of an end. The objects of actions, then, which are their ends, are certain goods. These goods are known first of all, since they are objects, and

---

38. *Q. D. De anima*, 16, ad 8 (Leonine ed., v. 24, 147, 410–14). "Et hoc est etiam commune in omnibus potentiis anime, quod actus cognoscuntur per obiecta, et potentie per actus, et anima per suas potentias."

39. I, 77, 3. "Ad actum autem potentiae activae comparatur obiectum ut terminus et finis, sicut augmentativae virtutis obiectum est quantum perfectum, quod est finis augmenti."

THE PROBLEM

only then do we come to know the actions, the potencies, and the nature. The epistemological dependence, then, begins with the good. We first know the good and only then do we know human nature.

Finnis's distinction between the ontological order and the epistemological order is not unusual. Ontologically, Neptune causes certain irregularities in the orbit of Uranus. Epistemologically, however, Le Verrier was first aware of the irregularities and then concluded to the existence of Neptune. Similarly, argues Finnis, ontologically the human good depends upon teleology. Epistemologically, however, we first become aware of the good and only then recognize teleology.

This position has an odd asymmetry. It originates from a supposed divide between is-statements and ought-statements. In the final analysis, however, it concludes that this divide is only one way. We cannot begin with an is-statement and move to an ought-statement, but evidently we can start with an ought-statement and conclude to an is-statement.[40]

The asymmetry appears to destroy the naturalistic fallacy in both directions. If we can move from the good, which is known in itself, to a conclusion concerning nature, then we should be able to reverse the procedure. Le Verrier first knows the irregularities of the orbit of Uranus and concludes to the existence of Neptune. Having discovered Neptune, however, he can reverse the procedure. Given the existence of Neptune, he can conclude to the irregularities. This reversal is typical in human reasoning. We first reason to the existence of a cause, but once this cause is discovered we reason to its effects.

Similarly, if we first of all reason to our nature from our practical knowledge of the good, we should be able to reverse the procedure, reasoning from the newly discovered nature to the nature of the good. Indeed, we unquestionably make this move. *Because* we have a mind, knowing the truth is good for us. Perhaps we first of all discovered the nature of our mind by way of our awareness that knowledge is good — as Finnis claims — but now we reverse the procedure and reason to the good. The shift from ought to is and back again goes both ways. The naturalistic fallacy is no fallacy, even by Finnis's reasoning.

Even if the naturalistic fallacy is not a fallacy, Finnis still might be

---

40. For a similar view, see Rhonheimer, *Perspective of Morality,* 268.

correct concerning the issue at hand, that is, we still might know practical truths before theoretical. Finnis's distinction, then, alerts us to a danger. When we find evidence of an inference we must be careful to ascertain what is being indicated, an ontological relation or merely an epistemological relation. When Le Verrier reasons, "A planet exists at this point in space *because* of irregularities in the orbit of Uranus," the "because" indicates not ontological causation but epistemological. The irregularities did not cause the planet to exist, but his knowledge of the irregularities caused Le Verrier to come to know that a planet exists.

These two might overlap, that is, "because" might indicate *both* epistemological and ontological causation. Such is the claim of those who oppose the new natural law theory. Nature is the ontological cause of the first precepts, a point admitted even by Finnis; because of our nature (ontological dependence) certain things are good for us. But also — claim the opponents of the new natural law theory — our knowledge of nature causes (epistemological dependence) our knowledge of the first precepts of the natural law. This last point is denied by Finnis and Grisez, and it is the focus of this study. We are trying to determine how we come to know the first precepts of the natural law. Do we arrive at them by way of is-statements?

1.3.3: Physicalism

The third argument is not directly an attack on the move from is-statements to ought-statements. Rather, it claims that those who (fallaciously) make the move end up with a certain kind of ethical theory. On the supposition that this ethical theory is unacceptable, the original move is deemed problematic. In short, this argument is something of a reductio ad absurdum.[41]

The unacceptable ethical theory is often called physicalism. It locates the moral good in mere natural or biological functioning. On this view, some physical activities are deemed good while others are designated as evil. In the domain of sexual activity, for instance, the physical act of contraception is evil while sexual activity that conforms with proper biological functioning is considered good.

A particularly egregious instance of this outlook is the so-called

---

41. This argument is most explicitly laid out by Lee, "Naturalist," 574–82.

THE PROBLEM

perverted function argument. It is morally evil, so the argument goes, to oppose a natural function. Since our reproductive organs function properly when they lead to reproduction, any attempt to thwart this proper functioning is morally evil. Consequently, contraception and other "sins against nature" must be recognized as morally abhorrent.

Why is physicalism an unacceptable ethical theory? Because it ignores the importance of the will for the moral good. The moral good is located in human actions, which are voluntary actions. Human acts are voluntary acts, and only as such can they be good or evil.

The attempt to show that Aquinas rejects physicalism often involves an emphasis upon reason — as opposed to nature — as the standard of human actions. "Physicalism" also recognizes the importance of reason, but it maintains that reason is not opposed to nature; rather, reason is important precisely because it discovers good and evil in nature. On this physicalist model, reason becomes a mere conduit, a messenger between nature and the will, relaying to the will the moral good found in nature; reason adds nothing to the good or evil already found in nature.

In contrast, thinkers such as Martin Rhonheimer emphasize that, for human beings, the directives of nature are nothing other than the directives of reason, that is, it is natural to human beings to follow the practical judgments of reason. This practical reason does not simply discover what lies in nature; it is constructive, directing to what does not yet exist, and therefore to that which cannot be found in nature. According to Rhonheimer,

> For Thomas this is a decisive point: for him, the natural law is not simply "discovered" by the reason, but rather "constituted" by the reason for an active *practical* understanding. Thomas understands the natural practical reason as a *law-giver* and not simply as an executory of the law.[42]

This third argument has many components, each of which might be called into question. First, one might question whether physicalism is all that objectionable; perhaps it can be made into an appealing moral theory. Second, one might question whether descriptivism is necessarily linked with physicalism; perhaps one can have a descriptive ethics, derived from what is the case, that nevertheless emphasizes the role

---

42. Rhonheimer, *Natural Law*, 5. See also Rhonheimer, "Pre-Rational Nature," 135.

THE PROBLEM

of the human will and the active role of reason. Third, one might also approach the argument textually, attempting to show that Aquinas did in fact claim to discover moral good and evil in nature.

We will take the latter two approaches. We will concede that physicalism is an inadequate moral theory and that Aquinas himself did not in fact hold it. Nevertheless, he did hold that we can arrive at ought-statements through our observations of nature, and he did so without diminishing the importance of will and reason.

1.3.4: From Knowledge to Action

The fourth argument for the independence of practical knowledge is the most enigmatic. In short, the argument claims that if we begin with speculative knowledge we will never get to action, which is the final upshot of practical knowledge.[43] Simply speaking, speculative knowledge does not move us to act.

It is difficult to determine where in the fourfold division this argument is operating. Does it mean that purely speculative knowledge will never arrive at action? Does it mean that materially practical knowledge can never get us to act? Does it mean that even virtually practical knowledge, which is still speculative in its end, will never lead to action? At this point the vague notions of "practical reason" are most unfortunate.

In some sense, no doubt, only purely practical knowledge moves us to act; it alone engages our will. Are we to conclude, then, that materially practical knowledge and virtually practical knowledge have no impact upon our actions?

Besides having the feel more of an assertion than an argument, this objection also has the handicap of being tied to the view of Aquinas only tenuously, that is, Thomas does not say that speculative knowledge is unable to lead to action. Aquinas does distinguish between speculative and practical knowledge, but this distinction is not a very promising avenue, since Aquinas himself says that speculative reason becomes practical by extension.[44]

At any rate, the argument raises an interesting question: How do

---

43. See Rhonheimer, *Perspective of Morality*, 116; Lee, "Naturalist," 570.
44. I, 79, 11, sed contra; II-II, 4, 2, ad 3.

THE PROBLEM

we move from knowledge to action? Any account of the natural law should be able to answer this question. How can my knowledge that pizza tastes good lead me to act? How does my knowledge that I ought to turn right in order to get to the pizza shop affect my action?

I.4
THE JOURNEY AHEAD

The journey from "is" to "ought" will follow four basic steps, corresponding to the four levels of reasoning. We will move step by step, beginning with purely speculative knowledge, moving to materially practical knowledge, then to virtually practical knowledge and finally to action. At the level of purely speculative knowledge we will look for a suitable object as a starting point. Taking a hint from Aquinas, we will examine natural inclinations. We will then determine how knowledge of natural inclinations might lead us to materially practical knowledge concerning the good. From there, we will move to virtually practical knowledge of how we ought to behave. Finally, we will examine how knowledge leads to action.

Before the journey begins, however, we will examine, in chapter 2, the crucial text of Aquinas. Grisez began the whole debate with a detailed examination of question 94, article 2 of the *Prima secundae*. More than any other text, this passage examines the beginnings of practical knowledge. It has served as the focus of a multitude of studies on our topic; indeed, it is not unreasonable to claim that more has been written on this one text of Aquinas, at least in recent years, than upon any other article Aquinas has written. We will not attempt a definitive interpretation of the text, which will indeed be the work of the whole book. Rather, we will cover the main topics that Aquinas addresses, mentioning various interpretations, eliminating some, and pointing out directions the text might take us.

Chapter 3 will find us in the beginning of our journey with purely speculative knowledge concerning natural inclinations; the nature of these inclinations must be examined in detail. Chapters 4, 5, and 6 will concern the materially practical knowledge of the good. Chapter 4 will consider how we come to know the good by way of natural inclinations; chapter 5 will examine texts of Aquinas in which he bases moral

THE PROBLEM

judgments upon nature; and chapter 6 will consider how the will and its inclinations enter our knowledge of the good. Chapters 7, 8, and 9 will concern virtually practical knowledge, the how-to knowledge of ought-statements. Chapter 7 will show how from knowledge of the good we can arrive at knowledge of what ought to be done; chapter 8 will consider how this knowledge might account for moral obligation; and chapter 9 will examine the first principles of the natural law, the ought-statements that are known immediately through their terms. Finally, chapter 10 will consider fully practical knowledge, how we move from knowledge to action.

2

THE TEXT

Question 94, article 2 of the *Prima secundae* asks whether there is one precept of the natural law or many. Ultimately, Aquinas will answer that there are many precepts to the natural law; nevertheless, these precepts are united into a single natural law by the very first precept, urging us to do good and avoid evil. Aquinas begins with a general explanation of first principles; he then looks at the very first principle in speculative reason and the very first principle in practical reason. Finally, he looks at the more particular principles of practical reason.

2.1
PER SE NOTA PROPOSITIONS

Aquinas has an extended treatment of what it means for something to be *per se nota,* that is, known in itself. By its very nature, the proposition "a whole is greater than one of its parts," is immediate, that is, it requires no proof and no proof can be given for it. Why? Because the connection between the subject term and the predicate term is immediate; no middle term could come between them. The predicate, says Aquinas, belongs to the very notion of the subject.

The example Aquinas gives is a rather straightforward analytic proposition: a human being is rational. The very definition of the subject term includes the predicate term. This is something like saying that a straight line is straight. The second example — that a whole is greater than its part — is not so obviously tautological, though it does not take much imagination to see how the predicate term might be included in the subject term.[1] All the other examples Aquinas gives, including the principle of noncontradiction, are more problematic.

---

1. See *In Metaphysicorum,* lib. 5, l. 21, n. 1098.

THE TEXT

2.1.1: Three Acts of the Intellect

Aquinas's analysis fits within the broader context of his teaching on the three acts of reason. Consider the syllogism examined earlier: all mammals have hair; all whales are mammals; all whales have hair. This is an example of the third act of reason, in which the mind begins with some knowledge — the premises — and concludes to something originally unknown. The syllogism is constituted by three propositions and each proposition is itself constituted by two concepts, a subject term and a predicate term. The proposition "mammals have hair," for instance, has the concept "mammals" as its subject term and the concept "have hair" (or "things having hair") as its predicate term. The proposition relates these two terms to one another, in this case indicating that they go together.

A proposition is an instance of the second act of reason, which Aquinas calls combining or dividing, since we can either unite the subject and predicate term or separate them, as in a negative proposition. The individual concepts are instances of the first act of reason (called simple apprehension), which is the grasp of the nature of something, such as "mammals" or "hair."

Propositions and their concepts can become rather involved, as even the example "a whole is greater than its part" indicates. The predicate term includes multiple concepts, such as "greater than" and "part." These conglomerate concepts are not at all unusual. The concept of a triangle includes the component concepts of "three," "having sides," and "figure." In addition, each of these concepts may be itself composite. For this reason, identifying *per se nota* propositions can be far from straightforward.

In a valid syllogism, the truth of the premises guarantees the truth of the conclusion. If indeed all mammals have hair, and if indeed whales are mammals, then necessarily whales have hair. Since one or both of the premises might be false, we might need to argue for the truth of the premises by way of other syllogisms. The premises of these new syllogisms might also need proof. And so it goes. Obviously, however, it cannot go on forever. We must know (or possibly, grant) the truth of some first premises, without any syllogistic proof. These premises are

THE TEXT

what Aquinas identifies as *per se nota*; they are known through themselves, without the need of syllogism.[2]

A syllogism is needed when the terms of a proposition do not relate immediately; then the subject term and the predicate term must be related by some third term, called the middle term. "Whale" must be related to "have hair" by way of the middle term "mammal." In contrast, the terms of a *per se nota* proposition relate to one another immediately, with no middle term.

In question 94, article 2, Aquinas informs us that the two terms relate immediately when the *ratio* of the predicate term belongs to the *ratio* of the subject term. What is meant by *ratio*? The word is translated as "intelligibility," "definition," "formality," "character," and more. Obviously, it is difficult to translate. Rather than translate it I prefer to define it at this point, and for the remainder of the book I will leave it untranslated.

The obvious straightforward meaning is "reason," but in this case and in others that we will encounter it has a more particular meaning. In this special usage, *ratio* indicates a concept, or more precisely the content of that concept, which is a certain nature or essence. We are aware of this content through the first act of the intellect, the act of simple apprehension. As Aquinas says, "The *ratio*, which is signified by a noun, is that which the intellect conceives concerning something and then signifies through a word."[3] Perhaps the best translation, then, would be "intelligible content"; it is the content of our ideas.

I have broached this basic material of logic, at the risk of being pedantic, because in our search for nonsyllogistic epistemological dependence, an understanding of propositions and the concepts that make them up will prove important. Aquinas himself emphasizes the role of concepts within *per se nota* propositions.

For our purposes, it is significant that our minds have two natural capacities. First, they can grasp certain *rationes*, the natures or characters of certain things. Second, they can see how these *rationes* relate to one another. When they relate in an immediate way, then the mind grasps the truth naturally.

2. *Expositio Posteriorum Analyticorum*, lib. 1, lect. 5.
3. I, 5, 2. "Ratio enim significata per nomen, est id quod concipit intellectus de re, et significat illud per vocem."

THE TEXT

We can grasp what it means to be a substance, what it means to be without a body, and what it means to be in a place. Then we can see how these ideas relate immediately to one another, that a substance without a body (that is, an angel) is in no place. Even this rather arcane proposition, then, which is known only to the learned, is naturally known. In effect, what is naturally known is known without deductive reasoning. It is the same as being *per se nota*.

2.1.2: Different Modes of Per Seity

Let us return to the text. Aquinas says that the predicate term of a *per se nota* proposition is contained within the *ratio* of the subject term. Such is Aquinas's depiction of a *per se nota* proposition whenever he broaches the topic. Nevertheless, there is reason to suspect that the matter may be more complicated. In his commentary on Aristotle's *Posterior Analytics*, Aquinas follows Aristotle in identifying four modes of being per se (without the "nota"). One of these (the third) does not concern propositions, but the other three involve modes of predicating or speaking per se. The first mode corresponds to Aquinas's description of the *per se nota* proposition, in which the predicate term is contained within the subject term. The second and fourth mode, however, are different.

The second mode is the opposite of the first. The subject term is contained within the predicate term.[4] An attribute contains within its definition the subject in which it resides, for example, "nose" falls in the very definition of "snub." When we predicate the attribute of the subject, then we have the second mode of predicating per se. In the proposition "A nose is snub," the subject term, "nose," is included within the predicate term, "snub."

Aquinas does not describe the fourth mode by way of the component terms; rather, he simply says that it concerns efficient causality and then gives an example: "That which is killed dies."[5] Plainly, the effect of death relates per se to the activity of killing; consequently, the predication that connects the effect and the activity involves a per se connection.

Aquinas relates these three different modes to the diverse Aristo-

---

4. *Expositio Posteriorum Analyticorum,* lib. 1, lect. 10, 39, 51–67.
5. *Expositio Posteriorum Analyticorum,* lib. 1, lect. 10, 40, 132–33, "quod interfectum interiit."

telian causes. The first mode concerns formal cause, for it predicates what belongs to the essence of a thing. The second mode concerns material cause, since the subject of the proposition is the material in which the attribute resides. As already mentioned, the fourth mode concerns efficient cause, and Aquinas adds, "other causes," which he had earlier designated as "extrinsic causes."[6] Since formal and material cause have already been covered, "other causes" might refer to final causality. In addition, it might include "efficient causality" in a rather extended sense, for example, an essence causes its attributes; such causality is not straightforward efficient causality, but perhaps it fits best under that heading.

As already mentioned, Aquinas consistently identifies the first mode of predicating per se with *per se nota* propositions, that is, with propositions known immediately or naturally. What of the second and fourth modes? Can they also involve *per se nota* propositions? Aquinas does not say. Indeed, he states that they are sometimes the conclusions of syllogisms, which would indicate that in these cases they are not *per se nota*.[7] Nevertheless, forceful reasons suggest that they can sometimes be *per se nota*.

First, Aquinas says that scientific demonstration concerns the proper attributes of a subject, for instance, using geometry one might try to determine the proper attributes of a triangle.[8] Since proper attributes do not fall within the essence of a thing — as the size of the interior angles (equaling two right angles) does not enter into the definition of a triangle — they must enter the syllogism by some mode of per seity besides the first. While the minor premise is in the first mode, the major premise must be in some other. Indeed, Aquinas explicitly states that sometimes the major premise is in the fourth mode.[9] Since the premises of a scientific demonstration must ultimately be *per se nota*, it follows that some *per se nota* propositions are not in the first mode.

Second, Aquinas's examples of the fourth mode seem to be *per se nota*. It is difficult to imagine, for instance, that we would have to prove Aquinas's example of the fourth mode: "that which is killed dies."

---

6. *Expositio Posteriorum Analyticorum*, lib. 1, lect. 10, 39–18.
7. *Expositio Posteriorum Analyticorum*, lib. 1, lect. 10, 40, 144–46.
8. *Expositio Posteriorum Analyticorum*, lib. 1, lect. 2, 10, 17–20.
9. *Expositio Posteriorum Analyticorum*, lib. 1, lect. 13, 50, 62–65.

THE TEXT

Third, the examples Aquinas gives in question 94, article 2 are far from clear-cut instances of the first mode. One example of something known to all is, "Those which are equal to one and the same thing are equal to one another."[10] How is the predicate term found within the subject term? Perhaps an account can be given, but it is far from pellucid.

One of Aquinas's examples seems possibly to be in the second mode. He says that the proposition "An angel is not in a place" is *per se nota*. Is the negation of place (the predicate term) contained within the *ratio* of an immaterial substance (angel), or is it the other way around? It would seem to be the latter. The *ratio* of "place" contains within it the (negation of the) subject; the very definition of "place" includes the subject in which it resides, namely, a material substance. We could make an exactly parallel proposition for the nose: "A nonnose is not snub."

Fourth, in his commentary on Aristotle's *Metaphysics,* Aquinas quite clearly states that the fourth mode includes immediate propositions, not derived from a syllogism. He states that a conclusion is said to be caused by the middle term, but that immediate propositions have no such cause. He then proceeds to say,

> To this manner [of "in itself"] is reduced the fourth mode of per seity given in the *Posterior Analytics,* in which the effect is predicated of its cause, as when it is said that that which is killed dies because of the killing, or that which is cooled cools or chills on account of the cooling.[11]

A final reason to suspect that some *per se nota* propositions are in the second or fourth mode of per se predication concerns the very subject matter of question 94, article 2. The very propositions Aquinas is working toward do not seem to fit within the first mode. McInerny, focusing upon the principle of noncontradiction and the first principle of practical reason, argues that Aquinas means exactly what he says, the *per se nota* propositions are all in the first mode.[12]

This conclusion seems reasonable as long as we focus simply upon the very first principles, such as the principle of noncontradiction. Un-

---

10. "Quae uni et eidem sunt aequalia, sibi invicem sunt aequalia."

11. *In Metaphysicorum,* lib. 5, lect. 19, n. 1056. "Et ad hunc modum reducitur quartus modus dicendi per se in posterioribus positus, quando effectus praedicatur de causa; ut cum dicitur interfectus interiit propter interfectionem, vel infrigidatum infriguit vel refriguit propter refrigerium."

12. McInerny, *Human Action,* 131–32. Gregory Stevens ("The Relations of Law and

THE TEXT

fortunately, it is difficult to imagine how propositions like "knowledge is good" or "knowledge ought to be pursued" can fit in the first mode. Presumably, neither "being good" nor "ought to be pursued" falls in the very definition of knowledge. Indeed, the causality involved with the good points us in the direction of the fourth mode. The good is an end; it is a kind of final cause. The fourth mode, then, may be more appropriate to the good than is the first mode, which concerns formal causality.

2.2

THE PRINCIPLE OF NONCONTRADICTION

Aquinas goes on to consider what "falls" in the apprehension of everyone, that is, those *rationes* that everyone comes to grasp. These first *rationes* are prior to any propositions, grasped by simple apprehension, that is, the first act of the intellect. Aquinas mentions only two. The first *ratio* of the speculative intellect is being; the first *ratio* of the practical intellect is good.

These first *rationes* give rise to the very first *per se nota* propositions. Concerning speculative reason, Aquinas notes, "Therefore, the first indemonstrable principle is that what is affirmed cannot at the same time be denied, which is founded [fundatur] upon the *ratio* of being and the *ratio* of non-being, and upon this principle all others are founded [fundantur]."[13]

Aquinas's formulation of the very first principle, sometimes called the principle of noncontradiction, is far from pellucid; it is not immediately clear how the predicate term is contained within the subject term. The *rationes* of being and of nonbeing, upon which it is said to be founded, are not even stated explicitly in the proposition. Elsewhere, he has a more straightforward formulation: "it is impossible for something to be and not to be at the same time."[14] In its most simple form, I suppose, the

---

Obligation," *Proceedings of the American Catholic Philosophical Association* 29 [1955]: 195–205, at 198–99) also argues for the first mode of predicating per se.

13. "Et ideo primum principium indemonstrabile est quod non est simul affirmare et negare, quod fundatur supra rationem entis et non entis, et super hoc principio omnia alia fundantur."

14. *In Metaphysicorum*, lib. 4, lect. 6, n. 606. "Impossibile est esse et non esse simul." See also *Expositio Posteriorum Analyticorum*, lib. 1, lect. 19, n. 3.

proposition would be phrased "being is not nonbeing." Clearly, then, the *ratio* of the predicate term (or its opposite) can be found in the subject term. Furthermore, the proposition is clearly founded upon being and nonbeing. Aquinas, however, chose a less transparent expression, phrasing it in terms of the mental acts of affirming and denying.

We need not worry how this formulation relates to the more primitive formulations he mentions elsewhere.[15] I wish only to note that Aquinas is not choosing to express his principles in their clearest and most straightforward manner. When we come to the principles of practical reason, then, we should not be surprised to find a similar lack of felicity.

2.3
NONSYLLOGISTIC EPISTEMOLOGICAL DEPENDENCE

A second and more significant feature of this passage is Aquinas's mention of two instances in which one idea is founded upon another. The first we have just noted, namely, that the principle of noncontradiction is founded upon its constitutive concepts, being and nonbeing. The second is a dependence of all other principles upon this very first principle. Neither instance can involve deductive syllogistic dependence, since in both cases we are dealing with *per se nota* principles, which cannot be reached through syllogism. We have, here, that which we seek: nonsyllogistic epistemological dependence.

Aquinas explains neither case, but the first instance seems fairly straightforward. A proposition is founded upon its constitutive concepts.[16] This must be true of every proposition ever formed, in the same manner in which a house depends upon the bricks that make it up. In the case of *per se nota* propositions, however, the dependence involves more than material components. The *rationes* that make up a *per se nota* proposition not only provide the stuff out of which the proposition is made; they also provide the content by which the truth

---

15. McInerny (*Human Action*, 198–204) has an account of the relation of diverse formulations of the principle of noncontradiction.
16. In "Natural Lights," 286, Dewan notes the dependence of per se propositions upon their terms.

of the proposition is recognized. They are not merely like rocks that the builder must somehow fit together into a house; they are more like proteins, which are so structured as to have a perfect fit with other proteins. The proteins lock together automatically. Similarly, the *rationes* of an immediate proposition lock together by their very nature. The truth of the proposition, then, follows immediately upon the grasp of its terms.

> The truth and knowledge of indemonstrable principles depends upon the *ratio* of their terms, for given the knowledge of what a whole is and what a part is, the knowledge that a whole is greater than its part follows immediately.[17]

Aquinas's second case of dependence is less clear; indeed, it will remain unclear. It involves the dependence of one proposition upon another proposition. This dependence, however, is not syllogistic. We readily recognize that in some sense the proposition "A whole is greater than its part" is founded upon the principle of noncontradiction. If we could both affirm and deny, then a whole would be greater than and less than its part. Explaining the details of this nonsyllogistic dependence, however, might prove difficult. At this point we can say that some propositions depend upon other propositions, not by way of syllogism.

What is most striking about this case is that it calls into question the position of the new natural law theory. Aquinas says that all principles are founded upon the first principle. All principles would seem to include both speculative and practical principles. The very first principle, however, is speculative. Consequently, all practical principles depend upon a speculative truth. It is difficult to see how one can read question 94, article 2 and reach the conclusion that practical reason is independent of speculative reason.

As we have already suggested, the implicit argument from disjunction is probably operative. The new natural law theory grants that practical reason depends upon speculative reason. This dependence, however, is only material, or so the argument goes. It does not imply any serious dependence, in which the very form and structure of practical reason depends upon speculative reason.

---

17. I-II, 66, 5, ad 4. "Veritas et cognitio principiorum indemonstrabilium dependet ex ratione terminorum, cognito enim quid est totum et quid pars, statim cognoscitur quod omne totum est maius sua parte."

THE TEXT

Before we return to Aquinas's exposition we should note a third kind of nonsyllogistic epistemological dependence. One concept or *ratio* can depend upon another. The passage actually contains an instance of it, but Aquinas does not advert to it. Clearly, the *ratio* of nonbeing depends upon the *ratio* of being. In a similar manner, the *ratio* of an immaterial being (an angel) depends upon the *ratio* of a material being, and the *ratio* of a triangle depends upon the *ratio* of a line.

We have seen, then, three kinds of nonsyllogistic epistemological dependence. First, a proposition depends upon the *rationes* that make it up; most especially, a *per se nota* proposition depends upon these *rationes* not only for its material constituents, but also for the very link that reveals its truth. Second, one proposition can depend upon another proposition. How? That is far from clear. Third, one *ratio* can depend upon another *ratio*.

2.4
THE FIRST PRINCIPLE OF PRACTICAL REASON

2.4.1: The *Ratio* of the Good

Aquinas goes on to say,

> Just as being is that which first falls in all of our awareness, similarly the good is that which first falls in the awareness of practical reason, which is ordered to activity, for every agent acts on account of an end, and the end has the *ratio* of the good. Therefore, the first principle in practical reason is that which is founded upon [fundatur] the *ratio* of the good, namely, that the good is what all things desire. Consequently, this principle is the first precept of the law, namely, that good should be done and pursued and evil should be avoided.[18]

Once again, we find the first kind of nonsyllogistic epistemological dependence, for the first principle of practical reason depends upon its constitutive *ratio,* namely, the good.

---

18. "Sicut autem ens est primum quod cadit in apprehensione simpliciter, ita bonum est primum quod cadit in apprehensione practicae rationis, quae ordinatur ad opus, omne enim agens agit propter finem, qui habet rationem boni. Et ideo primum principium in ratione practica est quod fundatur supra rationem boni, quae est, bonum est quod omnia appetunt. Hoc est ergo primum praeceptum legis, quod bonum est faciendum et prosequendum, et malum vitandum."

THE TEXT

The *ratio* of the good deserves further consideration. Aquinas says that every agent acts for an end, and he defines the good as that which all things desire. His universal teleology is evident here. Aquinas does mean *every* agent, not just human agents, and not even just conscious agents. Even a tree or a rock acts for an end. Likewise, Aquinas does mean that *all agents* desire the good. In this case, "desire" must not be taken literally; it refers to any tendency or inclination, even the tendency of the tree to grow or to reproduce.[19]

When Aquinas says, then, that the good is that which all things desire, he does not mean there is some one thing that every creature whatsoever desires. Of course, in his conception there will be such a being, for all creatures ultimately desire God. The definition of the good, however, refers to the separate good of each creature. The good of the tree is what it desires; the good of a cat is what it desires; the human good is what human beings desire.

> When it is said that the good is that which all things desire, it should not be understood as if every good is desired by everything; rather, whatever is desired has the *ratio* of the good.[20]

The first *ratio* that falls in practical reason is the *human* good.[21] The good of a tree, or the good of a cat, is not an *operabile*. The knowledge of these goods is speculative. The first principle of practical reason does not recommend that we pursue these goods, even though they fall under the definition of the good as Aquinas gives it.

One last point is worth noting concerning the *ratio* of the good, namely, it seems to exhibit the third kind of nonsyllogistic dependence discussed above, in which one concept depends upon another. In this case, the *ratio* of the good seems to depend upon the *ratio* of desire.

2.4.2: The First Precept of the Law

Let us make two more points concerning the first principle of practical reason. First, after introducing it, Aquinas makes clear that it is also the

---

19. See Stephen L. Brock, "Natural Law, the Understanding of Principles, and Universal Good," *Nova et Vetera* (English Edition) 9 (2011): 671–706, at 685.
20. I, 6, 2, ad 2. "Cum dicitur bonum est quod omnia appetunt, non sic intelligitur quasi unumquodque bonum ab omnibus appetatur, sed quia quidquid appetitur, rationem boni habet."
21. See Grisez, "First Principle," 184.

THE TEXT

first precept of the law. In other words, Aquinas does not have some broad category of practical reason, under which the natural law falls as a particular instance. Rather, to reason practically is to reason according to the natural law.

Second, the relation within the terms of the first principle is unclear. In what manner is the predicate term included within the subject term, or vice versa? If "desire" is taken to be the same thing as "pursuit," then we might imagine that the immediate proposition Aquinas has in mind can be spelled out as follows: "The good [that is, that which is desired] ought to be pursued [that is, it ought to be desired]."

Then we have a move, says Ralph McInerny, something like "from 'Snow falls in winter' to 'snow ought to fall in winter.'"[22] In order to avoid such nonsense perhaps we wish to assert that "to pursue" does not mean the exact same thing as "to desire," at least insofar as desire enters the definition of the good. Perhaps, suggests McInerny, "desirable" better captures the definition of the good.

This difficulty reveals an oddity about basic concepts. Although we are dealing with *rationes* that are grasped by almost everyone, and although we are dealing with propositions that are immediately known, nevertheless spelling out the details of these *rationes* and of these propositions can be very difficult. Indeed, we might feel more comfortable speaking about the workings of a car engine than about the definition of the good. We can get a firm handle on the former, while the latter seems elusive.

Part of the difficulty is that these basic terms have been stretched and used in a variety of ways, so that they now have many related meanings in our language. Sorting out these meanings can be challenging. Another difficulty is that we like to break concepts into component parts, but the most basic concepts have no parts. When my young daughter asks me to define words, the most basic words can prove more challenging than the more complex. I can define a house as a place where people live, but defining "place" is more problematic.

---

22. Ralph McInerny, "Naturalism and Thomistic Ethics," *Thomist* 40 (1976): 222–42, at 238.

THE TEXT

2.5
TWO INFERENCES

Aquinas next says that all other precepts of the natural law are founded upon this first precept. Once again, some *per se nota* propositions depend upon another *per se nota* proposition. Once again, Aquinas provides no explanation of this dependence.

What Aquinas says in the next sentence has possibly received more attention, in the recent literature, than anything else in Aquinas's corpus. I will break the sentence into three parts.

The good has the *ratio* of an end while evil has the *ratio* of its contrary,

for which reason all those things to which man has a natural inclination reason naturally grasps as goods

and *consequently* as to be pursued through activity and their contraries as evil and to be avoided.[23]

The sentence expresses two inferential relations, indicated here in italics. The exact nature of these relationships has been the subject of much dispute.

2.5.1: The First Inference

The first inferential relation, which is indicated by the words "for which reason," is far from straightforward, at least as presented in the text. Does it indicate an epistemological dependence or an ontological dependence? What move is being made, from what starting point and to what ending point?

The Latin for "for which reason" is *inde est quod,* which might be translated literally as "from whence it is that." The "whence" refers back to the entire previous phrase: "The good has the *ratio* of an end while evil has the *ratio* of its contrary." (Which phrase, in the Latin, is actually introduced by the word "because" making the inferential relation even more evident.)

What follows from this introductory phrase? The entirety of the

---

23. "Quia vero bonum habet rationem finis, malum autem rationem contrarii, inde est quod omnia illa ad quae homo habet naturalem inclinationem, ratio naturaliter apprehendit ut bona, et per consequens ut opere prosequenda, et contraria eorum ut mala et vitanda."

next clause: "All those things to which man has a natural inclination reason naturally grasps as goods." If we pull out "reason naturally grasps," then we are left with the proposition that is grasped, namely, "All those things to which man has a natural inclination are good." Since reason naturally grasps something insofar as it is *per se nota*, the inference might be restated, "Because the good has the *ratio* of an end, therefore, 'X is good' is *per se nota*," where X refers to the object of a natural inclination.

The first inference, then, seems to be epistemological rather than ontological. The "because" and "for which reason" indicate the cause of our coming to know. The character of the good as an end causes a natural knowledge.[24] Or, more precisely, our grasp of the character of the good as an end causes our grasp of certain things as goods.

If "X is good" is *per se nota*, then the subject term, that is, X, must in some manner contain the predicate term, which is the *ratio* of the good. The only thing that Aquinas tells us about X, however, is that it is the object of a natural inclination. Plausibly, then, Aquinas wishes us to see a connection — a per se connection — between being the object of an inclination and the *ratio* of the good.

Previously, Aquinas defined the good in terms of desire [*appetere*]; he now speaks of inclinations [*inclinatio*]. Is something new being said? It would seem not. Aquinas often interchanges inclination and desire.[25] In this context, natural inclination means natural desire, or vice versa. The good, then, could be defined as that to which all are inclined.

The predicate term of the proposition "X is good," then, includes within it the notion of inclination. The subject term, namely, X, is certainly connected with inclinations, for it is the object of a natural inclination. Might this connection create the link needed for a *per se nota* proposition? By knowing X as the object of a natural inclination do we thereby know it as good? That would explain the inferential relation in this text. *Because* the good has the notion of the object of an inclination (an end), by recognizing something as the object of an inclination, we recognize it as good.

---

24. Gomez-Lobo ("Naturalism," 243) correctly notes that Aquinas is not claiming that the inclinations account for something being good. See also Douglas Flippen, "Natural Law and Natural Inclinations," *New Scholasticism* 60 (1986): 284–316, at 297–301.

25. For example, *Summa contra Gentiles*, IV, cap. 9, n. 3; I, 59, 1.

THE TEXT

Indeed, if natural inclinations did not somehow help us see the *per se nota* connection with the good, then it is perplexing why Aquinas would even mention them. He is trying to show us that on account of the *ratio* of the good we have some immediate knowledge. If a natural inclination does not help us to see this connection, then why mention it within the inference? It would prove to be only a distraction.

The link between natural inclinations and our grasp of the good is further indicated by what he says immediately after the two inferences: "Therefore, the order of the precepts of the natural law will follow the order of natural inclinations."[26] The inclinations do not follow the precepts; rather, the precepts follow the inclinations. Something about the inclinations, then, seems to determine the content of the precepts.

The epistemological dependence involved is a dependence of a proposition upon its component terms. More precisely, it is the dependence of a *per se nota* proposition upon its intimately linked terms. In order to see the inference, we must know both the terms, so that we can see how they are connected. Aquinas tells us only one thing about the subject term, namely, it is the object of a natural inclination. This information, then, must help us to see the link between the subject and predicate terms. Indeed, this minimal information concerning the subject term does seem to forge a link with the only information Aquinas provides concerning the predicate term, namely, that the good has the *ratio* of an end, that is, it is the object of an inclination.

In short, Aquinas seems to be telling us that our propositional grasp of certain goods depends upon the apprehension (nonpropositional, in the first act of reason) of natural inclinations.

2.5.2: The Second Inference

We are still discussing a single sentence. We have spent so much time discussing the first inferential relationship that we may have forgotten that this sentence contains a second as well. After noting our immediate knowledge of certain goods, Aquinas goes on to say, rather cryptically, that "*and consequently* [we know these things] as to be pursued through activity and their contraries as evil and to be avoided."

---

26. "Secundum igitur ordinem inclinationum naturalium, est ordo praeceptorum legis naturae."

THE TEXT

What leaps out from a casual reading of this text is a pseudosyllogism. Aquinas has provided all the propositions, and even introduces the pseudoconclusion with "and consequently." The syllogism reads as follows:

The good ought to be pursued (the first principle of practical reason)

The object of [this] inclination is good (reached in the first part of this sentence)

Consequently, the object of [this] inclination ought to be pursued.

Nothing seems more obvious than this reading of the text.[27] Yet it is impossible. The "conclusion" cannot be a conclusion of a syllogism. Aquinas told us at the beginning of the article that the first precepts of the natural law are *per se nota*; consequently, they cannot possibly be reached by way of syllogism. How all of these propositions can be immediately known is difficult to see, since a middle term (good) is ready at hand.

If the "consequently" does not indicate syllogistic inference, then what does it mean? Presumably, it must refer to a nonsyllogistic epistemological dependence, of which we have considered three possibilities. The endpoint of this inference seems to be another kind of natural knowledge. Aquinas has just said that on account of our awareness of the good we come naturally to know that the objects of certain inclinations are good. He now says, "and consequently, [these objects are] to be pursued." It seems plausible to fill in as follows: and consequently, *we naturally apprehend* that these objects are to be pursued. This added detail is all the more plausible since we know, from what Aquinas has said previously, that the first precepts are indeed naturally apprehended.

⊷ 2.6 ⊶
THE ORDER OF INCLINATIONS

Aquinas closes his discussion with a consideration of the order of inclinations and the consequent order of precepts. He begins, "Therefore, the order of the precepts of the natural law will follow the order of natural inclinations." The expectation generated is for a moral order.

---

27. Gomez-Lobo ("Naturalism," 243) gives this syllogism and then claims, inexplicably, that it is not a strict syllogism because the minor premise cannot be derived from the major.

THE TEXT

What else should we expect for an order of precepts of law? The order that he proceeds to give, however, gives no hint of being a moral order; in every respect, it seems to be logical.

He divides the natural inclinations into three categories: those shared by all creatures, those shared by all animals, and those peculiar to human beings. Those shared by all creatures have to do with the good of our existence and the preservation of our existence. Those shared by all animals have to do with mating and the education of offspring. Those peculiar to human beings include the inclination toward society with others and the inclination to know the truth about God.

This brief list is not meant to be exhaustive.[28] A cursory examination reveals other natural inclinations mentioned elsewhere by Aquinas, such as a desire to know the future, an inclination to be subject to those who are superior to us, and a natural inclination to set aside time for necessary things such as sleep and worship of God.[29]

What are we to make of Aquinas's threefold division? The new natural law theory suggests that the classification is merely logical or metaphysical and has no practical implications for ethics.[30] Others have suggested that the classification lays out a hierarchy of goods and that this hierarchy helps us to reach particular moral judgments.[31] Even if the division is only logical, it does not follow that the basic goods are incommensurable, as the new natural law theory claims. The text itself simply does not say. It does not say whether the division is meant to be a moral division; it does not say whether there might be some other moral hierarchy.

---

28. See Finnis, *Aquinas*, 83.

29. II-II, 95, 1, ad 3, II-II, 85, 1, and II-II, 122, 4, ad 1 respectively.

30. Finnis, *Aquinas*, 81; Kevin Staley, "Metaphysics and the Good Life: Some Reflections on the Further Point of Morality," *American Catholic Philosophical Quarterly* 65 (1991): 1–28. See also Kevin L. Flannery, *Acts amid Precepts: The Aristotelian Logical Structure of Thomas Aquinas's Moral Theory* (Washington, D.C.: The Catholic University of America Press, 2001), 84–108.

31. See Ernest L. Fortin, "The New Rights Theory and the Natural Law: Natural Law and Natural Rights by John Finnis," *Review of Politics* 44 (1982): 590–612, at 602–4; Long, "Looking-Glass," 273–81; Long, "Autonomous Practical Reason," 174–76; Steven A. Long, *The Teleological Grammar of the Moral Act* (Naples, Fla.: Sapientia Press, 2007), 4; McInerny, "Principles," 14–15; McInerny, *Human Action*, 120–21, 137; Rhonheimer, *Perspective of Morality*, 92.

THE TEXT

2.7
CONCLUSION

Our examination of question 94, article 2, has come to a close. We have raised questions rather than answered them, or, at the very least, any answers we provided were tentative. We have noted that Aquinas discusses two kinds of nonsyllogistic epistemological dependence, and that a third kind is not difficult to glean from the text. We have seen the skeletal suggestion of a step from natural inclinations to the good, and from there to "oughts." What remains is to examine these steps in detail. We will begin, therefore, by inquiring what Aquinas means by natural inclinations.

3

INCLINATIONS

3.1
THREE POSSIBILITIES

In the last chapter we saw that natural inclinations play a central role in Aquinas's argument. Unfortunately, it is far from clear what Aquinas means by a natural inclination. Three possibilities suggest themselves. First, he might be referring to inborn emotional desires, what Aquinas would call passions of the soul. We say, for instance, that we have a natural sexual drive or that we have a natural desire to preserve our own lives.

Second, Aquinas might be referring to natural desires of the will. Aquinas considers the will, like the passions, to be a conscious desiring power. When we are aware of some good, we may then consciously desire it.

Third, Aquinas might be referring to nonconscious inclinations. A tree, for instance, has an inclination to grow or to reproduce. Human beings have such inclinations as well. Quite apart from consciousness, for instance, our bodies will transform nutrients and use them for maintenance and energy.

In general, Aquinas distinguishes three different kinds of appetites, corresponding to the three kinds of inclinations we have mentioned.[1] In question 94, article 2, Aquinas might be referring to any of these inclinations or perhaps to all three. We will explain each in a little more detail, and then we will try to determine to which natural inclinations Aquinas refers.

Both the will and the emotions are conscious inclinations, that is, they follow upon some awareness of the good. Before we can have an emotional desire for pizza we must be aware of something good about

---

1. See I, 59, 1; I, 80, 1 and I-II, 26, 1.

INCLINATIONS

pizza, for instance, its taste. The same can be said for the will. The two powers, the passions (or emotions) and the will, differ in the kind of knowledge that gives rise to them.

The passions follow upon sense knowledge, that is, knowledge of particulars derived from sensation. In contrast, the will follows upon intellectual knowledge. Since with our intellect we get beyond particulars and come to know universals, the will desires things not just in their particularity; rather, it desires them as this or that particular good but precisely insofar as they are good.

While we readily speak of natural desires in the emotions, we are not so eager to attribute natural desires to the will.[2] Part of the difficulty, no doubt, is that in the modern world we are reluctant even to concede the existence of the will and its desires. But even those who acknowledge that we have a power of willing may deny natural desires. Why? Because the will is conceived as free. What is free is not necessitated, but what is natural is necessary. If the will has natural desires, then it will be necessitated and not free.

Aquinas rejects this reasoning. The will can be both necessitated by natural desires and free. Of course, the will cannot be both necessary and free with regard to the same thing at the same time. Nevertheless, the will can have some necessary desires. Indeed, it *must* have some necessary desires. According to Aquinas, the will clearly has at least one natural inclination, namely, the desire for happiness or the ultimate end. Aquinas also attributes other natural inclinations to the will.

Just as the intellectual principles of knowledge are naturally known, so the moving principle of voluntary actions must be something naturally willed, which is the good in common, toward which the will naturally tends, as does any potency toward its object. This moving principle is also the ultimate end, which relates to things that are desired just as the first principles of demonstrations relate to things that are known. In general, all those that belong to the will according to its nature are naturally willed, for with the will we desire not only those things that pertain properly to the power of the will; we also desire those things that pertain to individual powers and to the whole human being.

2. Authors who acknowledge the natural inclinations of the will include Finnis, "Deriving Ought," 45; Stephen L. Brock, "Natural Inclination and the Intelligibility of the Good in Thomistic Natural Law," *Vera Lex* 6 (2005): 57–78; Lawrence Dewan, "Jacques Maritain and the Philosophy of Cooperation," in *Altérité vivre ensemble différents: approches pluridisciplinaires,* ed. Michel Gourges et al. (Montréal: Editions Bellarmin, 1986).

INCLINATIONS

It follows that human beings naturally will not only the object of the will but also other things that are fitting to the other powers, for example, knowledge of the truth, which is fitting to the intellect, to be and to live, and other things of this sort, which refer to one's natural existence. All of these fall under the object of the will as certain particular goods.[3]

When Aquinas speaks of natural inclinations, then, he might mean inclinations or desires of the emotions or he might mean desires of the will. A third possibility is rarely acknowledged.[4] He might be referring to inclinations or desires of other powers, besides the emotions and the will, powers such as the intellect or the power to see.

In English, it is very odd to say that something without awareness desires or loves. We do not say that a rock desires to go down or that a tree desires to grow. Aquinas recognizes that he is stretching words, but he is quite willing to speak of a nonconscious desire or love. Even at the nonconscious level, he thinks, we find some tendency to reach an endpoint, which suffices for the term "desire." This teaching is the teleology so repugnant to the modern mind.

The presence of one of the three appetites or inclinations does

---

3. I-II, 10, 1 "Et hoc manifeste apparet in intellectu, nam principia intellectualis cognitionis sunt naturaliter nota. Similiter etiam principium motuum voluntariorum oportet esse aliquid naturaliter volitum. Hoc autem est bonum in communi, in quod voluntas naturaliter tendit, sicut etiam quaelibet potentia in suum obiectum, et etiam ipse finis ultimus, qui hoc modo se habet in appetibilibus, sicut prima principia demonstrationum in intelligibilibus, et universaliter omnia illa quae conveniunt volenti secundum suam naturam. Non enim per voluntatem appetimus solum ea quae pertinent ad potentiam voluntatis; sed etiam ea quae pertinent ad singulas potentias, et ad totum hominem. Unde naturaliter homo vult non solum obiectum voluntatis, sed etiam alia quae conveniunt aliis potentiis, ut cognitionem veri, quae convenit intellectui; et esse et vivere et alia huiusmodi, quae respiciunt consistentiam naturalem; quae omnia comprehenduntur sub obiecto voluntatis, sicut quadam particularia bona." See also *De virtutibus*, 1, 5, ad 2.

4. Robert B. Ashmore ("Aquinas and Ethical Naturalism," *New Scholasticism* 49 [1975]: 76–86, at 77–78) seems to conceive only of conscious inclinations. See also Errol Harris, "Natural Law and Naturalism," *International Philosophical Quarterly* 23 (1983): 115–24, at 117–19. Finnis (*Aquinas*, 92–93) does acknowledge all three possibilities, although earlier, in *Natural Law* (64–69) he seems to have in mind only conscious inclinations of some sort or other; he refers to psychological states and to "urges." Grisez et al. ("Practical Principles," 108–9) acknowledge all three kinds of natural inclinations. Rhonheimer ("Practical Reason and the 'Naturally Rational': On the Doctrine of the Natural Law as a Principle of Praxis in Thomas Aquinas," in *The Perspective of the Acting Person: Essays in the Renewal of Thomistic Moral Philosophy* [Washington, D.C.: The Catholic University of America Press, 2008], 115) seems concerned with inclinations that are formed by reason; consequently, they must be conscious inclinations.

INCLINATIONS

not exclude the others. Human beings have the rational appetite of the will; at the same time, they have the sensitive appetite of the emotions. So also do human beings have nonconscious appetites, among which are included powers such as the intellect (with the intellect, we ourselves are conscious, but the intellect itself is a power that tends — without a conscious tendency — toward knowledge). Aquinas says, for instance, "It belongs to any power of the soul to desire its own good by a natural desire that does not follow awareness."[5] Elsewhere, he says,

> To desire with an animal appetite pertains only to the concupiscible power, but to desire with a natural desire pertains to any potency, for any potency of the soul is a certain nature and is naturally inclined toward something.[6]

The individual powers desire a determinate good.[7]

In question 94, article 2, then, Aquinas might very well be referring to all three of these natural inclinations. Unfortunately, the article itself provides little evidence one way or the other. A case can be made for each of the three, but each case is problematic. We will consider the arguments for each, beginning with the emotions, moving onto nonconscious inclinations, and concluding with the will.

3.2
THE EMOTIONS

3.2.1: Sexual Desire

Without argument many commentators seem to presume that the natural inclinations are natural emotional desires.[8] Someone might presume,

---

5. I-II, 30, 1, ad 3 "Unicuique potentiae animae competit appetere proprium bonum appetitu naturali, qui non sequitur apprehensionem."

6. *De veritate*, 25, 2, ad 8 (Leonine ed., v. 22, 734, 237–42). "Quod concupiscere appetitu animali ad solam concupiscibilem pertinent, sed concupiscere appetitu naturali pertinet ad quamlibet potentiam; nam quaelibet potentia animae natura quaedam est et naturaliter in aliquid inclinatur." See also I, 80, 1, ad 3.

7. *De veritate*, 22, 3, ad 5 (Leonine ed., v. 22, 619, 144–45). "Singulae potentiae appetunt bonum determinatum."

8. See Grisez ("First Principle," 180), who speaks of inclinations that we feel; see also Matava ("Moral Realism," 323), who excludes acts of will but refers to acts of appetites. See also Lee, "Naturalist," 572; Nicholas E. Lombardo, *The Logic of Desire: Aquinas on Emotion* (Washington, D.C.: The Catholic University of America Press, 2011), 114–17; R. Mary Hayden, "Natural Inclinations and Moral Absolutes: A Mediated Correspondence for Aquinas," *Proceedings of the American Catholic Philosophical Association* 64 (1990): 130–50, at 133–35.

INCLINATIONS

for instance, that the second category of inclinations listed by Aquinas — those shared with the animals and having to do with the reproduction of offspring — are emotional sexual desires. Aquinas, however, may have something else in mind, perhaps the inclinations of the will or perhaps the nonconscious inclinations. We, like the animals, have a power of reproduction, which is a kind of inclination toward the continuation of the species.

Aquinas does say that this second class of inclinations concerns what nature *teaches* all animals, implying a kind of knowledge. Obviously, however, this knowledge must be minimal in animals, especially in lower animals such as worms or insects. They do not have any ideas of "male" or "female." Nor do they have any idea of rearing their offspring, or even of their offspring reaching maturity.

In the following text, however, Aquinas indicates that for animals the real good involved here, namely, the continuation of the species, is aimed at only by a nonconscious inclination. Furthermore, he says that intellectual substances desire continued existence from their intellectual knowledge, which would imply a desire of the will. In either event, the desire for the continuation of the species is not an emotional desire.

> Those that do not have the power to maintain their individual existence forever, but only the power to perpetually preserve their existence according to the species, also naturally desire this perpetuation. In those things that have knowledge, however, a distinction may be made regarding this desire. Those that know existence only in the present desire to exist only at the present moment; they do not desire to exist forever, because they do not understand perpetual existence. Nevertheless, they desire the species to be perpetuated, but they do so without knowledge, for the power of generation, which is ordered to this end, is prior to knowledge and not subject to it. Those things that know and understand perpetual existence desire it with a natural desire. This applies to all intellectual substances.[9]

---

9. *Summa contra Gentiles*, II, cap. 55, n. 13 (Leonine ed., v. 13, 395). "Quorum autem principia non habent ad hoc virtutem, sed solum ad conservandum esse perpetuum secundum idem specie, etiam sic naturaliter appetunt perpetuitatem. Hanc igitur differentiam oportet et in his inveniri quibus desiderium essendi cum cognitione inest: ut scilicet illa quae non cognoscunt esse nisi ut nunc, desiderant esse ut nunc; non autem semper, quia esse sempiternum non apprehendunt. Desiderant tamen esse perpetuum speciei: tamen absque cognitione; quia virtus generativa, quae ad hoc deservit, praeambula est, et non subiacens cognitioni. Illa igitur quae ipsum esse perpetuum cognoscunt et apprehendunt, desiderant ipsum naturali desiderio. Hoc autem convenit omnibus substantiis intelligentibus."

INCLINATIONS

The desire to perpetuate the species is located, says Aquinas, in the power of generation and not in the power of the emotions; only the latter power has conscious inclinations, so Aquinas insists that the desire to perpetuate the species is without knowledge.

3.2.2: The Reply to the Second Objection

The inclusion of emotions among the natural inclinations seems to receive direct support from the reply to the second objection; as we will see, however, the reply actually provides support for all three kinds of inclinations. The objection is trying to argue that there is only one precept of the natural law rather than many precepts. It argues that the precepts can either be taken from human nature as a whole — in which case there will be only one precept, since there is one nature — or they can be taken from the parts of human nature, in which case there will be many precepts. But then, the objection continues, the natural law might relate even to the inclinations of the concupiscible emotions.

How is this an objection to multiple precepts? It is a reductio ad absurdum. Who could possibly hold that the natural law would involve the inclinations of the emotions? After all, are they not often lawless?[10] Are they not disordered as a result of original sin?[11]

Aquinas could have conceded the point. He could have replied by excluding emotions from the list of possible inclinations. But he did not. Rather, he says,

> All the inclinations of any part of human nature, for example, the concupiscible and irascible powers, pertain to the natural law insofar as they are ruled by reason, and they are reduced to the one first precept, as was said. In this manner, there are many precepts of the natural law in themselves, which nevertheless share in a single foundation.[12]

While this response appears to provide strong direct support in favor of the desires of the emotions, the appearance will prove deceptive.

---

10. See I-II, 91, 6.

11. Aquinas himself describes certain natural desires of the emotions as evil. See, for instance, *De malo*, 16, 2; *De veritate*, 25, 5, ad 8; *Sent.*, II, 39, 2, 2.

12. I-II, 94, 2, ad 2 "Omnes inclinationes quarumcumque partium humanae naturae, puta concupiscibilis et irascibilis, secundum quod regulantur ratione, pertinent ad legem naturalem, et reducuntur ad unum primum praeceptum, ut dictum est. Et secundum hoc, sunt multa praecepta legis naturae in seipsis, quae tamen communicant in una radice."

INCLINATIONS

The text does, however, provide indirect support for all of the different kinds of inclinations, for Aquinas seems to presume that the inclinations of all of the parts of human nature — including the will, the intellect, the power of reproduction, and so on — pertain to the natural law just so long as they are measured by reason.

3.2.3: Disordered Emotions

If the emotions seem to receive some direct support from the text, they are also undeniably problematic. The case against the emotions is precisely the case presumed by the objection just discussed, namely, the emotions are disordered. As such, how could they be central to the moral or natural law? Aquinas clearly states that the emotions are often directed toward evil. He even says that they have a *natural* inclination to evil, although he is probably using "natural" loosely.

> If anything has a natural inclination to what is simply speaking evil, it must be composed of two natures, of which the lower has an inclination to some particular good fitting to this lower nature but repugnant to the higher nature, from which the good of the whole should be judged. In human beings, for instance, there is a natural inclination to that which is fitting to the bodily senses against the good of reason.[13]

> Sensuality names these powers [the passions] insofar as they have a natural inclination of the sensitive part, which inclination is in opposition to reason and does not participate in reason.[14]

Emotional desires, then, cannot provide the basis for the natural law, apart from reason; they cannot provide the content for reason.[15] Rather, they themselves must be measured by reason, as Aquinas ex-

---

13. *De malo*, 16, 2 (Leonine ed., v. 23, 288, 230–38). "Vnde relinquitur quod cuicumque inest naturalis inclinatio ad malum simpliciter, quod hoc sit compositum ex duabus naturis, quarum inferior habeat inclinationem ad bonum aliquod particulare conueniens inferiori nature et repugnans nature superiori secundum quam attenditur bonum simpliciter, sicut in homine est inclinatio naturalis ad id quod est conueniens carnali sensui contra bonum rationis."

14. *De veritate*, 25, 5, ad 8 (Leonine ed., v. 22, 740, 168–71). "Sensualitas nominat has vires quantum ad inclinationem naturalem sensui, quae est in contrarium rationi, et non secundum quod participant rationem."

15. Nevertheless, Lombardo (*Logic of Desire*, 233) thinks that disordered desires can provide a legitimate, if incomplete, basis for determining how we should live.

INCLINATIONS

plicitly says. At most, then, these desires could be a kind of material shaped by the natural law, but not something, of themselves, belonging to the natural law.

3.2.4: Emotions: Actions versus Powers

The reply to the second objection, seemingly so forthright in asserting emotional desires as pertaining to the natural law, may mean something different. Aquinas may not be referring to the conscious desires of the emotions; rather, he may be referring to the inclination of the powers of the emotions.

As we have already seen, each power has a nonconscious inclination. Nevertheless, the distinction between the desires of the emotions and the inclination of the power of the emotions is far from perspicuous. When Aquinas speaks about parts of human nature, he usually refers to the body and the soul; derivatively, the parts of these are also parts of human nature, so that a hand and a foot are part of human nature, since these are parts of the body.[16] The parts of the soul are also parts of human nature. These include the powers of the soul, such as the intellect, the will, the power to reproduce, and the emotions. As powers, each of these has an inclination, a point that Aquinas applies to the concupiscible and irascible powers in the following text. "In any power of the soul there is a desire for its own good, for example, the irascible power desires victory and the concupiscible power desires pleasure."[17]

While each of the powers of the soul has a certain inclination, the acts of these powers are not properly called inclinations. The power of sight has an inclination to see, but the act of seeing is not itself called an inclination. The exception to this rule is the appetitive powers, namely, the emotions and the will. The acts of the will are themselves certain kinds of inclinations, and so too are the acts of the emotions.

It turns out, then, that the will both has a certain inclination, insofar as it is a power of soul, and has acts that are inclinations. The will is

---

16. See, for instance, *Sent.*, III, 21, 2, 1; I, 90, 4; I, 91, 4, ad 3; III, 19, 2; *Quodlibet* IX, 2, 1.
17. *De virtutibus*, 1, 4, ad 10 (Mandonnet, 224). "Nam in qualibet potentia animae est desiderium boni proprii; unde et irascibilis appetit victoriam, sicut et concupiscibilis delectationem. Sed quia concupiscibilis fertur in id quod est bonum toti animali simpliciter sive absolute; ideo omne desiderium boni appropriatur sibi." See also *Sent.*, III, 26, 1, 2, ad 3; I-II, 41, 3; *De veritate*, 25, 5, ad 8.

INCLINATIONS

a certain inclination to goodness itself, and the acts of the will are acts inclining to goodness itself.[18] Similarly, the concupiscible and irascible passions are powers and as such they have a certain inclination, but their activities are also inclinations.

When Aquinas says, then, "All the inclinations of any part of human nature, for example, the concupiscible and irascible powers, pertain to the natural law insofar as they are ruled by reason," his meaning is ambiguous. The parts of human nature seem to be largely the powers of the soul, each of which has an inclination belonging to it. Only the passions and the will also have further inclinations, which are the acts of the power. Furthermore, only these latter inclinations are conscious inclinations. The will itself, as a power of the soul, is also a kind of inclination, but not a conscious inclination. The acts of the will are conscious inclinations, but the will itself is a power with a nonconscious order to certain acts and certain ends.

When he refers to the concupiscible and irascible powers, then, Thomas might mean one of two things. First, the natural inclinations that pertain to the natural law might be the inclination that belongs to the power of the passions. Second, these natural inclinations might be the very activity of desiring, that is, the activities of the powers, which are also inclinations.

The reply to the second objection, then, is not a conclusive argument in favor of the emotions as pertaining to the natural law, *if* by emotion one means the act of desiring, which is what is typically meant. That is only one reading of the text, and perhaps the more doubtful reading, since the acts of the emotional desires (as opposed to the powers themselves) are often disordered.

3.3

NONCONSCIOUS INCLINATIONS

The reply to the second objection, examined above in relation to the emotions, strongly supports the conclusion that Aquinas had in mind at least some nonconscious inclinations. In that text Aquinas speaks about the inclinations of all of the parts of human nature. The parts of human

---

18. See Robert P. Sullivan, "Natural Necessitation of the Human Will," *Thomist* 14 (1951): 351–99, 490–528, at 490–528.

INCLINATIONS

nature include not just the passions; they include all of the other powers, such as the intellect or the power to reproduce. As we have seen, however, the inclinations belonging to these powers are nonconscious inclinations.

Another text also provides strong support for this conclusion. In question 94, article 4, Aquinas is trying to show that the natural law is the same for all men. The third objection argues as follows:

> To the law of nature pertains that to which man is inclined according to his nature, as has been said. But diverse men are naturally inclined to diverse things, some to the desire for pleasure, others to honors, and yet others to other things. Therefore, there is not one natural law for all men.[19]

The objector seems to have in mind conscious desires, either of the emotions or of the will. He may have in mind, however, the natural disposition toward these desires. In his reply, Aquinas once again insists that these inclinations, if they belong to the natural law, must be ordered according to reason.

> Since a man's reason rules and commands the other powers, so every natural inclination belonging to the other powers must be ordered according to reason, so that the same thing is right for all men in common, namely, that all their inclinations be directed by reason.[20]

For our present concern, what matters is Aquinas's reference to "other powers" besides reason. Reason commands other powers and other powers must be ordered according to reason. Which powers? No restrictions are given. Not just the inclinations of the emotions and of the will, it seems, but the inclinations of "other powers" generally must be ordered by reason.

What powers does reason command? Aquinas says that it commands the will and the sense powers, as well as all those things moved by the sense powers.[21] That includes the will and the passions most

---

19. I-II, 94, 4 arg. 3. "Ad legem naturae pertinet id ad quod homo secundum naturam suam inclinatur, ut supra dictum est. Sed diversi homines naturaliter ad diversa inclinantur, alii quidem ad concupiscentiam voluptatum, alii ad desideria honorum, alii ad alia. Ergo non est una lex naturalis apud omnes."

20. I-II, 94, 4, ad 3. "Sicut ratio in homine dominatur et imperat aliis potentiis, ita oportet quod omnes inclinationes naturales ad alias potentias pertinentes ordinentur secundum rationem. Unde hoc est apud omnes communiter rectum, ut secundum rationem dirigantur omnes hominum inclinationes."

21. I-II, 17, 5–9.

prominently; it also includes the sensitive knowing powers, such as imagination or memory; it includes the activities of the body that fall under voluntary motor control.[22]

Aquinas says that it does not include vegetative powers, such as taking in nutrients or growing, that is, we cannot command ourselves to start or stop growing.[23] Nevertheless, even here we have a measure of control, since we can choose to eat well or to eat poorly. Similarly, we can choose to engage or not to engage our power of reproduction, and we can direct it to this or that object, for instance, we can direct the power of reproduction to another human being or — in the case of bestiality — to an animal. A similar account holds for the external senses. If our eyes are open we cannot command ourselves to see or not to see, to see well or to see poorly, but we can command the movement of our eyes, thereby engaging and directing our power of seeing.

If the powers of the soul pertain to the natural law insofar as they are directed by reason, then clearly several powers are implicated. The will and the passions first of all, but many others besides, at least insofar as we can choose to engage them and direct them upon some object. The idea seems to be that if natural law commands us to pursue various goods, and if those goods are associated with the inclinations of various potencies, then our pursuit implies some control over those potencies. Natural law does not command us to start or stop growing, since that power does not fall under our control. It might, however, command us to eat, insofar as eating can engage the power to grow.

3.4

THE WILL

3.4.1: The Reply to the Second Objection, Yet Again

Both Stephen Brock and Lawrence Dewan argue that the natural inclinations discussed in question 94, article 2, are all inclinations of the will.[24]

---

22. See *De malo* 7, 6.
23. I-II, 17, 8.
24. See Dewan, "Philosophy of Cooperation"; Brock, "Natural Inclination"; Brock, "Natural Law," 679–80.

INCLINATIONS

What do these authors do with the texts that we have been examining? In fact, they find the texts in no way problematic. To the contrary, these texts are used by both Brock and Dewan in defense of their position.[25] How so?

Brock and Dewan actually make two claims. They chiefly wish to argue that the inclinations are not prerational; they are not, for instance, irrational inclinations of the emotions. Within their argument, the will enters only as a conclusion from this primary point: if the inclinations are rational, then they must be inclinations of the will, for the rational inclination is the will. Indeed, does not Aquinas say that the natural inclination of the intellectual nature is found in the will?

> It is common to all natures to have an inclination that is a natural desire or love, but this inclination is found in different ways in different natures, in each thing according to its own manner. Consequently, in the intellectual nature is found a natural inclination according to the will.[26]

Dewan correctly notes that the inclination of the whole intellectual nature is the will. We have seen, however, that human beings nevertheless have many inclinations besides those of the will, some of which are aptly described as natural inclinations. Must all of these be described as prerational? The reply to the second objection – as well as the parallel text two articles later – might well refer to the inclinations that belong to various powers, including the powers of the emotions. In that case, these inclinations would pertain to the natural law insofar as they are directed to a good understood by reason, and then some inclinations beyond the will would belong to the natural law.

These two texts, then, provide support for one aspect of the view of Brock and Dewan, namely, that the inclinations belong to the natural law through the intervention of reason. At the same time, the texts suggest evidence against another aspect of their view, namely, that the inclinations are all inclinations of the will.

---

25. See Brock, "Natural Inclination," 62; Dewan, "Natural Lights," 292, 27.
26. I, 60, 1. "Est autem hoc commune omni naturae, ut habeat aliquam inclinationem, quae est appetitus naturalis vel amor. Quae tamen inclinatio diversimode invenitur in diversis naturis, in unaquaque secundum modum eius. Unde in natura intellectuali invenitur inclinatio naturalis secundum voluntatem." Cited by Dewan in "Philosophy of Cooperation," 112; Dewan, "Natural Lights," 292, n. 27.

INCLINATIONS

3.4.2: Supporting Evidence

Despite the difficulties posed by these two texts, the position of Brock and Dewan receives indirect support.[27] While Aquinas never says that the natural inclinations associated with the natural law belong only to the will, he does speak, in certain places, as if he has no other inclinations in mind. For instance, when he discusses how rational creatures participate in the eternal law by way of inclination, he says,

> Every rational creature has a natural inclination to that which is in conformity with the eternal law, for we are innately disposed to virtue. This participation is imperfect — and in some manner corrupt — in those who are evil, in whom the natural inclination to virtue is perverted through a vicious habit.[28]

The natural inclination to virtue, which is possibly Aquinas's most frequent usage of the term "natural inclination," seems to be something of the will. Certainly, the nonconscious inclinations of various powers cannot be perverted through a vicious habit. At the very least, then, the inclinations associated with the natural law must include some inclinations of the will.

These inclinations, however, may not be conscious inclinations. Recall that every power has its own natural inclination, so that the passions have a natural inclination insofar as they are powers, and they also have conscious acts that are inclinations. Similarly, the acts of the will are inclinations, but the power of the will itself also has a nonconscious inclination. The natural inclination to virtue may well be this nonconscious inclination. When Aquinas speaks of it being diminished, he means simply that an obstacle is put in the way of it coming to act. What obstacle? The opposite disposition toward evil, namely, a habit toward sin.[29] For this reason, Aquinas claims that the natural inclination toward virtue remains even in those in hell, although it is never realized in act.[30]

---

27. For this sort of argument see Brock, "Natural Inclination," 63–64.
28. I-II, 93, 6. "Unicuique rationali creaturae inest naturalis inclinatio ad id quod est consonum legi aeternae; sumus enim innati ad habendum virtutes, ut dicitur in II Ethic. Uterque tamen modus imperfectus quidem est, et quodammodo corruptus, in malis; in quibus et inclinatio naturalis ad virtutem depravatur per habitum vitiosum."
29. See I-II, 85, 1 and 2.
30. *Sent.*, II, 39, 3, 1, ad 5; I-II, 85, 2, ad 3.

INCLINATIONS

~ 3.5 ~

A BRIEF SUMMARY OF THE CASE

We have seen that when Aquinas speaks of natural inclinations in question 94, article 2, three possibilities emerge. He might be speaking of conscious inclinations of the emotions, conscious inclinations of the will, or nonconscious inclinations of the various powers of the soul and of the soul itself. The text itself provides few clues, but a reply to an objection speaks about the inclinations of all the parts of human nature, indicating a multiplicity. Two articles later Aquinas speaks about the inclinations of the other powers besides reason. What, then, are we to conclude?

The conscious inclinations of the emotions are themselves often disordered and could not possibly belong to the natural law unless they themselves were already guided by reason, as would follow from one reading of Aquinas's reply to the second objection. Prerational conscious emotions, then, do not seem to be what Aquinas has in mind. Did he have in mind, then, rational conscious emotions?

Not necessarily. Aquinas may not be speaking of the conscious desires of the emotions. Instead, he may be speaking of the inclination that belongs to the power of the emotions, for all powers, even the passions and the will, have a certain nonconscious inclination belonging to them. Only these two powers also have further inclinations in their very actions, for their actions are also inclinations; in contrast, the acts of the intellect or of the power of seeing are not inclinations. When Aquinas says that the inclinations of the parts of human nature must be measured by reason, he may be referring to the inclination belonging to the power of the passions, not to the inclinations that are further actions of the passions themselves.

What of nonconscious inclinations? Does Aquinas mean to include the inclinations that belong to the various powers of the soul and to the soul itself? It seems likely. Aquinas speaks in a blanket manner about the inclinations of all of the parts of human nature and about the inclinations of the other powers beyond reason.

Still, it must be acknowledged that the texts are inconclusive. We must, then, leave the question open-ended for the time being. Perhaps a deeper understanding of the good will help to determine the precise

INCLINATIONS

nature of the inclinations associated with this good. Before we proceed to discuss the good in detail, however, we should consider what role the inclinations might play in the big picture of our knowledge of the natural law. What alternatives have been presented?

3.6
THE CLASSICAL PICTURE

In what might be called the classical picture, we begin with God, who has a plan for his creation.[31] He then institutes this plan, in the creative act, through the various inclinations that he gives to creatures.

> Every inclination of anything, whether natural or voluntary, is nothing other than a certain impression from the first mover, just as the inclination of an arrow to a target is nothing other than an impression from the archer. Consequently, all those things that act, either naturally or voluntarily, move to that to which they are divinely ordered as if from their own impetus. Therefore, God is said to order all things sweetly.[32]

Aquinas calls these impressed inclinations a participation in law:

> Since law is a certain rule and measure it can be in something in two ways. In one way, as in the one measuring and ruling, which is proper to reason, so that in this way law is only in reason. In another way, as in the one measured and ruled, and in this way the law is in all those things that are inclined toward something on account of the law, so that any inclination coming from some law can be called a law, not essentially but by way of participation.[33]

In this case, the inclinations found in creatures are a participation in the eternal law, the law in the mind of God expressing his plan for creation.

---

31. For an example of this view, see Long, "Autonomous Practical Reason"; Fulvio Di Blasi, *God and the Natural Law: A Rereading of Thomas Aquinas* (South Bend, Ind.: St. Augustine's Press, 2006).

32. I, 103, 8. "Omnis inclinatio alicuius rei vel naturalis vel voluntaria, nihil est aliud quam quaedam impressio a primo movente, sicut inclinatio sagittae ad signum determinatum, nihil aliud est quam quaedam impressio a sagittante. Unde omnia quae agunt vel naturaliter vel voluntarie, quasi propria sponte perveniunt in id ad quod divinitus ordinantur. Et ideo dicitur Deus omnia disponere suaviter."

33. I-II, 90, 1, ad 1. "Cum lex sit regula quaedam et mensura, dicitur dupliciter esse in aliquo. Uno modo, sicut in mensurante et regulante. Et quia hoc est proprium rationis, ideo per hunc modum lex est in ratione sola. Alio modo, sicut in regulato et mensurato. Et sic lex est in omnibus quae inclinantur in aliquid ex aliqua lege, ita quod quaelibet inclinatio proveniens ex aliqua lege, potest dici lex, non essentialiter, sed quasi participative."

INCLINATIONS

Since everything subject to divine providence is ruled and measured by the eternal law, it is plain that all things share in some manner in the eternal law, namely, insofar as from its impression they have inclinations toward their proper acts and ends.[34]

Human beings, like every other creature, have their own natural inclinations, which we have been considering in this chapter.

Up to this point, all parties of the dispute are in agreement. The disagreement concerns the role of these inclinations in our knowledge of the natural law. According to what might be called the classical view, we know these natural inclinations in us, which knowledge is purely speculative, and we thereby come to know the eternal law, so that our knowledge is a kind of participation in the eternal law.

In general, we come to know the things of God through his effects; in this case, we know the divine will through the effects of the natural inclinations he has implanted in creatures, especially the inclinations found within ourselves.[35] Elsewhere, Aquinas affirms that we know the will of God by natural inclinations:

> What is willed by God, with respect to his antecedent will, is known to us from natural inclinations, but what he wills with the consequent will is made known to us through revelation or through activities.[36]

---

34. I-II, 91, 2. "Unde cum omnia quae divinae providentiae subduntur, a lege aeterna regulentur et mensurentur, ut ex dictis patet; manifestum est quod omnia participant aliqualiter legem aeternam, inquantum scilicet ex impressione eius habent inclinationes in proprios actus et fines." The eternal law should not be confused with the revealed laws of the Old and New Testament, not all of which can be known through natural reason. The eternal law is the plan of God, as it exists in his own mind, whether or not he chooses to reveal it.

35. Aquinas refers to this sort of reasoning — from effects back to God, their cause — when he replies to an objection claiming that the eternal law cannot be known, since we cannot know what is in God. He replies that the things of God are known to us through their effects. See I-II, 93, 2, ad 1.

36. *Sent.,* I, 48, 1, 4, ad 1 (Madonnet, v. 1, 1090). "Volitum divinum, quantum ad voluntatem antecedentem, est nobis notum ex ipsa naturali inclinatione; sed volitum voluntatis consequentis innotescit nobis vel per revelationem vel per operationem." Finnis's claim (*Natural Law,* 48–49, 404), then, that according to Aquinas (Finnis cites I, 46, 2), "The will of God, so far as it concerns creatures (such as mankind), cannot be discovered by reasoning," is false with regard to the antecedent will. We can also know the conditional will of God; given that God has chosen to create a certain nature, he must will what belongs to that nature, for example, if he makes a rational nature, then he must make it with reason and will. Consequently, by knowing what belongs to a nature created by God, such as our own, we can know God's will; by knowing our natural inclinations, which belong to

INCLINATIONS

In summary, then, God has a plan, called the eternal law, which he impresses upon creatures by way of natural inclinations. Human beings become aware of this plan through its effects, which are the natural inclinations. Humans become aware of the plan as it applies to themselves through their own natural inclinations. This knowledge is called the natural law.

On this view, the epistemological dependence moves from knowledge of the inclinations, which is a kind of speculative knowledge, to knowledge of human goods, which is materially practical, and finally to knowledge of what ought to be done, which is virtually practical. We first know natural inclinations and we thereby know what ought to be done.

Not all agree with this account, however. The new natural law theory denies this epistemological dependence, claiming that knowledge of the good and of what ought to be done depends upon no prior knowledge, especially not speculative knowledge. If the classical view is to make its case, then, it must give an account of how we come to know the good through natural inclinations, to which topic we now turn our attention.

---

our very nature, we can know the will of God. In some sense, of course, Finnis is correct. We cannot know, for instance, what God wills in the future. Nor can we know the details of what God wills in any concrete instance. After the fact, for instance, we can know that God has willed that the sun rise, but we cannot know all that he seeks to accomplish in this effect.

4
GOOD

In this chapter, we hope to take our first step from the realm of purely speculative knowledge into practical knowledge. From knowledge of natural inclinations we hope to arrive at the materially practical knowledge of the good. The greatest obstacle to this step is a false conception of practical reason. In chapter 1, we saw that Peter Geach proposed descriptivism in opposition to prescriptivism. The latter view claims that the term "good" — and therefore practical knowledge — does not describe any attribute in the good object; rather, the speaker uses it to express his attitude toward the object. In contrast, Geach claims that the word "good" is descriptive. Like the word "yellow," it describes some feature of the object.

If speculative knowledge and practical knowledge both describe the world, then the step from one to the other seems a small matter. It is just a question of what feature in the world is being described. Such seems to be Aquinas's conception of materially practical knowledge; it differs from speculative knowledge only in what object happens to be focused upon. But if speculative knowledge and practical knowledge have entirely different relations to the world, such that speculative knowledge describes the world but practical knowledge is an expression of the agent, then the step from one to the other seems rather large.

Consequently, we must first consider descriptivism. If the term "good" describes something about the world, then what exactly is it picking out? It is certainly not so straightforward as the term "yellow." Defending descriptivism is only the first step. Once it is granted that "good" describes the world, it is still not clear how we move from speculative knowledge of things like inclinations to materially practical knowledge of the good. In the final two sections of this chapter, therefore, we will examine this intellectual move from speculative to practical knowledge.

GOOD

4.1

DESCRIPTIVISM

4.1.1: Artifacts

Peter Geach has argued that "good" is a descriptive term.[1] It describes the way things are. Obviously, however, it does not pick out some simple attribute like the color red. While the color red is the same in a knife or in a hammer, what is good for a knife may not be good for a hammer. Still, Geach claims, something common can be found between diverse uses of "good": a good knife and a good hammer are both complete in their kind.

The point is more evident with artifacts. A good knife and a good hammer have quite diverse attributes. The good knife must be sharp; the good hammer must be heavy and blunt. Nevertheless, something the same is meant by calling both of them good, for both are good insofar as they are complete. A dull knife lacks something of its completion. A sharp hammer would be incomplete in its ability to pound. Similarly, the completion of the lens of an eye requires that it be transparent; the completion of the lid of an eye requires that it be opaque.

This notion of completion depends upon the idea of function. Because the function of the knife is to cut, it is completed by being sharp, through which it cuts well; because the function of the hammer is to pound, it is completed through that by which it pounds well. The various attributes by which something is complete differ. For one thing, the attribute of being sharp makes it complete; for another, the attribute of being dull makes it complete. In either event, completion is whatever helps to realize the function or purpose.

To describe a knife or a hammer as good, then, is to describe something about it. The function included within this description appears to be built into our idea of many artifacts.[2] A chair, for instance, is for sitting upon. Although the word "chair" picks out a family resemblance of diverse objects, the purpose of sitting seems hard to separate from the notion of a chair. Is an old tree stump a chair, since it can be

---

1. See Geach, "Good and Evil."
2. Foot ("Moral Beliefs," 216) speaks of functional words or terms that are defined with a function built into them.

GOOD

used for sitting? No, for it was not made with the purpose of sitting, unless someone cut the tree stump for that purpose, in which case we might begrudgingly call it a chair.

"Good chair" describes a real state of affairs in the world. It describes a certain thing with a certain function, and it describes this thing insofar as fulfilling or completing that function. The function is itself a kind of direction or movement of the thing to some goal or end. It is fulfilled or completed if the end is achieved or realized.[3]

The purposes of artifacts do not originally belong to the artifacts. We make a knife in order to cut, but the purpose of cutting is not some attribute that we can find in the knife; the purpose is in us. When we describe something as a knife, then, we are not just describing its attributes; in part, we are describing the purpose we have for these attributes.

Ultimately, however, we ascribe the purpose to the artifact as if the purpose belongs to it; only as such do we describe the artifact as good. If someone happened to find a sharp rock, by which he cut, we would not describe the rock as good in its kind. It might be good as useful, but we would not say it is a good instance of a rock, the way we would say that a sharp knife is a good instance of a knife. Although we recognize that the person has the purpose of using the rock to cut, this external purpose does not affect our judgment concerning the good. Why? Because we do not suppose that the purpose belongs to the rock. In contrast, we do suppose that the purpose of cutting belongs to what it means to be a knife. Only as such can we describe a sharp knife as good in its kind.

4.1.2: Things in Nature

Natural things also have purposes, as the purpose of an eye is to see and the purpose of a heart is to pump. These purposes, it seems, are not externally attributed to the things by some maker, as is the case with artifacts (unless one wishes to say that the purpose is really in God). The description of an eye includes its purpose; unlike the knife, however, the purpose truly belongs to the eye.

The meaning of "good" for these natural things appears to be no

---

3. For the link between function and the good see McInerny, "Naturalism," 228–34.

different than for artifacts. It means that the thing has a purpose, and that it realizes this purpose. We ascertain whether an eye is good by knowing what an eye is, including its purpose, and determining whether this particular eye realizes its purpose or in some way falls short of the full realization of its purpose.

Modern science speaks of the purpose of an eye, but generally scientists shy away from such language, claiming that there are no purposes in nature. Aquinas has no such qualms. Natural things do have purposes. Furthermore, these purposes, or functions, are found in inclinations.[4] Indeed, the words "function" and "inclination" are better than "purpose," since "purpose" does seem to imply a person putting the thing to use for some end. Like a purpose, an inclination is a movement to some end, but the inclination is internal to the thing, at least if the inclination is natural.

In the *De veritate,* Aquinas distinguishes between two ways in which something can be directed to an end. Those that have knowledge of the end, namely, human beings, can direct themselves; those lacking knowledge of the end can be directed by something that does have knowledge, as an arrow is directed to a target by an archer. Aquinas then further divides the latter category.

> This direction from another can happen in two ways. Sometimes, that which is directed toward the end is impelled and moved by the one directing but it itself does not acquire a form (from the one directing) through which the direction or inclination belongs to it. Such an inclination is violent, as the arrow is inclined by the archer to a determinate target.
>
> Sometimes, however, that which is directed or inclined toward an end acquires (from the one directing or moving) a form through which the inclination belongs to it. Such inclination will be natural.... In this way all natural things are inclined to that which is fitting to them, having in themselves some principle of their own inclination on account of which the inclination is natural, so that in some manner they go toward their proper ends of their own accord, and are not only led toward the ends.[5]

---

4. On the contrast between "purpose" and "end," see Francis Slade, "Ends and Purposes," in *Final Causality in Nature and Human Affairs,* Studies in Philosophy and the History of Philosophy, vol. 30 (Washington, D.C.: The Catholic University of America Press, 1997). See also Robert Sokolowski, "What Is Natural Law? Human Purposes and Natural Ends," *Thomist* 68 (2004): 507–29.

5. *De veritate,* 22, 1 (Leonine ed., v. 22, 613, 152–74). "Sed hoc dupliciter contingit:

GOOD

Aquinas's teleology clearly asserts itself. Without this teleology, nothing is really good or bad in nature.[6] Perhaps we might ascribe purpose to things in nature, the way we ascribe purpose to artifacts we make. In Aquinas's view, that would make all things like the arrow. Any purpose or inclination would be external and violent; the inclination would not really belong to the thing, and neither would the thing really be good.

A knife does not truly have a purpose of its own; in this respect, it is more like the arrow propelled to the target than like an eye with its own inclination to see. The knife is simply metal shaped in a certain way. If this metal has no purpose, then it has no good. The word "knife" picks out this shaped metal together with a purpose of cutting; as such, we can speak of a good knife. But if the purpose does not belong to the metal, then neither does the goodness. The purpose does pick out something real, but it is not in the metal. It indicates something about the person who uses the metal, or the person who made the shaped metal, or the society that generally uses this metal in certain ways.

If nature does truly move to an end by some internal principle, then things in nature can be truly good. An eye, for instance, is good insofar as it realizes its function of seeing. The term "good" picks out a state of affairs. It describes the state of the eye in relation to its function, which is part of what the eye really is. As such, the knowledge of a good eye is speculative.

---

quandoque enim id quod dirigitur in finem solummodo impellitur et movetur a dirigente, sine hoc quod aliquam formam a dirigente consequatur, per quam ei competat talis directio vel inclinatio; et talis inclinatio est violenta, sicut sagitta inclinatur a sagittante ad signum determinatum. Aliquando autem id quod dirigitur vel inclinatur in finem consequitur a dirigente vel movente aliquam formam per quam sibi talis inclinatio competat; unde et talis inclinatio erit naturali.... Et per hunc modum omnes res naturales in ea quae eis conveniunt sunt inclinata, habentia in se ipsis aliquod suae inclinationis principium, ratione cuius eorum inclinatio naturalis est, ita ut quodam modo ipsa vadant et non solum ducantur in fines debitos."

6. Peter Tumulty ("A Contemporary Bridge from Facts to Values: But Will Natural Law Theorists Pay the Toll?" *International Philosophical Quarterly* 28 [1988]: 53–63) emphasizes that without functional concepts in nature we will have no account of the good, and the move from is to ought will be unbridgeable. Unfortunately, his functional nature is much too culturally bound.

GOOD

4.1.3: What Is Described in the Perfection

In his analysis of the meaning of "good," Peter Geach focused upon "a good x" (where x represents some thing such as a knife or an eye); he considered all other meanings of "good" as derivative upon this first meaning.[7] We first of all understand "a good knife" and only then come to understand that "being sharp is good for a knife." The first meaning, then, applies to the completed thing, a composite idea consisting of the thing itself—which must have some function—and its completion, which will typically be an attribute or attributes of the thing.

The composite good, that is, the completed thing, most easily satisfies the requirements of descriptivism, which is probably why Geach focused upon it. Most people will readily concede that calling a knife "good" provides some description of the knife.[8] Yet when Aquinas speaks of the good as that which all things desire, he is not typically referring to the completed thing; rather, he is referring to the completion.[9] He refers not to the good knife but to the sharpness, which is good for the knife. It is unclear, however, in what way calling sharpness "good" describes something about being sharp. After all, being sharp is not good for a hammer.

In a sense, then, goodness does not seem to be an absolute quality. Being sharp is good for a knife but not for a hammer. The description "good" must involve a relation to the subject. When we call "being sharp" good for a knife, we are not saying something about "being sharp" simply in itself; we are saying something about it in relation to a knife.

At the same time, calling a completion good does not seem to be like saying that an object is to the right or to the left of someone. If I describe a knife as "on your right," then I seem to be expressing noth-

---

7. Schultz-Aldrich ("Revisiting Aquinas on 'Naturalism': A Response to Patrick Lee," *American Catholic Philosophical Quarterly* 77 [2003]: 114–31, at 118) attributes this view to Aquinas.

8. Probably for this reason Rhonheimer concedes an "ontological" meaning of "good" that corresponds with Geach's descriptivism (*Perspective of Morality*, 127–43). We can talk about good knives and good eyes, all of which are self-contained descriptions, but all of which are irrelevant, in themselves, with regard to the human good. The truly human practical good, claims Rhonheimer, is not something found in nature and it cannot be discovered through functions or inclinations. It is found first of all in human reason itself.

9. See, for instance, I, 26, 2; I-II, 1, 7; *In Physic.*, lib. 1, lect. 15, n. 7; *In De caelo*, lib. 2, lect. 4, n. 5; *In De divinis nominibus*, cap. 11, lect. 1.

ing more than a relation. "Being on the right" involves nothing inherent in the knife at all. In contrast, being good seems to involve more than simply a relation.

Being good is more like being visible, which is also a relational term, for something is visible only in relation to the power of sight. On the other hand, "being visible" is not like "being to the right." In order to be visible, an object must have certain inherent attributes. In contrast, something can be to the right and in the next moment be to the left (because the person has turned around) with no inherent change in the object itself.

Ultimately, an object is visible because it has the attribute of being colored. "Being visible," however, does not mean simply to be colored. Rather, it means that an object has the attributes necessary (whatever they might be) to serve as the object of the act of seeing; or perhaps, it has the necessary attributes to cause the act of seeing.

In a similar manner, to describe a completion as good refers to some real attributes, but precisely insofar as these attributes relate to the subject that has a certain function. "Being sharp" is the sort of thing that can complete the function of a knife but cannot complete the function of a hammer. "The *ratio* of good consists in this, that something completes another after the manner of an end."[10]

The good, then, is relative to a certain function; nevertheless, it is not entirely relative. It is not like a person's favorite color or "being to the right." It is like being visible. The function has certain requirements, and a good "object" has those attributes, inherent to itself, which can fulfill those requirements. When we describe a completion as good, we are saying something about it, not merely something about an agent; it truly does have what it takes to complete a certain kind of function.

For this reason, Aquinas says that the good is a certain kind of cause, namely, final cause, and he equates the good with the end.[11] The very fact of desire, or inclination, indicates that a thing does not exist for itself; it is moving to achieve something beyond itself. By itself, it

---

10. *De veritate*, 21, 2 (Leonine ed., v. 22, 596, 61–63). "Ratio boni in hoc consistat quod aliquid sit perfectivum alterius per modum finis."

11. For a thorough treatment of final causality, see Richard J. Connell, *Nature's Causes* (New York: Lang, 1995), 183–227.

is not its own reason to be; it is incomplete and finds its completion in some end. As McInerny puts it, "Trying-to-get presumably involves something one has not got. Appetition thus suggests a want or lack, a negation, in the subject of appetite, of the one trying to get."[12] Consequently, desire is the most fundamental indicator of an end. Desire might be called the first effect of final causality.

The desire, however, is not arbitrary. It depends upon some real attributes in the thing desired. The thing must have what it takes to complete the individual in some manner or other. We do not simply desire things whimsically, and then call them good. Rather, we have some potential that needs completion, and only objects having the attributes necessary for completion can be desired and called good.

To put matters differently, the desire itself has a character. It is not simply like an arrow-pointer facing first west, then north, then east, and finally south; the pointer is indifferent in itself which direction it faces. Not so for desire or inclination. The desire arises from what is lacking in the agent. The agent has a certain character that moves out toward what fulfills it. Its character, then, and the character of its desire, depends upon the object of desire.

Up to this point, then, we have explained descriptivism. Discovering the descriptive character of the good, however, is only our first step. We must next determine how we come to know the good. Is it by way of speculative knowledge? Before we turn to this question, however, one objection should be addressed. It will seem to some that the term "good" cannot possibly be descriptive, since it concerns not that which is but that which is to come to be.

4.1.4: Speculative Knowledge of What Is Not the Case

If the good is some feature of reality that can be described, then we should expect to know it with speculative reason. Or rather, it will be speculative in all regards, except that the object happens to be something that human actions can bear upon; it will be practical according to object but speculative according to mode and end; in short, it will be materially practical. The new natural law theory claims, however,

---

12. McInerny, "Naturalism," 239.

GOOD

that our knowledge of the good is not speculative in mode, for it does not describe what is; rather, it determines "what is-to-be." Patrick Lee and others claim that the good cannot be known by speculative reason because the good does not yet exist.[13] While speculative knowledge knows what is, practical knowledge has a special domain of that which is-to-be.

This objection seems to have an odd implication: we have two separate kinds of knowledge concerning the human good. On the one hand, we have the knowledge of that which is to be, which is practical knowledge. On the other hand, we can still call human goods "good" even after they exist and so fall within the domain of speculative knowledge.

Anna might begin, for instance, by desiring knowledge of the natural law. This knowledge does not yet exist, and so she calls it good, as that which is-to-be. Eventually, she acquires the knowledge, and the knowledge now exists. Does she cease calling it good? Clearly not. But why not? It no longer falls under the domain of that which is-to-be. It seems, then, that she must call it good in a different sense, in a speculative sense, in a sense that concerns what *is* rather than that which is not yet. In our ordinary conversations, however, we do not recognize any such shift in meaning. When we call knowledge good before it exists and then also after it exists, we think that we mean the same thing.

Lee's mistake is twofold. First, he supposes that practical knowledge concerns that which is-to-be; second, he supposes that speculative knowledge concerns that which exists in the world. In fact, practical knowledge sometimes concerns that which is to be and sometimes that which now exists; similarly, speculative knowledge sometimes concerns that which now exists and sometimes that which is-to-be.

When the different levels of practical knowledge are not properly distinguished, then one might easily suppose that practical knowledge always concerns that which is to be. After all, virtual practical knowledge tells us how something (often, ourselves) ought to act, for instance, a builder ought to lay the foundation of the house first. Usually, however, when we speak about how something ought to act, we are speaking of the future.

Not all practical knowledge, however, is virtual practical knowl-

---

13. Lee, "Naturalist," 571.

edge. Currently, we are discussing our knowledge of the good, which is materially practical. This knowledge sometimes concerns what is not now the case, but it sometimes concerns what is in fact the case. If an eye is good and we describe it as such, we are not describing what is-to-be; we are describing what is now.

Some practical knowledge, then, concerns what is now the case; conversely, some speculative knowledge concerns what is not now the case. We can have purely speculative knowledge of dinosaurs. Similarly, we can know what it means to sit, even for a person who is now standing. In both these cases our knowledge comes from previous existence, but it concerns something not now existing.

We can also have speculative knowledge of the future, for instance, we might know when a solar eclipse will occur. Upon what is this speculative knowledge based? Ultimately, it is based upon something that now exists. Aquinas says that we know the future through the inclinations of the current causes.

> To know the future in its cause is nothing other than to know the present inclination of the cause to its effect. Properly speaking, then, it is not knowledge of the future but of the present.[14]

By our knowledge of the current positions of the earth and moon, together with our knowledge of how they are inclined to move, we project into the future, foreseeing a solar eclipse.

Similarly, our knowledge of a nonexistent good, a good that has yet to come into existence, is known through the current inclinations found in a thing. An eye has the inclination or function of seeing. This inclination belongs even to a blind eye, an eye that is defective and cannot now see. The goodness of the blind eye, then, exists in a way; it does not fully exist, but it exists in the inclination. Consequently, we can have speculative knowledge of a good eye, even if the eye itself is not yet good. We will further examine this knowledge of what is not yet the case when we look at ought-statements in chapter 7.

---

14. *De malo,* 16, 7 (Leonine ed., v. 23, 316, 249–53). "Cognoscere futurum in causa sua nichil est aliud quam cognoscere praesentem inclinationem cause ad effectum; unde hoc non proprie est cognoscere futurum, set presens." See also I, 86, 4; *Sentencia De sensu,* tract. 2, lect. 1 n. 8.

GOOD

4.2

THE MOVE FROM SPECULATIVE TO PRACTICAL

4.2.1: Finnis and the Order of Knowing

It is one thing to note that the good is descriptive; it is another thing to give an account of how it is known. Do we come to know it by way of purely speculative knowledge, for example, by way of our understanding of natural inclinations? Or do we come to know it only by first knowing what ought to be.

Finnis wishes to use the latter approach.[15] He argues that we begin by knowing the end of an action, and then know the action, from which we know the power (which would seem to include the inclination of that power) and then the nature. Since the end is the good, the good is known with practical knowledge, not with speculative knowledge. Since the end or the good is the first thing known, practical knowledge must be the beginning point, prior to our knowledge of action, power, and nature.

Finnis applies his teaching only to human nature. The importance of the end is ignored for our knowledge of nonhuman nature. Yet surely this oversight is the greatest weakness of Finnis's argument. Aquinas's statement is meant to be taken universally: for any operation, whether human or otherwise, we must first know its object and thereby know the action, from which we know the power and the nature. This epistemological truth applies to trees and beavers as much as to human beings. Clearly, however, our knowledge of trees and beavers is speculative; it is entirely independent of practical knowledge. Consequently, the move from end to action to power to nature does not require practical knowledge. If this is true for beavers, then why not also for human beings?

For this reason, Philippa Foot takes an approach diametrically opposed to Finnis's. She begins by observing good in nature, and then considers the human good as a particular instance of the natural good.[16] We will follow Philippa Foot, examining how we come to know the good in nature, and then we will see whether the human good can also fit this pattern.

---

15. See Finnis, "Deriving Ought."
16. Philippa Foot, *Natural Goodness* (Oxford: Clarendon, 2001), 25–51.

GOOD

4.2.2: Beavers and Trees

Let us consider beavers. We observe them gnawing away at tree trunks. What are they doing? Are they trying to get nutrients from the tree? Are they drilling through the wood to get at insects? Are they trying to cut down the tree? We will not know until we know what is the end of the activity. Where does it cease? If the beaver were getting nutrients from the tree, then he would not cease his activity when the tree falls down; he would continue gnawing at the fallen tree. As it is, when the tree falls down, he ceases that activity. He may begin gnawing off branches, or he may begin pulling the tree toward the river, or he may begin gnawing another tree. Since the activity ceases when the tree falls over, it seems herein lies the end of the activity; consequently, the activity is identified through this end. It is not an activity of eating or of searching for insects; it is an activity of cutting down a tree.

As Aquinas says, then, we understand the nature of the activity only by first knowing its end. Our understanding so far is fairly limited, since we do not know why the beaver is cutting down trees. Further observation reveals that the overall activity of the beaver upon trees terminates with the construction of a dam. With this end in view, we better understand the activity. Even then, however, the dam makes no sense unless we know its end; how does the beaver use the dam? To provide shelter from dangers and to provide a ready access to food. Now we are getting to the heart of the matter. We are getting to the true end of all of the activity.

Our knowledge concerning beavers and their ends is in no way practical. We do not learn the end of the beaver's activity by some kind of special practical knowledge. We learn it through simple observation.[17] Our knowledge is speculative from beginning to end.[18]

The same point applies to trees. We observe that trees produce nuts. Why? What is the end of producing nuts? Is it to draw squirrels into its branches? Does it provide some kind of protection? The answer to this question requires observations, perhaps rather long-range observations; we must observe what happens to the nut. Ultimately, we

---

17. Brock ("Natural Law," 686) also suggests that we know inclinations in nature by observing regular behavior.
18. See McInerny, *Human Action*, 190.

GOOD

can determine that the end of the nut is another tree. We might be led down various dead ends, since many nuts do not end up becoming new trees; often, for instance, they become nutrients for squirrels.

Only when we come to recognize that nuts have the end of producing another tree do we understand that the production of nuts is itself part of the act of reproduction. From knowing the nature of this activity, we come to know a power of the tree, namely, the power to produce its own kind. By knowing this power, we come to know the nature of the tree; it is self-moving or living.

Obviously, I have left out multiple steps in the reasoning.[19] For our purposes, what matters is that all of this reasoning depends upon knowing the endpoint. Without knowing that some activities of the tree end in the production of another of its species, we could not know the nature of those activities, nor the nature of the power that underlies them, nor ultimately the nature of the tree as a living organism. Once again, however, none of this knowledge is practical. We come to understand the end of the activity through purely speculative reasoning.

4.2.3: A Reversal

It would seem, then, that the approach of Finnis, of moving from end to action, is amply confirmed through experience. A more detailed analysis of the beaver, however, will reveal a reversal in our knowledge, in which we move from inclinations to the good. Our knowledge of the good turns out to be a two-step process: first, we move from the end to inclination and second, we move from inclination to the good. Let us consider the beaver once again.

We begin by observing change: trees are felled. We recognize that this change cannot come from itself; what does not previously exist (trees lying on the ground) cannot make itself to exist. If the change does not come from itself, then it must come from another; indeed, "another" is simply what is not the thing itself.

At this point, we have recognized the need of some external ef-

---

19. We take the end of nuts for granted, but to see how far wrong we can go on such matters, consider that Aquinas thought the purpose of a tree producing leaves was to hide and protect its fruit (see *Sent.*, IV 44, 1, 2, qc. 2; *Summa contra Gentiles*, III, cap. 3, n. 9; *Quodlibet* VIII, 3). To discover the end of leaves is indeed a difficult matter, requiring knowledge of microscopic activities.

ficient cause. We then might begin to look for this source of change. Exactly how we identify a particular source is a difficult question, and we are often mistaken in our conclusion. Nevertheless, before we have identified the source, we know that there must be some source. The change is not from itself; it must be from something else. In short, our search for causes does not begin, as Hume claims, by the observation of repeated concurrence. Rather, we have already recognized the need for a cause before we look to repeated concurrence as a possible indication of what that cause is.

At some point, we come to recognize the felled trees as arising from a beaver. We now have two things and something like a relation between them: the felled trees, a beaver, and the relation of origination. In short, we know that the felled trees arise from beavers.

When we know a relation we implicitly know its correlative. By knowing one term of the relation, we come to know the other.

> When we understand one thing as referring to another, then we must at the same time understand the opposite relation on the part of the other, for example, knowledge depends upon what is able to be known.[20]

We might first know "double" and then come to recognize "half." By knowing "six is two times three," we also know "three is one-half six." We do not derive one proposition from the other, at least not syllogistically. Nevertheless, our knowledge of the latter proposition depends upon our knowledge of the former. We have, then, nonsyllogistic epistemological dependence between propositions.

Likewise, by knowing that the felled trees arise from a beaver, we know the correlative, namely, that a beaver is the source of the felled trees. At this point we have come to understand the activity of the beaver, for an activity is nothing other than a change arising from some agent.[21] We are not yet at the level of inclination, but so far our reasoning has followed the rule of moving from end to action. We first of all know the felled trees, which turns out to be the end, and only then do we come to know the action.

We next come to understand better that which is the source of the

---

20. *De veritate*, 4, 5 (Leonine ed., v. 22, 131, 117–21). "Non potest intelligi aliquid referri ad alterum quin cointelligatur etiam respectus oppositus ex parte alterius, ut patet in scientia quae dependet ad scibile." See also *Summa contra Gentiles*, II, cap. 13, n. 3.

21. See *In Physic.*, lib. 3, lect. 5.

GOOD

action, in our case, the beaver. If the beaver is the source of the activity, then it must be moving toward the felling of trees; it must in some manner be directed to felled trees. If the beaver acts — or any source acts — then it cannot be an isolated object; it must be moving beyond itself, for that is what it means to act. We are now getting below the surface. At the surface, we see the activity of the beaver; under the surface, we recognize that there must be some source propelling toward this activity. We have now reached power and inclination. Once again, we are following the pattern of moving from end to action to power.

At this point, however, the epistemological flow reverses. By recognizing that I am going to Chicago, we come to understand Chicago as the end of my trip; similarly, by grasping that the beaver is moving toward felled trees, we come to understand felled trees as the end of the beaver. By grasping one relation — the movement toward felled trees — we grasp the correlative — that felled trees are being moved toward; it serves as an end.

We can now see that we do not begin knowing the effect *as an end*; we know it simply as a change. Only later do we come to understand it as an end. We first know felled trees as a change; only after we have come to understand that the beaver is the origin of this change do we also understand this change as the end of an activity. Furthermore, only when we dig under the surface, getting at the inclination of the agent, do we come to understand the effect as the end of an agent.

The single endpoint — felled trees — is an end in two ways. It is an end of activity and it is an end of the beaver; it is the end of the activity of the beaver and it is the end of the inclination of the beaver. In both cases, the end is known after that of which it is the end, that is, after the activity or the inclination. At the same time, the activity and the inclination are known after the end. How can our knowledge of the end both precede and follow our knowledge of activity? Only because one aspect of the end precedes activity and another aspect follows activity. First we know the end simply as a change or effect; subsequently, we come to know the end precisely as an end.

Ultimately, then, two approaches are followed. Activity and inclination are known by the end; at the same time, the end is known by inclination. How is a vicious circle avoided? The appearance of circularity can be avoided by rephrasing each approach. First, activity and inclination are known by the effect, which happens to be the end but is not known as an end. Second, we come to know the end as an end through inclination. "While considering form and end absolutely — since form itself is the end — form considered in itself is prior to a consideration of it as the end of something else."[22] Since the end enters *practical* knowledge only when it is known as an end, it would seem to follow — if the same reasoning applies to the human end — that speculative knowledge of inclinations precedes practical knowledge.

We have not yet reached the stage in which we know the effect as good; we know it as an end of activity and as an end of inclination, but we do not know it as that which completes inclination. Before we look at this final step, we should present a text of Aquinas in which he lays out three aspects of final cause. The first two aspects we have just seen; the third is the good. First, the final cause is the end of some efficient causality; second, the final cause is the end of some inclination; third, the final cause is the good.

Final cause indicates three things. First, it is the terminus of motion, through which it is opposed to the principle of motion, which is the efficient cause. Second, it is the first thing in intention, for which reason it is said to be "that for the sake of which [or the cause for which]." Third, it is desirable in itself, for which reason it is called good, for the good is that which all things desire.[23]

How do we take the final step and come to understand felled trees as good for the beaver? We have already examined this step when we discussed our knowledge of the good. Since the beaver is moving toward the effect, we understand that the beaver in himself is incomplete; he is completed (in part) through the effect of felled trees. We then come to understand felled trees as having what is needed to complete the beaver, that is, we understand felled trees as good. Just as we first grasp that we see color, and then we recognize that color has in it what it takes to be seen, so we first recognize the beaver desiring, and then we see that something in the object itself is desirable, something

---

22. *De veritate,* 21, 3, ad 3 (Leonine ed., v. 22, 599, 108–11). "Sed absolute considerando formam et finem, cum ipsa forma sit finis, prior est ipsa forma in se considerata quam secundum quod est alterius finis."

23. *In Metaphysicorum,* lib. 1, lect. 4, n. 71. "Causam finalem per tria notificat; scilicet quia est terminus motus, et per hoc opponitur principio motus, quod est causa efficiens: et quia est primum in intentione, ratione cuius dicitur cuius causa: et quia est per se appetibile, ratione cuius dicitur bonum. Nam bonum est quod omnia appetunt."

GOOD

about it has what it takes to complete the agent desiring. The desire is not arbitrary, but seeks what is found in the object, in felled trees. Ultimately, then, our knowledge of the good does not precede our knowledge of efficient causality, including the inclination of such causality. To the contrary, we can know the good only when we see it as the end of some agent. "Clearly, the good implies the *ratio* of an end. Nevertheless, the *ratio* of the good presupposes the *ratio* of the efficient cause and the *ratio* of formal cause."[24]

4.2.4: Metaphysics

Up to this point we have considered the good of beavers and trees; we have not considered the human good, which might prove to be different, as Finnis seems to think. Before we proceed to discuss how we come to know the human good, we should consider a common objection. Admittedly, the objection concerns the human good, but it can be answered with the material just covered, which concerns our knowledge of the good in natural objects. The objection claims that we cannot know the good by way of knowing nature, for then we would have to do metaphysics before we could come to know ethics. Or if metaphysics is not singled out, then the objection claims that some sort of difficult speculative investigation, whether metaphysics or natural philosophy or something else, is required before we can know what is good for us.[25] We must, so the objection goes, "establish" the good first, before we know what we ought to do.[26]

This objection argues soundly against any view that would say we must do metaphysics or natural philosophy before we can discover the good. Finnis correctly notes that ethics cannot be reduced to natural science, logic, or technology.[27] On the other hand, the objection goes wrong insofar as it implies (without asserting) that practical knowledge of ethics is not caused by speculative awareness.

Veatch distinguishes between the science of metaphysics and an

---

24. I, 5, 4. "Manifestum est quod bonum rationem finis importat. Sed tamen ratio boni praesupponit rationem causae efficientis, et rationem causae formalis."

25. See Grisez, "First Principle," 194, 196; Grisez, "Practical Principles," 102; George, "Human Nature," 32; Rhonheimer, *Perspective of Morality,* 266; Mark C. Murphy, *Natural Law and Practical Rationality* (Cambridge: Cambridge University Press, 2001), 14.

26. Lee, "Naturalist," 568; see also 573.

27. Finnis, *Aquinas,* 22.

awareness of metaphysical principles.[28] Science is a systematic investigation of some reality; in contrast, awareness need not be systematic. I can be aware that I see colors without doing a scientific investigation of the power of sight. Both science and awareness can fit under the umbrella term "knowledge," and both can be "speculative," that is, they involve no knowledge of how to bring something about. By denying the need for speculative *science*, however, one does not thereby successfully deny the need for speculative awareness of some aspects of human nature.

Observations of the world around us will be necessary for our knowledge of the good. We are not born knowing the purpose of the sexual act; this knowledge usually comes from others, but it must have initially come from observations. It does not follow that a systematic scientific investigation is needed in order to know the good of reproduction.

Indeed, some goods will be known after minimal observation. As we will see, our awareness of our inclination to know the truth — with the consequent knowledge of the good — follows rapidly upon our first intellectual judgments. This awareness does not require a scientific comprehension of the intellect as an immaterial power that knows by abstraction; it requires only the indistinct awareness of our own knowledge and of our ability to know. These observations, which lead to our knowledge of the good, should not be tendentiously described as metaphysics. Observations — even observations in metaphysical realms (or nonmaterial realms) — are not the same as scientific analyses.

After observing the behavior of beavers, we grasp that they fell trees and are in some manner moving toward the felling of trees. Have we done natural philosophy? If so, its minimal nature should pose no obstacle to an immediate grasp of the good. Once we have grasped what the beaver is moving toward, we also grasp its good.

From beginning to end our reasoning remains in the domain of speculative reason. Furthermore, our knowledge of the good of beavers comes at the end of a line of thought that includes other notions, most importantly, the notion of inclination. If a similar reasoning process

---

28. Veatch, "Is-Ought Question," 299–300; Dewan ("Natural Lights," 290) makes a similar distinction between metaphysics as a fully realized cultivation of the mind and the seeds of wisdom. See also McInerny, *Human Action*, 197–8.

GOOD

can be found for human beings, then knowledge of the human good will also come last. Practical knowledge will be the ending point, not the beginning point.

4.3
KNOWING THE HUMAN GOOD

4.3.1: An Epistemological Rift

Is our knowledge of the human good and of human nature different from the knowledge of the beaver and its good? Do we have some kind of special practical knowledge that precedes our knowledge of human nature? Finnis seems to suggest as much. His epistemological universe has a major rift running down its middle. Our knowledge of human nature is one thing; our knowledge of the rest of nature is another.[29] We know human nature only through some prior practical knowledge; presumably, the same does not apply to beavers and trees.

The most forceful argument in defense of Finnis and this epistemological rift comes from Ralph McInerny, who poses it against himself after dismissing Finnis's argument from the order of knowledge.[30] Unfortunately, McInerny never adequately responded to his own objection. The problem is as follows: if knowledge of action precedes knowledge of the end as end and of the good as good — as we have suggested for the beaver — then there must be some human action that precedes our knowledge of the human good (as our knowledge of the end qua end of the beaver follows upon some awareness of the activity of the beaver). Human action, however, follows upon practical reason with its grasp of the good. In the end, then, we are left with a circle. We must have human action before we can grasp the good; at the same time, we must have practical knowledge of the good before we can act.

The same difficulty does not apply to the beaver, since the activity of the beaver, which precedes our knowledge of its good, need not follow upon practical reason. Indeed, its activity does not follow upon any reason at all, and certainly not upon the reason of the individual ob-

---

29. Rhonheimer (*Perspective of Morality*, 183) explicitly makes a divide between our knowledge of nonhuman nature and of human nature, because, he says, reason (unlike nature) is open to diverse conceptions of the good.

30. McInerny, *Human Action*, 190; for a response, see Lee, "Naturalist," 573–74.

GOOD

serving the behavior of beavers. The epistemological rift arises, then, because the conditions for observing activity are different for beavers and for human beings. In order to observe the activities of beavers, no practical reason is required; in order to observe the activities of human beings, practical reason is presumed, in order that there be some activity to observe. At least some practical reason, then, must have preceded the very first observation of human action. It seems to follow that practical reason cannot arise from our speculative knowledge of human action.

In order to overcome this difficulty, we will propose that our knowledge of the human good does presuppose human activity, but not fully human activity; it supposes the human activity following upon nonconscious inclinations. We will begin, in this chapter, by examining a suggestive text of Aquinas. In the next chapter, we will see that Aquinas generally follows the procedure of discovering the human good through our nonconscious natural inclinations.

4.3.2: An Interesting Text

A text connecting our knowledge of desire and the *ratio* of the good comes in an article asking which concept is prior, the truth or the good. The second objection argues that the good is in things while truth is in the intellect; since what is in things is prior to what is in the intellect, it follows that the good is prior to the truth. Aquinas's reply indicates that the question is all about what is prior in the intellect; priority in things is irrelevant. He is concerned with which concept (or *ratio*) is prior, not with which reality is prior. He explains as follows:

> That is prior in *ratio* which arises first in the intellect. But the intellect first of all grasps being; second, it grasps that it understands being; third, it grasps that it desires being. Consequently, first is the *ratio* of being, second the *ratio* of the truth, and third the *ratio* of the good, even though the good is in things.[31]

The text clearly lays out two series and evidently a corresponding dependence. First we know being; second, we know that we understand

---

[31]. I, 16, 4, ad 2 "Secundum hoc est aliquid prius ratione, quod prius cadit in intellectu. Intellectus autem per prius apprehendit ipsum ens; et secundario apprehendit se intelligere ens; et tertio apprehendit se appetere ens. Unde primo est ratio entis, secundo ratio veri, tertio ratio boni, licet bonum sit in rebus."

GOOD

being; finally, we know that we desire being. Correspondingly, the *ratio* of being depends upon the first grasp, namely, our grasp of being; second, the *ratio* of truth depends upon the second thing we know, namely, our very act of understanding being; finally, the *ratio* of the good depends upon the third thing we know, namely, our desire of being.

This last dependence fits the analysis of the good presented in this chapter. Upon grasping desire we can grasp that something is good. Aquinas does not seem to be saying the reverse, that upon grasping the good we come to understand desire.

Does this text help us get around Finnis's difficulty? That depends upon what it means to "desire being." If the desire is a desire of the will, then we are left with Finnis's difficulty. Any desire of the will presupposes an awareness of the good, and therefore could not give rise to it.[32] Another possibility presents itself, however. The desire might be a nonconscious desire; it might be the desire of the intellect itself.

Elsewhere, Aquinas speaks about knowing powers *desiring* the object known; these powers do not desire the object as they exist in nature but as they come to exist in the power itself, in the very act of knowing. He says, for instance, "The power of sight naturally desires the visible object only for its own act, namely, so that it can see."[33] Likewise, Aquinas speaks of the intellect desiring the intelligible object: "The intellect naturally desires the intelligible object insofar as it is intelligible, for the intellect naturally desires to know and the senses to sense."[34]

Furthermore, in the Latin Aquinas uses, the reflexive (*se*), which indicates that the same subject both desires and apprehends the desire. That subject is *intellectus*. Now *intellectus* usually refers to the power of the intellect, but it can refer to the intellectual nature or the intellectual soul. In this text, however, Aquinas is concerned with what exists in the intellect; he is concerned with *rationes*. It seems likely, then, that just as the power of the intellect knows itself to know, so also the power of the intellect desires and then knows itself desiring.

---

32. Dewan ("Natural Lights," 292–97) interprets this text as concerning the desire of the will. For more details of Dewan's position, see Dewan, "Philosophy of Cooperation."

33. I, 78, 1, ad 3. "Visus appetit naturaliter visibile solum ad suum actum, scilicet ad videndum."

34. *Q. D. de anima* 13, ad 11 (Leonine ed., v. 24, 121, 440–43). "Intellectus quidem naturaliter appetit intelligibile ut est intelligibile. Appetit enim naturaliter intellectus intelligere, et sensus sentire."

GOOD

In a similar text from the *Sentences* Aquinas is unmistakably speaking about the power of the intellect, for he has distinguished this power from others (that still belong to the intellectual soul) in that it knows the quiddity of things. He speaks for some time about how the intellect knows what something is. He then goes on to consider how the intellect (for he indicates no change in the subject) knows the existence of certain things. One of these things is the inclination of the intellect itself.

The intellect knows that something exists in the intellect itself from the inclination which it (the intellect) has to some acts: which inclination it knows from this, that it bends back upon its own acts when it knows itself to be operating.[35]

The text from the *Summa,* then, can be interpreted after the manner of the beaver. The intellect first knows being. Second, it is aware of its own act of knowing being (from which it knows "truth"). Third, it is aware of its own tendency toward being. Finally, from this awareness, the intellect comes to know the good. We have finally reached materially practical knowledge.

The good, in this instance, is "my" good, that is, we have been speaking about the intellect grasping this or that, so we might suppose that the good we perceive is the good of the intellect, and in a sense it is; more properly, however, it is the good of the individual. Talking about the intellect grasping something is only a manner of speaking. More precisely, the individual grasps something by way of his intellect. I first grasp being, by way of my power of the intellect. I then perceive that I understand being, again by way of my intellect. Finally, I perceive that I, through my intellect, am moving toward the understanding of being. This being, or this understanding, completes *me,* insofar as I have an intellect.

Our knowledge concerning ourselves is fundamentally the same as our knowledge concerning the beaver. The same basic steps take place. We have, it seems, a greater certainty for ourselves. We have an immediate awareness of some of our own actions, whereas the activity of the

---

35. *Sent.,* III, 23, 1, 2 (Mandonnet, v. 3, 702). "Cognoscit aliquid in seipso esse ex inclinatione quam habet ad aliquos actus: quam quidem inclinationem cognoscit ex hoc quod super actus suos reflectitur, dum cognoscit se operari."

beaver is reached as a conclusion after much observation. Ultimately, however, our good, like the good of the beaver, is recognized as the object of an inclination that we have come to see in our perception of the world.

The two cases differ, of course. The knowledge of the good of the beaver is entirely speculative, while the knowledge of the human good is materially practical. Its practical nature, however, is incidental. It is, like our knowledge of the beaver, an awareness of the way things are. It just happens that the object is the sort of thing concerning which we might act. In the initial awareness, however, we simply know the truth concerning the good; its influence upon action will come later.

4.3.3: The Natural Human Good and Physicalism

Have we met Finnis's objection? One nagging doubt remains. Finnis claims that human actions are different from beaver actions because human actions presuppose practical knowledge. As such, the observation of human actions cannot possibly be a condition for practical knowledge; to the contrary, practical knowledge must precede any observation of human actions.

In our response, we have relied upon nonconscious inclinations, such as the inclination of the intellect toward the truth. These natural inclinations, because they are not conscious, do not presuppose any awareness (in the one with an inclination), whether speculative or practical. Observations of such inclinations and the actions that arise from them do not presuppose practical reason. Consequently, they can give rise to practical knowledge.

Finnis might find this response unsatisfactory. The actions corresponding to nonconscious inclinations are not fully human actions, for human actions are voluntary. The very first acts of the intellect, which arise from nature apart from the will, are not voluntary, so that they are not fully human. Perhaps the upshot of basing our knowledge of the human good upon such incomplete human acts will be the ethical view of physicalism. The human good perceived through such nonconscious inclinations will not be truly human. These inclinations will give us proper functioning biology, but they will not give us moral good and evil.

GOOD

The response to this objection will be twofold. On the one hand, it will be textual, involving an attempt to show that Aquinas does indeed "derive" the human and moral good from nature. On the other hand, it will be conceptual, involving an analysis of the will and what its inclinations can contribute to our knowledge of the human good. The first approach will be addressed in chapter 5 and the second in chapter 6.

5

NATURE

The objection concerning physicalism claims that descriptivism, in which good and evil are discovered in the world around us, leads to the objectionable ethical view called physicalism, in which the human good is reduced to biology and the human will is left out of the picture. In chapter 1 we suggested two avenues of response to this objection. First, one could attempt to show that Aquinas himself often bases moral good or evil upon nature. Second, one could attempt to show that descriptivism need not necessarily lead to physicalism; one can discover moral good and evil in nature and yet allow for a proper role of the will and reason. The first avenue is the subject of this chapter. The second approach will be taken up in two parts, first with regard to the will and then with regard to reason. The role of the will within Aquinas's naturalism will be discussed in the next chapter; finally, the constructive role of reason will be addressed in Chapter 9.

5.1
PRINCIPLES OF INTERPRETATION

If in fact the human good is discovered through our knowledge of nature, in particular, through our speculative knowledge of natural inclinations, then we should expect Aquinas to draw this connection, at least sometimes, when he is discussing particular goods. Beyond doubt Aquinas says that humans should follow nature and that the human good is what is according to nature. These sayings, however, are open to an alternate interpretation, friendly to the new natural law theory. What is according to nature, on this reading, is simply whatever practical reason dictates.[1] Why? Because the nature of man is to be rational.

---

1. See Martin Rhonheimer, "The Cognitive Structure of the Natural Law and the Truth of Subjectivity," in *The Perspective of the Acting Person: Essays in the Renewal of Thomis-*

NATURE

The nature of anything is most of all the form from which it takes its species. Man has his species through his rational soul. Therefore, what is contrary to the order of reason, is properly contrary to the nature of man insofar as he is man; what is according to reason is according to the nature of man insofar as he is man.[2]

What is according to nature, then, has nothing to do with a knowledge of some nature besides reason itself. Reason is the nature. Whatever practical reason dictates — from its own starting points — is according to human nature.

According to Martin Rhonheimer, for instance, "For practical reason to be 'based on that which is according to nature' thus means for it to be *'based on principles that are known naturally.'*"[3] Nature, in these contexts, does not refer to some biological teleology, but "'nature' here is something given in and with some natural form of exercise of reason."[4] Indeed, Rhonheimer thinks that those who refer to natural ends have confused natural law, which is simply the dictates of natural reason, with an account of natural law. Natural law itself does not come from nature (besides the nature of reason); it is self-standing, not needing any natural teleology as a foundation. It is "a cognitive reality inserted in the human soul which unfolds precisely through the first and spontaneous judgments of practical reason itself."[5]

If we are to contradict this interpretation of Rhonheimer, we must find texts that clearly refer to some nature besides reason. Ideally, they will refer to nature as realized in some nonconscious inclinations. Such texts, it is supposed, are difficult to find. They tend to crop up in discussions of sexual ethics, although Finnis concedes a similar text concerning lying.

---

tic Moral Philosophy (Washington, D.C.: The Catholic University of America Press, 2008); Rhonheimer, *Perspective of Morality*, 161–67, 183–85.

2. I-II, 71, 2. "Sed considerandum est quod natura uniuscuiusque rei potissime est forma secundum quam res speciem sortitur. Homo autem in specie constituitur per animam rationalem. Et ideo id quod est contra ordinem rationis, proprie est contra naturam hominis inquantum est homo; quod autem est secundum rationem, est secundum naturam hominis inquantum est homo."

3. Martin Rhonheimer, "Natural Law as a 'Work of Reason': Understanding the Metaphysics of Participated Theonomy," *American Journal of Jurisprudence* 55 (2010): 41–77, at 61.

4. Ibid.

5. Rhonheimer, "Work of Reason," 62.

NATURE

Perhaps the most telling text explicitly distinguishes between what is according to reason and what is according to nature.

> There is a determinate species of lust where there occurs a special character of deformity making the sexual act unsuitable, which can happen in two ways. In one way, because it is repugnant to right reason, which is common to all sins of lust; in another way, because, beyond this, it is repugnant to the very order of the nature of the sexual act fitting to the human species, which is then called a sin against nature.[6]

If reason is contrasted to nature, then it is difficult to see how nature can simply be the nature of reason, as Rhonheimer claims. Aquinas goes further, asserting that reason itself is based upon nature:

> The principles of reason are those that are according to nature, for reason, presupposing those things that are determined by nature, disposes other things insofar as it is fitting.[7]

These texts are difficult to finesse in light of the new natural law theory. Consequently, Lee concedes that these passages pose some difficulty for his interpretation, but he thinks that these passages are anomalies.[8] Aquinas typically — so Lee argues — bases his ethical account on the basic goods known immediately by reason, with no reference to nonrational nature.

Finnis concedes that these texts, on the surface, are problematic; in addition, Aquinas's treatment of lying seems to rely upon an end independent of reason. He argues, however, that Aquinas simply omitted to fill in the details of the moral principles he is using.[9]

Rhonheimer takes a similar approach, although he does not seem

---

6. II-II, 154, 11. "Ibi est determinata luxuriae species ubi specialis ratio deformitatis occurrit quae facit indecentem actum venereum. Quod quidem potest esse dupliciter. Uno quidem modo, quia repugnat rationi rectae, quod est commune in omni vitio luxuriae. Alio modo, quia etiam, super hoc, repugnat ipsi ordini naturali venerei actus qui convenit humanae speciei, quod dicitur vitium contra naturam."

7. II-II, 154, 12. "Principia autem rationis sunt ea quae sunt secundum naturam, nam ratio, praesuppositis his quae sunt a natura determinata, disponit alia secundum quod convenit."

8. Lee, "Naturalist," 586–87. Daniel Nelson (*The Priority of Prudence: Virtue and Natural Law in Thomas Aquinas and the Implications for Modern Ethics* [University Park, Pa.: Pennsylvania State University Press, 1992], 121–23) also claims that Aquinas is inconsistent on this point. Paterson ("Non-Naturalism," 181) argues that this interpretation is ridiculous; Aquinas is clearly consistent on the point.

9. Finnis, "Deriving Ought," 50–52.

to concede that the texts pose even a surface difficulty for his interpretation. He claims that when Aquinas speaks of nature as a standard, he means to say nature insofar as it has been deemed good by reason.[10] Other parts of nature are irrelevant to morality because reason has not deemed them to be relevant.[11] In short, reason is the true standard and nature is introduced only because reason has said that it should be.

These principles of interpretation can conveniently whitewash any difficult text. It is always possible to say, "In this text Aquinas was being inconsistent," or "In that text Aquinas did not lay out his principles," or "That use of 'nature' refers to nature as determined by reason, even though Aquinas does not explicitly say so." Furthermore, these principles of interpretation are difficult to gainsay. Perhaps Aquinas is inconsistent, and certainly, he does not always explicitly state the principles he is using. It is nearly impossible to disprove any of these approaches.

The only promising countermeasure is brute force. If the texts can be piled one on top of the other, then it becomes less and less likely that Aquinas is simply reasoning inconsistently with his fundamental principles; it becomes less likely that he would — in all of these many instances — remain silent about his fundamental principles, while speaking in a manner apparently opposed to them. If the texts are numerous enough, then it will begin to appear that a reliance upon nature — without hidden principles — permeates the thought of Aquinas.

We should raise two caveats before looking to the texts of Aquinas. One common misunderstanding of natural law supposes that moral norms are derived from regularities; natural law is simply the assertion that what happens frequently or for the most part ought to happen.[12] It should be abundantly clear by now that Aquinas did not use this concept of nature. Aquinas follows Aristotle in recognizing that nature is an inherent principle of movement. As a consequence, but not as a defi-

---

10. Rhonheimer, "Pre-Rational Nature," 145–51.

11. Aquinas, however, seems to think otherwise. As we will see in the first text quoted below, Aquinas says, "Just as for the whole, so also for its parts one must consider that *every* part of man, and all of his actions, ought to attain their required ends" (emphasis added). Every part of man is involved, not simply those parts deemed ahead of time as good according to reason.

12. Rhonheimer (*Perspective of Morality*, 183) equates what is natural to what happens for the most part. Ashmore ("Ethical Naturalism," 81) also seems to utilize a kind of statistical notion of human nature. In contrast, Foot (*Natural Goodness*, 30–33) is careful to identify a teleological notion of nature rather than a statistical notion.

NATURE

nition, what nature moves toward will likely happen for the most part. In our own investigation of nature, then, we might begin with regularities, for example, we might observe what beavers regularly do. Such regularities, however, can never be the final determination of nature. Aquinas believed, for instance, that on account of original sin human beings act with regularity against nature, with sinful desires and sinful actions.

Finally, some of the texts we will be examining involve a move from nature to virtual practical knowledge, rather than to materially practical knowledge. In short, the texts go beyond the stage we have so far reached. Nevertheless, these texts are best discussed at this point, since they are being raised mainly to show a dependence of practical knowledge upon nature. Whether that practical knowledge be materially practical or virtually practical is of little consequence. In either event, Aquinas will appear to be a physicalist.

5.2
SEXUAL ETHICS

5.2.1: *Summa contra Gentiles*

Aquinas is most forthright in the *Summa contra Gentiles*. He begins with a general principle that all of the parts of the human being (reflecting the text examined earlier, concerning all of the parts of human nature) must attain their ends.

> The good of anything is that it attain its end while its evil is found in diverging from the required end. Just as for the whole, so also for its parts one must consider that every part of man, and all of his actions, ought to attain their required ends.[13]

He applies this principle to the power of reproduction, as realized in the male semen. For the semen more than expulsion is sought, for it is expelled for use in reproduction, to which sexual relations are ordered. But human generation would be in vain if the required nurturing did not follow, for the offspring would not survive if the required nurturing were taken away. Consequently, the emission of the semen ought

---

13. *Summa contra Gentiles*, III, cap. 122, n. 4 (Leonine ed., v. 14, 378). "Est autem bonum uniuscuiusque quod finem suum consequatur: malum autem eius est quod a debito fine divertat. Sicut autem in toto, ita et in partibus hoc considerari oportet: ut scilicet unaquaeque pars hominis, et quilibet actus eius, finem debitum sortiatur."

NATURE

to be ordered so that the appropriate reproduction can follow, as well as the raising of the offspring.[14]

He is identifying the end of ejaculation, in the same manner as when we considered the end of a tree producing a nut. And just as we discover what is good for the tree, or for the beaver, by recognizing the end at which its actions aim, so we come to recognize the good of sexual activity through its end.

Aquinas continues,

> From which it is plain that every emission of semen from which reproduction cannot follow is contrary to the human good, and if it is done voluntarily, then it is a sin. I speak of the manner in which reproduction cannot follow by its very nature [secundum se], for example, every emission of semen without the natural union of male and female, for which reason these sins are called sins against nature.[15]

From recognizing the end of ejaculation and sexual activity, we come to recognize that when this action is carried out in opposition to this end, then it is evil.

The argument continues with an examination of nature beyond the human realm.

> Likewise, it is contrary to the human good if the semen is emitted such that reproduction can follow but there is an obstacle to the appropriate rearing of the child. In some animals the female alone suffices to raise the offspring, in which case the male and female do not remain together after sexual activity, as is plain in dogs. In contrast, for some other animals the female does not suffice for raising the offspring, in which case the male and female remain together for a time after sexual activity, to the point needed for the raising and training of the offspring, as is plain in certain birds.[16]

---

14. *Summa contra Gentiles*, III, cap. 122, n. 4 (Leonine ed., v. 14, 378). "Non hoc autem solum quaeritur in semine, sed ut emittatur ad generationis utilitatem, ad quam coitus ordinatur. Frustra autem esset hominis generatio nisi et debita nutritio sequeretur: quia generatum non permaneret, debita nutritione subtracta. Sic igitur ordinata esse seminis debet emissio ut sequi possit et generatio conveniens, et geniti educatio."

15. *Summa contra Gentiles*, III, cap. 122, n. 5 (Leonine ed., v. 14, 378). "Ex quo patet quod contra bonum hominis est omnis emissio seminis tali modo quod generatio sequi non possit. Et si ex proposito hoc agatur, oportet esse peccatum. Dico autem modum ex quo generatio sequi non potest secundum se: sicut omnis emissio seminis sine naturali coniunctione maris et feminae; propter quod huiusmodi peccata contra naturam dicuntur."

16. *Summa contra Gentiles*, III, cap. 122, n. 6 (Leonine ed., v. 14, 379). "Similiter etiam oportet contra bonum hominis esse si semen taliter emittatur quod generatio sequi possit,

NATURE

He then applies these observations to human beings.

Plainly, however, in the human species the woman is not at all sufficient to raise the children alone, since many things are required for the necessities of human life that cannot be managed by one person alone. Therefore, it is fitting to human nature that after sexual relations a man should remain with the woman, not leaving her at once and having relations with anyone he pleases, as happens with those who fornicate.[17]

This conclusion concerning fornication does not appear to be *per se nota* to everyone; rather, Aquinas's detailed reasoning indicates that this conclusion is either derived syllogistically or at least that it is *per se nota* only to the learned.[18] In any event, the reasoning is based upon what is known concerning the ends of nature. As stated previously, ejaculation is ordered not simply to reproduction but also to raising the child; consequently, it is permissible only within the context fit for raising children. What is that context? For human beings, both the man and the woman must remain present to raise the child.[19]

Aquinas's argument to this effect involves a detailed examination of animal behavior in nature, and he will continue his analysis in the next paragraph, which we need not quote. This use of nature, however, does not concern our case. It does not establish the ends and goods of a

---

sed conveniens educatio impediatur. Est enim considerandum quod in animalibus in quibus sola femina sufficit ad prolis educationem, mas et femina post coitum nullo tempore commanent, sicut patet in canibus. Quaecumque vero animalia sunt in quibus femina non sufficit ad educationem prolis, mas et femina simul post coitum commanent quousque necessarium est ad prolis educationem et instructionem: sicut patet in quibusdam avibus."

17. *Summa contra Gentiles*, III, cap. 122, n. 6 (Leonine ed., v. 14, 379). "Manifestum est autem quod in specie humana femina minime sufficeret sola ad prolis educationem: cum necessitas humanae vitae multa requirat quae per unum solum parari non possunt. Est igitur conveniens secundum naturam humanam ut homo post coitum mulieri commaneat, et non statim abscedat, indifferenter ad quamcumque accedens, sicut apud fornicantes accidit."

18. Elsewhere (*De malo*, 15, 2, ad 3), Aquinas indicates that the norm against fornicating is not one of the first principles of the natural law, but it is known to the learned through reasoning. In general, he holds that the precepts of the Decalogue are not self-evident. See Randall Smith, "What the Old Law Reveals about the Natural Law According to Thomas Aquinas," *Thomist* 75 (2011): 95–139; James M. Jacobs, "The Precepts of the Decalogue and the Problem of Self-Evidence," *International Philosophical Quarterly* 47 (2007): 399–415.

19. McInerny (*Human Action*, 141–50) gives a detailed account of the manner in which marriage can be called natural.

NATURE

human being; rather, it helps to recognize the best means of achieving these ends, which have been previously established. For our purposes, what matters is that Aquinas is building upon what he has said concerning the end of sexual activity.

The next paragraph is particularly embarrassing for Grisez, in part because he misinterprets Aquinas as claiming that walking on one's hands is a sin.[20]

Nor should we suppose it to be a small sin when someone expels semen outside the required ends of generation and education, just because it is a small sin, or no sin at all, when someone uses a part of his body for some other purpose than that to which it is ordered according to nature, for example, when someone walks on his hands or does something with his feet which ought to be done with his hands. Through these disordered usages the human good is little impeded; in contrast, the disordered emission of semen is opposed to the good of nature, namely, the preservation of the species.[21]

Elsewhere in the *Summa contra Gentiles* Aquinas speaks of reproduction being directed by nature, and he refers to the end in reference to a natural inclination of nature.

Insofar as reproduction is ordered to the good of nature, which is the continuation of the species, it is directed toward the end by nature inclining into this end; in this manner, it is said to be a duty of nature.[22]

5.2.2: *De malo*

This line of reasoning—from the nature of sexual acts to their good and evil—is not reserved to the *Summa contra Gentiles*. I need not repeat the details of the argument, but it is worth quoting passages from

---

20. Germain Grisez, *Contraception and the Natural Law* (Milwaukee: Bruce Publishing Company, 1964), 28–29, esp. n. 13.

21. *Summa contra Gentiles*, III, cap. 122, n. 9 (Leonine ed., v. 14, 379). "Nec tamen oportet reputari leve peccatum esse si quis seminis emissionem procuret praeter debitum generationis et educationis finem, propter hoc quod aut leve aut nullum peccatum est si quis aliqua sui corporis parte utatur ad alium usum quam ad eum ad quem est ordinata secundum naturam, ut si quis, verbi gratia, manibus ambulet, aut pedibus aliquid operetur manibus operandum: quia per huiusmodi inordinatos usus bonum hominis non multum impeditur; inordinata vero seminis emissio repugnat bono naturae, quod est conservatio speciei."

22. *Summa contra Gentiles*, IV, cap. 78, n. 2 (Leonine ed., v. 15, 246). "Unde oportet quod huiusmodi generatio a diversis dirigatur. - Inquantum igitur ordinatur ad bonum naturae, quod est perpetuitas speciei, dirigitur in finem a natura inclinante in hunc finem: et sic dicitur esse naturae officium."

NATURE

other texts in which the role of nature is evidently expressed. In the *De malo,* for instance, Aquinas says,

> That every [use of the reproductive organs outside of the act of marriage] is disordered in itself is apparent because all human acts are said to be disordered when they are not proportioned to the proper end. For example, eating is disordered if it is not proportioned to the health of the body, to which the act of eating is ordered as to an end. Since the end of using the reproductive organs is the generation and education of offspring, every use of these organs that is not proportioned to the generation of offspring, and to their due education, is of itself disordered, for example, every act of these organs outside the union of male and female is manifestly unfit for the generation of children.[23]

Aquinas proceeds to give the same argument against fornication as we have seen in the *Summa contra Gentiles,* which we need not reproduce here.

In a reply to an objection, Aquinas provides the following familiar argument; in the *De malo,* however, Aquinas speaks of an "end intended by nature."

> The Philosopher says that semen is excess material in relation to the act of nourishing but that it is needed for the generation of offspring. Therefore, every voluntary emission of semen is illicit unless it is suitable for the end intended by nature.[24]

In the next article, Aquinas also speaks of "the intention of nature with respect to the reproduction and education of offspring in the act of the fornicator."[25]

---

23. *De malo,* 15, 1 (Leonine ed., v. 23, 270, 124–41). "Quandoque uero cum inordinatione concupiscentie est etiam inordinatio ipsius actus exterioris secundum se ipsum; sicut contingit in omni usu genitalium membrorum preter matrimonialem actum. Et quod omnis talis actus sit inordinatus secundum se ipsum apparet ex hoc quod omnis actus humanus dicitur esse inordinatus qui non est proportionatus debito fini; sicut comestio est inordinata, si non proportionetur corporis salubritati` ad quam ordinatur sicut ad finem. Finis autem usus genitalium membrorum est generatio et educatio prolis; et ideo omnis usus predictorum membrorum qui non est proportionatus generationi prolis et debitae eius educationi, est secundum se inordinatus. Quicumque autem actus predictorum membrorum est preter commixtionem maris et feminae manifestum est quod non est accommodus generationi prolis."

24. *De malo,* 15, 1, ad 4 (Leonine ed., v. 23, 271, 222–27). "Philosophus dicit in eodem libro, semen est superfluum quidem quantum ad actum nutritiuae, set quo indigetur ad generationem prolis, et ideo omnis uoluntaria emissio seminis est illicita nisi secundum conuenientiam ad finem a natura intentum."

25. *De malo,* 15, 2, ad 12 (Leonine ed., v. 23, 276, 333–36). "Et ideo licet in aliquo casu

NATURE

This "intention of nature" is connected to the natural law in Aquinas's commentary on the *Sentences*.

An action is said to be against the natural law when it is not proportioned to the required end, either because it is not ordered toward that end by the action of the agent or because it lacks the proportion to that end by its very nature. Since the end that nature intends in sexual activity is the reproduction and raising of offspring, someone can take pleasure in sexual activity insofar as he seeks this good. But if anyone uses sexual activity for its pleasure but does not refer it to the end intended by nature, then he acts contrary to nature.[26]

What is this intention of nature and where does it come from? The contrast, it seems, is to the intention of the person acting, that is, to the conscious goals that the person has. In the *Summa*, Aquinas explains the intention of nature in the following manner:

To intend is to tend into another, which [tendency] is in both the mover and the thing moved. In this manner, that which is moved to an end by another is said to intend the end; thus, nature is said to intend an end, as if it is moved to its end by God, as an arrow by an archer.[27]

Furthermore, for nature to intend an end is just to have a natural inclination to something: "It is possible for a natural agent to intend an end without deliberation, and to intend this is nothing other than to have a natural inclination into something."[28] It would seem, then, that nature intends, in this case, by the nonconscious inclination associated with the power of reproduction.

---

possit saluari intentio nature in actu fornicario quantum ad generationem prolis et educationem."

26. *Sent.*, IV 33, 1, 3, qc. 1. "Actio dicitur esse contra legem naturae, quae non est conveniens fini debito, sive quia non ordinatur in ipsum per actionem agentis, sive quia de se est improportionata fini illi. Finis autem quem natura ex concubitu intendit, est proles procreanda et educanda; et ut hoc bonum quaereretur, posuit delectationem in coitu; ut Augustinus dicit. Quicumque ergo concubitu utitur propter delectationem quae in ipso est, non referendo ad finem a natura intentum, contra naturam facit."

27. I-II, 12, 5. "Intendere est in aliud tendere; quod quidem est et moventis, et moti. Secundum quidem igitur quod dicitur intendere finem id quod movetur ad finem ab alio, sic natura dicitur intendere finem, quasi mota ad suum finem a Deo, sicut sagitta a sagittante."

28. *De principiis naturae*, cap. 3 (Leonine ed., v. 43, 42, 38–41). "Possibile est agens naturale sine deliberatione intendere finem. Et hoc intendere nichil aliud erat quam habere naturalem inclinationem ad aliquid."

NATURE

5.2.3: *Summa theologiae*

The same sort of arguments appear in the *Secunda secundae*. Lee concedes that Aquinas makes these arguments from nature, but he claims it is an aberration, departing from Aquinas's usual procedure. He might find some consolation in the following text, since Aquinas notes that at least some sexual sins derive from a repugnance to right reason, rather than a repugnance to nature.

> There is a determinate species of lust where there occurs a special character of deformity making the sexual act unsuitable, which can happen in two ways. In one way, because it is repugnant to right reason, which is common to all sins of lust; in another way, because, beyond this, it is repugnant to the very order of the nature of the sexual act fitting to the human species, which is then called a sin against nature.[29]

The reference to right reason, however, actually provides no balm for Rhonheimer and the new natural law theory. In the very next article Aquinas explains that reason is based upon those things that are determined by nature. "The principles of reason are those that are according to nature, for reason, presupposing those things that are determined by nature, disposes other things insofar as it is fitting."[30]

This account matches Aquinas's actual procedure perfectly. He argues for the evil of fornication — which is a matter that belongs to right reason rather than to nature — based upon the nature of the sexual act. Because the reproductive act is ordered not only to reproduction but also to the raising of the offspring, sexual relations must be had in that context appropriate for the raising of offspring. We use a fair amount of reasoning to determine that context, but the very condition of the context — that sexual relations must be fit to maintain this order to education — is set by nature. This idea of basing right reason upon the things of nature is noted elsewhere: "Plainly, human acts can be ruled

---

29. II-II, 154, 11. "Ibi est determinata luxuriae species ubi specialis ratio deformitatis occurrit quae facit indecentem actum venereum. Quod quidem potest esse dupliciter. Uno quidem modo, quia repugnat rationi rectae, quod est commune in omni vitio luxuriae. Alio modo, quia etiam, super hoc, repugnat ipsi ordini naturali venerei actus qui convenit humanae speciei, quod dicitur vitium contra naturam."

30. II-II, 154, 12. "Principia autem rationis sunt ea quae sunt secundum naturam, nam ratio, praesuppositis his quae sunt a natura determinata, disponit alia secundum quod convenit."

NATURE

by the rule of human reason, which is taken from the created things that man naturally knows."[31]

Aquinas explains the "divide" between reason and nature as follows:

> A lustful act can be said to be against nature in two ways. First, absolutely, because it is contrary to the nature of all animals. In this manner, every lustful act outside the context of the union of male and female is said to be against nature, insofar as it is not proportioned to reproduction, which is made, for every species of animal, through the union of both sexes. In another way, something is said to be contrary to nature because it is contrary to the nature proper to human beings, to whom it belongs to order the act of reproduction to the necessary education; in this manner, all fornication is contrary to nature.[32]

> Human nature can refer to that which is proper to human beings, and in this way all sins, insofar as they are opposed to reason, are also contrary to nature. It can also refer to that which is common to human beings and other animals, and in this way certain special sins are said to be contrary to nature, for example, sexual activity between males is opposed to the union of male and female, which is natural to all animals, and is called, in a special way, a sin against nature.[33]

In other words, the "divide" is a matter of how we use the word "nature." In either event, nature, in the sense of certain ends set by our natural powers, is at the bottom of it all.[34]

---

31. I-II, 74, 7. "Manifestum est autem quod actus humani regulari possunt ex regula rationis humanae, quae sumitur ex rebus creatis, quas naturaliter homo cognoscit."

32. *De malo*, 15, 1, ad 7 (Leonine ed., v. 23, 272, 141–53). "Actus luxurie potest dici contra naturam dupliciter : uno modo absolute, quia scilicet est contra naturam omnis animalis : et sic omnis actus luxurie preter commixtionem maris et femine dicitur esse contra naturam in quantum non est proportionatus generationi, que in quolibet genere animalis fit ex commixtione utriusque sexus ; et hoc modo loquitur Glosa. Alio modo dicitur esse aliquid contra naturam quia est contra naturam propriam hominis cuius est ordinare generationis actum ad debitam educationem, et sic omnis fornicatio est contra naturam."

33. I-II, 94, 3, ad 2. "Natura hominis potest dici vel illa quae est propria homini, et secundum hoc, omnia peccata, inquantum sunt contra rationem, sunt etiam contra naturam, ut patet per Damascenum, in II libro. Vel illa quae est communis homini et aliis animalibus, et secundum hoc, quaedam specialia peccata dicuntur esse contra naturam; sicut contra commixtionem maris et feminae, quae est naturalis omnibus animalibus, est concubitus masculorum, quod specialiter dicitur vitium contra naturam."

34. In *Summa contra Gentiles*, III, cap. 123, n. 3 Aquinas refers to fornication as against human nature; in n. 4 Aquinas refers to divorce as contrary to nature.

NATURE

⊷ 5.3 ⊶

GOOD AND EVIL IN OTHER DOMAINS

5.3.1: Eating and Drinking

Is the reference to nature as the basis of good and evil an anomaly, reserved to Aquinas's treatment of sexual ethics? A cursory examination reveals otherwise. In a text quoted above, Aquinas clearly used the same reasoning for the ethics of eating and drinking: "Eating is disordered if it is not proportioned to the health of the body, to which the act of eating is ordered as to an end." The same line of reasoning appears in the *Summa contra Gentiles*.

> The consumption of food can be a sin only to the degree that it is opposed to the rectitude of the will, which can happen because of an opposition to the proper end of food, for example, someone, on account of the pleasure found in the food, might use foods that are opposed to the health of the body, either on account of the kind of food or of the quantity of food.[35]

Aquinas does not provide the details, but it is not difficult to imagine how the discovery might go. Through observation we can determine that the purpose of eating is the maintenance of the body. Once that purpose is determined — through speculative reason — then we know what is the end and good of eating. At issue, here, is the nonconscious inclination of the power of nourishing, which we engage through the act of eating.

In the *Sentences* Aquinas provides some interesting details regarding eating. He begins with general reflections upon the relation between natural law and nature.

> The natural law is nothing other than a conception naturally impressed upon men by which they are directed to act appropriately in their own actions, either as they apply to the nature of the genus, for example to reproduce, to eat, and things of this sort, or as they apply to the nature of the human species, for example, to reason and such things. *Every performance of an action unsuitable to the end that nature intends in some activity is said to be against the natural law.*[36]

---

35. *Summa contra Gentiles*, III, cap. 127, n. 4 (Leonine ed., v. 14, 390). "Non igitur ciborum sumptio secundum se potest esse peccatum, nisi quatenus repugnat rectitudini voluntatis. Quod quidem contingit uno modo, propter repugnantiam ad proprium finem ciborum: sicut cum aliquis, propter delectationem quae est in cibis, utitur cibis contrariantibus corporis saluti, vel secundum speciem ciborum, vel secundum quantitatem."

36. *Sent.*, IV, 33, 1, 1. "Lex ergo naturalis nihil est aliud quam conceptio homini nat-

NATURE

The italicized sentence (my emphasis) indicates the universal character of this approach. Looking to the end intended by nature as a guide for the good or evil of actions is a general rule that can be applied to many diverse cases.

Aquinas continues by making a distinction between primary and secondary ends, a distinction that does not appear in later writings, but is certainly consistent with his later thought. Finally, he concludes with some general principles of how these diverse ends of nature relate to precepts of the natural law.

> If an action is unsuitable to the end by entirely prohibiting the principal end, then it is prohibited directly by the natural law with a primary precept of the natural law, which precepts are, for things to be done, like the common conceptions in speculative matters. On the other hand, if it is opposed to a secondary end in some manner, or even if it is opposed to the principal end by making its accomplishment difficult or less suitable, then it is prohibited not by a primary precept of the natural law but by a secondary, which precepts are derived from the first.[37]

Clearly, Aquinas has identified various ends of nature, and from these he has moved to precepts of the natural law.

Further along in this text, Aquinas notes that the sexual act also has a secondary end, namely, the mutual support of the spouses. It is good to keep in mind this secondary end when considering other texts, some of which we have quoted, that seem to allow no other purpose for the sexual act besides reproduction.

5.3.2: Manual Labor

The focus upon the natural order of various bodily functions also arises when Aquinas considers the question whether the precepts of the law

---

uraliter indita, qua dirigitur ad convenienter agendum in actionibus propriis, sive competant ei ex natura generis, ut generare, comedere, et hujusmodi; sive ex natura speciei, ut ratiocinari, et similia. Omne autem illud quod actionem inconvenientem reddit fini quem natura ex opere aliquo intendit, contra legem naturae esse dicitur."

37. *Sent.*, IV, 33, 1, 1. "Si ergo actio sit inconveniens fini quasi omnino prohibens finem principalem, directe per legem naturae prohibetur primis praeceptis legis naturae, quae sunt in operabilibus, sicut sunt communes conceptiones in speculativis. Si autem sit incompetens fini secundario quocumque modo, aut etiam principali, ut faciens difficilem vel minus congruam perventionem ad ipsum; prohibetur non quidem primis praeceptis legis naturae, sed secundis, quae ex primis derivantur."

NATURE

require manual labor. The question carried great significance for Aquinas, since the Dominicans were criticized because they did not require manual labor. Aquinas's response is nuanced. Some of the reasons for manual labor are really just reasons for any kind of labor. The one that truly does lead to a precept of the law concerning manual labor, however, is only for human beings in general, and not for every individual human being. The section of the argument that concerns us reads as follows:

> Insofar as manual labor is ordered to acquiring food, it seems to belong to a precept, for which reason it is said in the first letter to the *Thessalonians*: "work with your hands, as we have commanded you." This precept belongs not only to the positive law but to the natural law as well, for those belong to the natural law to which man is inclined by his nature. As is plain from the very disposition of the body, however, man has a natural order to manual labor, for which reason it is said in *Job* that "man is born for labor as a bird is born to fly."[38]

The natural order to labor, then, does not depend upon some primary underived "ought"; it depends upon the disposition or ordering of the body. We are looking here at something like what Aquinas calls the locomotive power, the ability to move our bodies. This power is directed toward accomplishing various tasks.

Aquinas proceeds to give an involved argument, akin to the one that we saw concerning fornication, contrasting other animals to human beings. While other animals have the proper bodily parts to achieve their various tasks, we have hands, which are a kind of generic tool to achieve a variety of tasks under the guidance of reason.

5.3.3: The Intellect

This line of reasoning, in which some order is discovered through the nature of some power, is not reserved to bodily goods, such as sex and food; Aquinas uses it in a wide range of areas. Most often, perhaps,

---

38. *Quodlibet* VII, 7, 1 (Leonine ed., v. 25, 35, 115–25). "Secundum autem quod ordinatur ad uictum quaerendum, sic uidetur esse in praecepto; unde dicitur I ad Thess. IV, 11: operamini manibus uestris, sicut praecepimus uobis. Nec solum in praecepto iuris positiui, sed etiam iuris naturalis: illa enim sunt de lege naturali ad que homo ex suis naturalibus inclinatur; sicut autem ex ipsa dispositione corporis patet, homo naturalem ordinationem habet ad opus manual, propter quod dicitur Iob, V, 7: homo ad laborem nascitur, et auis ad uolandum."

NATURE

Aquinas refers to the potency of the intellect. He says, for instance, "The truth, insofar as it is the end of intellectual operation, is contained under the good as a certain particular good."[39]

When he argues concerning the ultimate end and good of human life he does not refer to some free-standing practical knowledge; rather, he repeatedly refers to the nature of the intellect itself.

> If human beatitude is in operation, then it must be the highest human operation, which will be that operation belonging to the highest power with respect to its highest object. But the highest power is the intellect, and its highest object is the divine good, which is not the object of the practical intellect but of the speculative. Consequently, happiness consists most of all in this operation, namely, in contemplation of the divine.[40]

The follow-up argument, quoted below, is even more forceful, and comes as close as we might hope to a statement that the dependence to which Aquinas refers is epistemological. He says "for which evidence," indicating a kind of epistemological support. What is that support? Nothing from practical reason; everything from speculative reason. Furthermore, when Aquinas seeks a basis for identifying the completion of the intellect, he uses the word *attenditur,* which has something of the sense of a mental drawing of attention. In this text, Aquinas does speak of wonder, a natural desire that belongs, no doubt, to the will. Nevertheless, that desire depends upon the nature of the intellect, with the incomplete realization of the intellect's own end.

> Ultimate and complete beatitude can be realized only in the vision of the divine essence, *for which evidence* two things should be considered. First, man is not perfectly happy when he still desires and seeks something. Second, the completion of any potency is taken from [*attenditur*] the *ratio* of its object. The object of the intellect, however, is what-something-is, that is, the essence of a thing. Consequently, the completion of the intellect is realized to the degree that it knows the essence of any thing. Therefore, if an intellect knows the es-

---

39. *De malo,* 6, 1 (Leonine ed., v. 23, 149, 336–38). "Et ipsum uerum, in quantum est finis intellectualis operationis, continetur sub bono ut quoddam particulare bonum."

40. I-II, 3, 5. "Si beatitudo hominis est operatio, oportet quod sit optima operatio hominis. Optima autem operatio hominis est quae est optimae potentiae respectu optimi obiecti. Optima autem potentia est intellectus, cuius optimum obiectum est bonum divinum, quod quidem non est obiectum practici intellectus, sed speculativi. Unde in tali operatione, scilicet in contemplatione divinorum, maxime consistit beatitudo." See also *Super de causis,* pr.

NATURE

sence of any effect through which it is unable to come to know the essence of the cause (or know what the cause is), then the intellect is not said to grasp the cause simply speaking, although by way of the effect it can know that the cause exists. Consequently, when a man knows an effect, and he knows that it has a cause, then a natural desire remains in him to know the nature of the cause. That desire is wonder, which is the cause of inquiry.[41]

In other places, Aquinas simply refers to the completion, end, or good of the intellect, in a manner that parallels his discussion of the end of sexual activity.

Truth is the good of the intellect, and not the good of an appetitive power; therefore, every virtue that perfects the intellect excludes falsity entirely, since it belongs to the *ratio* of virtue that it relates only to what is good.[42]

The will desires those things that belong to the intellect, and many other things as well. Consequently, the truth, according to its proper *ratio*, which is the perfection of the intellect, is a certain particular good, insofar as it is something desirable.[43]

5.3.4: Other Powers

Looking beyond the intellect toward other powers, we can begin with a text that returns us to the question of sexual ethics. In the *De malo*, an objection suggests that fornication is a sin either by reason of the power from which it arises, or from its material, or from its end. The power turns out to be not the power of reproduction but the concupiscible

---

41. I-II, 3, 8. "Ultima et perfecta beatitudo non potest esse nisi in visione divinae essentiae. Ad cuius evidentiam, duo consideranda sunt. Primo quidem, quod homo non est perfecte beatus, quandiu restat sibi aliquid desiderandum et quaerendum. Secundum est, quod uniuscuiusque potentiae perfectio attenditur secundum rationem sui obiecti. Obiectum autem intellectus est quod quid est, idest essentia rei, ut dicitur in III de anima. Unde intantum procedit perfectio intellectus, inquantum cognoscit essentiam alicuius rei. Si ergo intellectus aliquis cognoscat essentiam alicuius effectus, per quam non possit cognosci essentia causae, ut scilicet sciatur de causa quid est; non dicitur intellectus attingere ad causam simpliciter, quamvis per effectum cognoscere possit de causa an sit. Et ideo remanet naturaliter homini desiderium, cum cognoscit effectum, et scit eum habere causam, ut etiam sciat de causa quid est. Et illud desiderium est admirationis, et causat inquisitionem."

42. II-II, 1, 3, ad 1. "Verum est bonum intellectus, non autem est bonum appetitivae virtutis, ideo omnes virtutes quae perficiunt intellectum excludunt totaliter falsum, quia de ratione virtutis est quod se habeat solum ad bonum."

43. II-II, 109, 2, ad 1. "Voluntas appetit ea quae pertinent ad intellectum, et multa alia. Unde verum, secundum rationem propriam, qua est perfectio intellectus, est quoddam particulare bonum, inquantum est appetibile quoddam."

NATURE

power, since the action we are concerned with is an act of consciously desiring sex. Fornication cannot be sinful on this account, the objector argues, because it is natural (presumably, natural to desire sex).

Aquinas's response provides little guidance for our concern, except that he does address the concupiscible power, which like the other powers has a certain nature. The concupiscible power is ordered not just to pleasure but to pleasure under the guidance of reason. In chapter 3 we questioned the manner in which the passions might relate to natural inclinations, either according to the nature of the passions as a power or according to their actions, which are also inclinations. This passage seems to favor the importance of the concupiscible power: "A lustful act is a sin by reason of the potency, insofar as the concupiscible power is not contained under the order of reason."[44]

In the *Summa contra Gentiles* we discover that this order of reason derives from nature, which orders pleasure to necessary actions; the overall purpose of the concupiscible power is thereby more clearly seen. Aquinas is explaining why there will be no sex and eating in heaven, and he has the following to say about these activities in this life.

> It is disordered and vicious to use food and sex only for pleasure and not for the necessity of sustaining the body or reproducing offspring. The reason for this is as follows. The pleasures taken in these actions are not the ends of the actions; rather, the reverse is the case, for nature orders the pleasures of these actions toward the action, so that animals do not cease from these actions, so necessary for nature, on account of the work involved, which would happen if they were not enticed by pleasure. Therefore, it is a perverse and indecent order when these actions are performed only for the sake of pleasure.[45]

In many places we do not find Aquinas providing particular examples of the good associated with some power and its end; rather, he makes general statements about powers having some end and good.

---

44. *De malo*, 15, 1, ad 3 (Leonine ed., v. 23, 271, 211–13). "Actus luxurie est peccatum ratione potentie, in quantum scilicet concupiscibilis non continetur sub ordine rationis."

45. *Summa contra Gentiles*, IV cap. 83, n. 9 (Leonine ed., v. 15, 264). "In hac autem vita inordinatum et vitiosum est si quis cibis et venereis utatur propter solam delectationem, et non propter necessitatem sustentandi corporis, vel prolis procreandae. Et hoc rationabiliter: nam delectationes quae sunt in praemissis actionibus, non sunt fines actionum, sed magis e converso; natura enim ad hoc ordinavit delectationes in istis actibus, ne animalia, propter laborem, ab istis actibus necessariis naturae desisterent; quod contingeret nisi delectatione provocarentur." See also *Summa contra Gentiles*, IV cap. 83, n. 11.

NATURE

These diverse statements can be summed up in the following line, "Any potency has some end, which is its good."[46] Other passages are worth quoting for emphasis. He identifies the good as follows:

> Because the prudent person is said to deliberate well simply speaking, he must deliberate concerning those things that are ordered to the human good simply speaking. This good consists in the completion of the soul, which has its ultimate completion in the required operation of the potencies of the soul.[47]

Likewise, in the following passage, Aquinas identifies the good through each potency.

> Since it is the mover of all other powers of the soul, the will must relate to the objects and acts of all other powers insofar as they have the character of good, for the required act of each potency is its good. Therefore, the contemplative life consists in an act of a cognitive power received by the affective power.[48]

In a parallel text, Aquinas gives the examples of the intellect and the power of sight.

> The will moves the intellect and all other powers, for in all active potencies ordered to one another, that potency which refers to the universal end moves the potencies that refer to particular ends.... But the object of the will is the good and end in common. In contrast, any potency relates to some proper good appropriate to it, for instance, vision relates to the perception of colors and the intellect to the knowledge of the truth.[49]

---

46. *De veritate*, 14, 2, ad 6 (Leonine ed., v. 22, 443, 336–38). "Quaelibet potentia habet aliquem finem qui est bonum ipsius."

47. *Sent.*, III, 33, 2, 2, qc. 1 (Mandonnet, v. 3, 1053). "Et quia prudens dicitur bene consiliativus simpliciter, oportet quod consilietur de his quae sunt ordinata ad bonum hominis simpliciter. Hoc autem consistit in animae perfectione, cujus ultima perfectio est debita operatio potentiarum animae."

48. *Sent.*, III, 35, 1, 2, qc. 1 (Mandonnet, v. 3, 1177). "Voluntas autem cum sit motor omnium potentiarum animae, oportet quod ad objecta et actus omnium potentiarum se habeat, prout habent rationem boni, quia unusquisque actus debitus cujuscumque potentiae est, bonum est. Et ideo vita contemplativa consistit in actu cognitivae virtutis praeacceptatae per affectivam."

49. I, 82, 4. "Voluntas movet intellectum, et omnes animae vires; ut Anselmus dicit in libro de similitudinibus. Cuius ratio est, quia in omnibus potentiis activis ordinatis, illa potentia quae respicit finem universalem, movet potentias quae respiciunt fines particulares.... Obiectum autem voluntatis est bonum et finis in communi. Quaelibet autem potentia comparatur ad aliquod bonum proprium sibi conveniens; sicut visus ad perceptionem coloris, intellectus ad cognitionem veri. Et ideo voluntas per modum agentis movet omnes animae potentias ad suos actus, praeter vires naturales vegetativae partis, quae nostro arbitrio non subduntur."

NATURE

In the next passage, Aquinas is concerned with the freedom of the will, but he first recognizes that the will is necessitated by its own natural inclination to beatitude. Every power of the soul has its own desire for its own particular good. The will is different, in that it seeks the good of the whole animal.

> A natural appetite is in every power of the soul and in every part of the body with respect to its own proper good, but the animal appetite, which is a determinate good, to which the inclination of nature does not suffice, belongs to some determinate potency, either the will or the concupiscible power. As a result, all other powers of the soul are necessitated by their objects, apart from the will, because every other power has, with respect to its object, a natural appetite only.[50]

5.3.5: Other Natural Inclinations

Finally, we have texts in which Aquinas speaks about natural inclinations and the good, or about natural inclinations and precepts. Sometimes he merely indicates a relationship between these two, but the direction of the relationship is unclear. In some texts, however, it is difficult to see how the direction that Aquinas wishes to express could be anything other than the move from the natural inclination to practical knowledge. We should note that many of the following texts might well be referring to inclinations of the will. In some of them, however, there is a clear connection with nonconscious inclinations. At the very least, then, these texts indicate the flow of thought from inclination to the good, whether that inclination belongs to the will or to nature in the strict sense of nonconscious inclination.

When asking whether an obligation to offer sacrifice to God belongs to the natural law, he says,

> Just as in natural things those that are naturally inferior are subject to the superior, so also natural reason dictates to man, according to a natural inclina-

---

50. *Sent.*, III, 27, 1, 2 (Mandonnet, v. 3, 862). "Appetitus naturalis inest omnibus potentiis animae et partibus corporis respectu proprii boni; sed appetitus animalis qui est boni determinati, ad quod non sufficit naturae inclinatio, est alicujus potentiae determinatae, vel voluntatis vel concupiscibilis. Et inde est quod omnes aliae vires animae coguntur a suis objectis praeter voluntatem; quia omnes aliae habent appetitum naturalem tantum respectu sui objecti."

NATURE

tion, that he should show honor and subjection, in the proper manner, to that which is above him.[51]

The natural inclination is not according to the dictate of reason; to the contrary, the dictate of reason is according to the natural inclination.

A similar move — from inclination to dictate of reason — is implied (with the inferential term "consequently") when Aquinas discusses the dictate to set aside time for God.

There is in man a natural inclination to set aside some time for anything that is necessary, for example, for refreshments for the body, sleep, and things of this sort. Consequently, men should set aside some time, according to the dictate of natural reason, for the refreshment of the spirit, by which the mind of man is refreshed in God.[52]

In the following text, Aquinas argues that something is against a natural inclination, and *consequently* it is a sin.

It is naturally impressed upon everyone to love his own life and those things that are ordered to it, but in the proper manner, so that these things are loved not as if the end is realized in them but insofar as the use of them is on account of the ultimate end. As a result, when someone fails from the proper manner of loving himself it is against a natural inclination and consequently it is a sin.[53]

Finally, Aquinas argues that it is a greater evil for a child to turn against his father than for a father to turn against his child. Why? Because of the relative strengths of the natural inclinations in either direction.

The natural love of a father for his child is to be understood according to the natural inclination of affection to benefit oneself, but the love of a son for his

---

51. II-II, 85, 1. "Sicut autem in rebus naturalibus naturaliter inferiora superioribus subduntur, ita etiam naturalis ratio dictat homini secundum naturalem inclinationem ut ei quod est supra hominem subiectionem et honorem exhibeat secundum suum modum."

52. II-II, 122, 4, ad 1. "Inest enim homini naturalis inclinatio ad hoc quod cuilibet rei necessariae deputetur aliquod tempus, sicut corporali refectioni, somno et aliis huiusmodi. Unde etiam spirituali refectioni, qua mens hominis in Deo reficitur, secundum dictamen rationis naturalis aliquod tempus deputat homo."

53. II-II, 126, 1. "Inditum autem est unicuique naturaliter ut propriam vitam amet, et ea quae ad ipsam ordinantur, tamen debito modo, ut scilicet amentur huiusmodi non quasi finis constituatur in eis, sed secundum quod eis utendum est propter ultimum finem. Unde quod aliquis deficiat a debito modo amoris ipsorum, est contra naturalem inclinationem, et per consequens est peccatum."

NATURE

father is to be understood according to the natural inclination to subject himself to his father. This latter inclination is not less than the first; to the contrary, it is greater. As a result, a greater evil arises when a human being turns away from this latter inclination than arises when he turns away from the former.[54]

5.4
A SUMMARY OF THE CASE

These texts are sufficient to indicate that Aquinas's identification of the good through certain natural ends, given to us in our diverse powers, is not anomalous. It is not reserved for sexual ethics, and it is not reserved to the power of reproduction. When Aquinas wishes to identify some good we find him looking to nature. Without exception he fails to mention some hidden principles of reason preceding nature. In fact, he leaves the distinct impression that nature precedes reason; reason discovers its principles from nature.

Is he merely providing us with the ontological basis of what we already knew through independent practical knowledge? We have no reason to think so. We have seen that Aquinas thinks that the good is a final cause, and that we know this cause through its effect, which is desire or inclination. The character of this inclination is grasped through observations of where activities end. This line of thinking, when it applies to beavers or trees, is purely speculative. For human beings, it is speculative until the final step, in which the good is discovered and we have materially practical knowledge.

Finally, while we can find a host of examples of Aquinas arguing toward the good from nature; the opposite move — from the good to nature — is absent. Or rather, since it is entirely possible that Aquinas makes the move somewhere I have missed, we can say, at least, that this Finnis-like move is rare to nonexistent. Of course, one or two such cases, if they were discovered, would not prove Finnis's case. On either account — on Finnis's view or on the classical view — our reasoning

---

54. *Sent.*, III, 29, 1, 7, ad 1 (Mandonnet, v. 3, 942). "Unde amor naturalis ad filium attenditur secundum inclinationem naturalem affectus ad benefaciendum sibi, sed amor filii ad patrem attenditur secundum inclinationem naturalem ad subjiciendum se ei; et haec inclinatio non est minor quam prima, immo major. Unde majorem malitiam oportet advenire ad hoc quod homo avertatur ab ista inclinatione quam a prima."

can always be reversed. We can come to understand what the good is from nature, and then understand what nature must be, given a certain good.

We have every reason to suppose, then, that Aquinas presents us with multiple examples of an epistemological dependence, moving from a natural inclination, or an intention of nature, to practical knowledge, either knowledge of the good or of a precept. Of course, the dependence is also ontological. Aquinas does not make the distinction between the two. He has no need to, since the dependence moves in the same direction both for our knowledge and for the reality in things.

According to Rhonheimer, "In the world can be found neither justice nor friendship nor virtue; nor can one find matrimony or anything similar."[55] What one can find, however, is a natural union founded upon the power of procreation, a union realized in a human way through the will. One finds these things as one discovers the future, as contained in potency in our inclinations.

All of these things are found in nature, not as if they grow without will, like a new sapling. Their coming to be involves choices of the will, and insofar as the will is opposed to nature, these things are not found in nature. But their very nature — what they are as opposed to their coming to be — is found in nature. The fulfilling union of male and female is found, in potency, in our natural inclinations. That we tend to the continuation of the species by way of union of male and female, and that this union is carried out through the will, and that this union must be directed to the maturity of the offspring — all of this is found in nature. It is there to be discovered, and if it were not discovered, then the will could not move toward it.

---

55. Rhonheimer, *Natural Law*, 17.

6

THE WILL

We hope to discover what the will contributes to our knowledge of the good. Somehow, the will must be central to ethics, for any good activity that does not ultimately arise from the will is not moral activity. Properly functioning digestion is indeed good for a human being, but it is not a moral good. If the goods that Aquinas discovers through our natural inclinations are simply goods of nonconscious inclinations, then it seems that they are disconnected from the human or moral good. In short, physicalism seems to follow from the use of nature exhibited in the last chapter.

This chapter hopes to overcome this apparent deficiency by looking to the distinctive inclinations of the will. We must first establish what these distinctive inclinations are. Unfortunately, the discovery of these inclinations will prove to be a difficult task. Compelling reasons will suggest that the will has no distinctive inclinations; it merely reflects and echoes what is first known through other inclinations. Consider the inclination of the will toward the good of knowledge. We first know that knowledge is good not through the will but through the nonconscious inclination of the intellect; only then does the will begin to desire knowledge, with its own natural inclination. Since any desire of the will presumes some awareness of the good, the desires of the will cannot themselves give rise to that awareness.

Consequently, this chapter will begin with a consideration of the arguments that suggest the will has no distinctive contribution. These arguments will reveal the limitations of what the will can contribute. The next section, however, will indicate that the will does in fact provide a unique contribution, namely, it is the inclination of the whole person to his united good. After we examine the precise nature of this contribution, we will then be able to address the objection concern-

THE WILL

ing physicalism, which claims that naturalism (the view that bases our knowledge of the good upon nature) must leave out the will. To the contrary, we will suggest, nature includes the will.

The chapter will close with a broader topic, moving beyond the concerns of the will. The last section will seek to bring closure to the entire discussion of material practical knowledge found in chapters 4, 5, and 6, by addressing the question of the *per se nota* character of our knowledge. In question 94, article 2, Aquinas implies that we have per se knowledge of certain goods; for example, the statement "knowledge is good" is not derived by syllogism but is known immediately. Before we proceed to discuss virtual practical knowledge, in chapter 7, it would be worthwhile considering how these sorts of statements concerning basic goods are *per se nota*.

6.1
THE WILL AS UNORIGINAL

The most compelling reason to suppose that the will contributes no inclinations of its own follows upon the nature of the will as a conscious inclination. The will is inclined only to what is known as good, and we know what is good by way of inclinations. It seems to follow that all inclinations of the will are derivative. This initial argument is supplemented by a kind of argument by elimination. An examination of inclinations that seem to arise uniquely from the will reveals that these inclinations, as well, are derivative. We will begin, then, with the argument concerning the derivative nature of the inclinations of the will.

6.1.1 Inclinations of the Will Are Derivative upon Other Inclinations

The inclinations of the will always follow upon some awareness of the good; consequently, we must first be aware of the good — by first knowing some other inclination — before the will itself is inclined to that good. For every natural inclination from another part of human nature, the will has its own corresponding natural inclination; the intellect is inclined to know the truth, and so also is the will inclined toward knowledge. The will, it seems, always provides an echo inclination, but does it provide any original inclinations of its own?

THE WILL

Every inclination, and therefore every power, has an end and a good for its object. Most inclinations, however, do not tend to this object precisely as good; rather, they move to the good under some other formality. The intellect, for instance, moves to the truth. The truth is itself a good, but the intellect moves to it under the formality of true, and not as good.

The same object, such as an apple, might be the object of the nourishing power, the power of taste, the intellect, and the will, but it will correspond to each under a different formality. The nourishing power is directed to it insofar as it is sustenance, the power of taste insofar as it is sweet, the intellect is directed to it insofar as it is true, that is, insofar as it is known as a certain being, and the will insofar as it is good. Since the apple is good in many respects — it is nourishing, sweet, and known as true — the will can be directed to it in diverse ways. The good corresponding to each of the different powers, with its inclination, can serve as the object of the will.

Each of the inclinations of the diverse powers reveals different aspects of good in the apple. But what of the will itself? That is, the apple is good insofar as it corresponds to the power of nourishing, the power of taste, and the intellect, but is it good insofar as it corresponds to the will itself? On the face of it, it would seem not. Or, at the very least, the will does not first of all seek the apple insofar as it is the object of its own inclination; it seeks the apple insofar as it is the object of other inclinations.

Most precisely, we can say that the first object to which the will tends cannot be a good corresponding to its own inclination; it must be a good corresponding to some other inclination. Retrospectively, perhaps, an object might also be desired precisely insofar as it is loved by the will. Primarily, however, it will be the object of the will's desire under some other formality of goodness; the will first desires the apple because it is nourishing, and then desires it insofar as it fulfills the will itself. For this reason, Aquinas insists that the first thing desired by the will cannot itself be an act of will.[1] The priority Aquinas speaks of here

---

1. *Summa contra Gentiles,* III, cap. 26, n. 9 (Leonine ed, v. 14, 71). "In omnibus potentiis quae moventur a suis obiectis, obiecta sunt naturaliter priora actibus illarum potentiarum: sicut motor naturaliter prior est quam moveri ipsius mobilis. Talis autem potentia est voluntas: appetibile enim movet appetitum. Obiectum igitur voluntatis est prius naturaliter

THE WILL

is a logical priority, not just a temporal priority. The act of the will cannot precede its object.

6.1.2: Are There Inclinations Unique to the Will?

Some natural inclinations, however, seem like they can have no other source besides the will. For the most part, the inclinations mentioned in question 94, article 2, can be easily identified with some nonconscious inclination. Only one inclination poses difficulty: the inclination to live in society. Since it is peculiar to human beings, it must be found either in reason or in the will. It is difficult to see, however, how the intellect could have an inclination toward living in society. It seems, then, that this inclination is in the will. At least one inclination in the will, then, does not seem to be simply an echo of other inclinations.

Searching beyond question 94, article 2, may provide other such inclinations. Aquinas speaks of two fundamental precepts of the natural law, to love God above all and to love one's neighbor as oneself. These precepts must be founded upon corresponding natural inclinations toward a love of God and others. Since it is with the will that we love, it seems that these natural inclinations must be in the will.

Finally, the sheer multiplicity of natural inclinations, together with the dearth of powers from which nonconscious inclinations might arise, suggests the need for conscious inclinations distinct from prior nonconscious inclinations. Aquinas lists a multitude of inclinations, such as the inclination to subordinate oneself to a superior, the inclination to set aside time for needed activities, and the inclination to know about the future. Plausibly, some of these might not be natural inclinations in the manner intended by Aquinas in question 94, article 2. On the other hand, many of them unquestionably are the sort of natural inclinations that Aquinas associates with the natural law. It seems unlikely that all of these inclinations can be linked with some nonconscious inclination. Some of these homeless inclinations, then, may find their home in the will.

In the next three subsections (6.1.3, 6.1.4, and 6.1.5) we will address the three cases mentioned above, namely, the inclination to live in so-

---

quam actus eius. Primum igitur eius obiectum praecedit omnem actum ipsius. Non potest ergo actus voluntatis primum volitum esse."

THE WILL

ciety, the inclination to love God and others, and the multiplicity of inclinations, although we will treat them in reverse order. In each case, we will see that the will need not be implicated in these natural inclinations, that is, the multiplicity of inclinations can be explained without the will, and likewise the inclination to love God and love others, and the inclination to live in society, can be identified with some other power besides the will.

6.1.3: Multiple Ends for a Single Power

The difficulty concerning the multiplicity of natural inclinations may depend upon a false assumption. What is that assumption? That to a single potency must correspond only a single natural inclination. What if, to the contrary, a single potency has multiple natural inclinations? The single power of reproduction, for instance, is directed both to the existence of offspring and to mature offspring. This single power, then, has multiple inclinations, or perhaps it has a single inclination to which multiple goods are associated.

How does a single power incline to multiple ends? In the case of the power of reproduction, it seems that the two ends differ as the incomplete and the complete. The complete end toward which reproduction inclines is the mature human being; the incomplete end is simply the initial existence of a new human being.

This pattern appears elsewhere. As we have already seen, the intellect inclines toward the truth. The truth concerning any effect, however, is not fully or completely realized until one knows all about its causes. Consequently, the intellect is also inclined to know the truth concerning the first cause. Is this a distinct inclination? No, it is the same inclination, differing according to the incomplete and the complete. Any single truth about anything less than the first cause is an incomplete realization of the tendency of the intellect. We might suspect, as well, that the inclination to know about the future, mentioned by Aquinas, is also just an aspect of the inclination of the intellect (or perhaps, in this case, "natural" inclination is being used loosely, since Aquinas does not associate it with a specific good or precept).[2]

---

2. The distinction between what is complete or perfect and what is incomplete, however, poses another difficulty. How do we divide diverse goods? After all, there are many incomplete stages. Does each incomplete stage generate a distinctive good? Is the power of

THE WILL

6.1.4: Love of God and Others

Even if the sheer number of natural inclinations does not demand distinctive conscious inclinations, we are still left with some inclinations that seem unavoidably connected with the will, such as the natural inclination to live in society and the natural inclinations to love God and to love others.[3]

Even these inclinations, however, will prove problematic in our search for a distinctive contribution of the will. There can be no doubt that the inclinations to love God and to love others are found in the will. The question before us, however, is whether there is yet some more foundational source. Do the inclinations to love God and others, which are found in the will, depend upon some other inclinations, some non-conscious inclinations? It seems they must. We could not be inclined — in the will — to these goods without perceiving them as good; the perception of the good, however, depends upon some inclination; therefore, some other inclination must precede the natural love of the will.

Lawrence Dewan points out that the inclinations to love God and others belongs to the first category of inclinations, those shared with all beings.[4] When Aquinas argues that the love of God and others is a natural love, he claims that it is a love shared by all beings.[5] Similarly, the love we have for other human beings (as revealed through the parallel love of one angel for another) corresponds to a natural inclination found in all things. Indeed, this love is based upon the natural inclination to love oneself.[6]

In human beings, of course, the love of God and others is realized most fully in the love of the will. Nevertheless, this love arises only because we grasp, with our intellect, that God is our good and that others

---

reproduction directed to the good of a new human being, the good of a one-year-old, the good of a five-year-old, and so on? Aquinas gives us only two goods, the existence of the offspring and the maturity of the offspring. Why only these two goods?

3. Aquinas, in I-II, 100, 3, ad 1, says that the most general precepts of the natural law include the precepts to love God and to love one's neighbor. These are self-evident, and by implication they must involve some natural inclination.

4. Dewan, "Philosophy of Cooperation," 115–17; see also Lawrence Dewan, "Natural Law in the First Act of Freedom: Maritain Revisited," in *Wisdom, Law, and Virtue* (New York: Fordham University Press, 2008), 238.

5. I, 60, 5.

6. I, 60, 4.

THE WILL

are united with us in the good. We recognize that we belong naturally to God. This recognition ultimately seems to depend upon the recognition that we are caused by God, for an effect belongs to its cause.[7]

It would be a mistake to suppose that there is some nonconscious inclination to seek our own good. There is not any one such inclination. Rather every inclination of every creature seeks its own good. The intellect is inclined to the good of the person, namely, knowing the truth; so also is the power to grow inclined to the good of the person; and so on. An inclination is always toward some good of the subject.

What is less apparent, but which follows from what has just been said, is that every inclination is directed to the common or shared good. Obviously, some inclinations might be more immediately directed to the common good than others; nevertheless, all must be directed to the common good. At the very least, any inclination to any good must be ordered to the common good that is the divine good. Even the inclination to nourishment, which is clearly directed most immediately to the individual, must ultimately be ordered to the common good.

More immediately and more evidently the inclination associated with reproduction is directed to a common good, namely, to the common good of the species. In particular, it is directed to the preservation and perpetuity of the species. As we have already seen, Aquinas says that all things are inclined to a perpetual existence. Intellectual beings are inclined consciously, with an awareness of what eternal existence might mean; other beings are inclined nonconsciously. Earlier, we argued that the power of reproduction is directed to two ends, to the existence of a new individual and to this individual's maturity. Now we see that it is further directed to another end, namely, to the continued existence of the species. Indeed, Aquinas says that generation is also ordered to the continued existence of the nation.[8]

Even the inclination toward nourishment shares in the goal of preserving the species, for by preserving its individual existence an animal also preserves the existence of the species. The inclination is not sim-

---

7. Consequently, the love of God poses a special difficulty as a first precept. If we must first prove that God exists, then it does not seem that the precept to love God could possibly be *per se nota* to everyone. Dewan ("First Act of Freedom"), however, argues that the precept is available to everyone, because the knowledge of God is available without strict proof.

8. *Summa contra Gentiles*, IV, cap. 78, n. 2.

THE WILL

ply to the existence of this individual as an individual; it is toward the existence of this individual as a member of the species. Furthermore, through an inclination to its own existence, an animal is also inclined to those that are united with it. Finally, through its inclination to its own existence, an animal is also inclined to the good of the cause of its existence, namely, to God. Aquinas expresses this idea succinctly: "By desiring their own completion everything desires God himself, insofar as the completion of all things is a likeness of the divine being."[9]

It follows that the will can find the love of God, and the love of others, in all inclinations. Or rather, reason perceives these goods through its awareness of all inclinations, and the will can then follow. Love, properly speaking, belongs to the will, but an inclination to the divine good, to the good of the species, and to the good of others in the species is not distinctive of the will. It is found in all inclinations to all goods. This love in the will, then, is based upon prior nonconscious inclinations.

It has become evident that when Aquinas speaks of natural inclination, he sometimes refers to a formality of an inclination or inclinations. The natural inclination to seek the good of the whole and the inclination to seek one's own good are not inclinations distinct from others; they are aspects of every inclination. Aquinas also speaks of a natural inclination to set aside time for sleep, refreshment, and so on. Is the inclination to set aside time for sleep distinct from the inclination to sleep, or is it an aspect of the inclination to sleep?

6.1.5: Living in Society

We are left with only the inclination to live together in society. Aquinas informs us that this inclination is peculiar to human beings. Consequently, it must belong to some power peculiar to human beings, that is, it must belong to either intellect or will or perhaps both. Since the intellect seems an unlikely candidate, we are left with the will.

There is some dispute over the precise nature of this inclination. Is it an inclination simply to friendship with other human beings, that is, an inclination to associate with others? Or is it, more precisely, an

---

9. I, 6, 1, ad 2. "Omnia, appetendo proprias perfectiones, appetunt ipsum Deum, inquantum perfectiones omnium rerum sunt quaedam similitudines divini esse."

THE WILL

inclination to live in civil or political society? Dewan argues for the latter.[10] Why? Because, as we have just seen, the natural love of others is common to all creatures.

Whether Dewan is correct or not, it seems that this inclination need not be associated exclusively with the will. The intellect is a power inclined to a certain good, namely, knowledge of the truth. It is inclined to this good not simply as an isolated individual good but as a common or shared good. The inclination, we might say, is to know the truth not simply as an individual but as a human being, or as a rational creature. This inclination, as we have seen, is realized most fully in the knowledge of God. This knowledge is realized more fully yet in union with others, that is, by knowing together with others we know more fully or more completely. The intellect itself, then, might be said to have an inclination not simply to know the truth but to know the truth together with others.

As with any natural inclination, there will be a corresponding inclination in the will. The question before us is not whether we find some natural inclination in the will to live in society; the question is whether this inclination is found originally, or only, in the will, or whether it is first of all found in some nonconscious inclination, through which the good is first discovered, and upon which discovery the inclination of the will follows. It now appears that we cannot eliminate this latter possibility.

Given the general principle that an inclination of the will must follow upon some awareness of the good; and given that we are aware of the good by way of some natural inclination; it seems to follow that the inclination to live in society cannot arise originally in the will. In that case, our discovery of this good would wait upon the inclination of the will, but at the same time the inclination of the will would wait upon the discovery of the good. Since this inclination can conceivably be found in the intellect, prior to the inclination of the will, it seems that we must turn toward this option.

---

10. Lawrence Dewan, "St. Thomas, John Finnis, and the Political Good," *Thomist* 64 (2000): 337–74.

THE WILL

✦ 6.2 ✦
THE CONTRIBUTION OF THE WILL

We are left with no inclination peculiar to the will. All conscious inclinations of the will echo some prior nonconscious inclinations, found in other powers. This leaves us with a rather odd view of the will. It is a power with no peculiar inclination of its own. Why, then, have this power? Surely, there must be some distinctive inclination of the will. In this section, we will identify the contribution of the will and then examine how it affects our judgment concerning the human good.

6.2.1: The Good of the Whole Person

Recall that the same object, such as an apple, can be the object of diverse powers, such as taste, the intellect, and the will; the single object corresponds to the different powers under different formalities, for instance, the power of taste is directed to the apple according to its flavor, and the intellect is directed to the apple according to its essence. We noted that the diverse inclinations, from the diverse powers, reveal different aspects of good. The apple is nourishing, which we know as the end or term of the power of growth or maintenance; the apple is sweet, which we know as good from the power of taste; and the apple is known as true by the intellect. The will alone, it seems, corresponds to no particular good aspect of the apple; it responds to all of the particular goods revealed through the other inclinations.

The will does, however, relate to the apple under a distinctive formality, namely, insofar as the apple is good. The apple is good insofar as it relates to the intellect, to the nourishing power, and to the power of taste, but none of these powers relate to the apple precisely insofar as it is good. The intellect relates to the apple insofar as it is known as true; this truth is itself a good, but the intellect does not move toward it as good. Similarly, the nourishing power moves into the apple insofar as it is sustenance, which sustenance is a certain good; nevertheless, the nourishing power does not move toward it precisely as good. Only the will moves to an object precisely as good.

The good of which we speak is the good of the person. As we have seen, the good always relates to some subject. Being sharp is the good

THE WILL

of a knife and not the good of a hammer, which is good by being blunt. The will is not inclined to the good of a tree or to the good of a beaver, except insofar as these things in some way might be good for a human being. The goods to which the will is inclined, then, must be goods of the person.

When we perceive knowledge of the truth as a good, we perceive it as a good of ourselves, as a whole person; we do not perceive it simply as the good of some power. Aquinas says that the intellect knows its own act of knowing; more precisely, the person, by way of his intellect, knows his own act of knowing and his own tendency toward the truth. Ultimately, it is not the intellect that knows; it is the person who knows, by way of the intellect.

The person may have some indistinct notion that he knows and inclines by way of a principle within himself, a principle distinct from that by which he tends toward other ends, such as the end of knowing colors. He does not, however, have some clear notion of the power of the intellect, and he certainly has no clear understanding of the nature of that power. Such understanding comes, if at all, after much reflection. His initial awareness is simply an awareness that he knows the truth by way of some principle within him, and that, similarly, he tends toward knowing the truth.

This initial awareness engages the will, which by its nature tends to the good of the person. Since it is the person that inclines to know the truth (and not just some potency) knowledge is a good of that person. It completes or perfects him; it acts as a final cause, giving reason for his activity. Upon awareness of this good, therefore, the will spontaneously desires the truth. So it is with other goods corresponding to other natural inclinations. Each falls under the general object of the will, which is the good of the person.

Since the will is directed toward all these goods insofar as each is a good of the person, we may conclude that only the will is directed to the whole good of the person. Each inclination is directed to some particular good, but the will is directed to each and every good. The object of the will is the good in common; it is not just some singular good but the whole good of the person. Consequently, the will can be called the inclination of the whole person.

THE WILL

The intellect, even if it has an inclination toward something, does not name the inclination of the man; in contrast, the will does name the inclination of the man. Consequently, whatever is done according to the will is done according to the inclination of the man.[11]

The will, then, seems to provide at least one distinctive inclination, an inclination that is not merely an echo of other inclinations. Only the will, with its inclination, aims at the whole good of the person. This general good includes under it many particular goods, such as knowledge of the truth and the continuation of the species. With our wills we naturally desire these goods precisely insofar as each belongs to the whole good of the person. Although the goods of knowledge, existence, reproduction, and so on, are all partial goods of the whole person, there is no inclination for the overall good of the person, or rather, only the will provides this inclination.

6.2.2: The Manner of Attaining the Human Good

The will, then, does have a distinctive inclination of its own, but this inclination does not provide the content for a new good. The will alone is inclined to the good of the person. More precisely, the will is inclined to the good just insofar as it is the good of the person. The intellect happens to be directed to the good of the person but it is not directed to this good precisely as good of the person.

The will does not provide a distinctive good, but it does provide a distinctive way of inclining or moving toward the human good. Indeed, with the will alone we move toward it *as good*; with the will alone we move toward it as a human person. The only way that we can move toward the whole human good precisely as our human good is through the inclination of the whole person, which is the will.

Since the goods following upon natural inclinations are typically activities of the person, and since the will is the inclination of the whole person, it follows that these activities are truly fulfilling of the person only insofar as they arise from the will. By itself, knowing the truth does not complete the individual; rather, *voluntarily* knowing the truth does.

---

11. *De veritate*, 22, 5, ad 3 (Leonine ed., v. 22, 624, 238–43). "Intellectus enim etsi habeat inclinationem in aliquid non tamen nominat ipsam inclinationem hominis, sed voluntas ipsam inclinationem hominis nominat. Unde quicquid fit secundum voluntatem fit secundum hominis inclinationem."

THE WILL

The particularly human way of realizing an inclination is through the will.[12] An individual *voluntarily* chooses to engage in sexual relations; he *voluntarily* chooses to raise his children. Only as such is the natural inclination to new life realized in a human way. Nonconscious reproduction would not fulfill the human inclination. The inclination, after all, is an inclination of the person, but as we have seen, the will is the inclination of the whole person. If reproduction is to arise from the individual, then, it must arise voluntarily.

The peculiarly human way of realizing a union is through love in the will. The spouses who unite to raise their children, for instance, are fully united, as human, only if they are united in love. The inclination to new life, and to mature life, involves a union of activity; the couple must be united in the physical act of sexual intercourse and then they must be united in the activities of raising the child. These activities truly provide a union, and are truly ordered to the human good as good, only insofar as they arise from the will.

The picture that unfolds involves two stages. First, the intellect recognizes some nonconscious inclination of the person, such as the inclination of the intellect to know the truth; the intellect then perceives a human good. At this point, the second stage begins, for the will, presented with its object, has a corresponding natural inclination to this good, for instance, a voluntary desire to know the truth. Following upon this natural inclination of the will, reason then perceives that the truth is fully good for the individual insofar as it is realized voluntarily.

The good of a pen is to write; this writing, however, must be its own activity, arising from its own causality. A pencil writing in no way completes the pen. Similarly, the human good is realized from the person's own causality. This causality, if it is truly his own, initiates in his will. The human good, then, is not realized in a well-functioning reproductive power. Rather, the human good is found (in part) in voluntary reproductive activity. Being voluntary or involuntary is not simply a matter of determining whether a person is responsible for a good or evil; it enters into the very definition of the good. If reproduction is truly a human good, then it is carried out voluntarily. Furthermore, it is carried out with the affective union of love, for such is the human way of realizing the causal union of male and female.

12. See McInerny, "Principles," 4–5.

THE WILL

For Aquinas, the will and the power it moves are wedded into a single inclination moving to a single good. There is no good of a power independent of the person and his will, to which the will must respond. Neither is there an independent will, seeking goods apart from human activities embedded in human powers. Rather, there is a movement of the whole person, will and power united, toward some good.

According to the new natural law theory, descriptivism has forgotten about the will, because it has focused upon nature. The argument presupposes an opposition between nature and will. Certainly, we can use the word "nature" in this way. In the most profound sense, however, Aquinas holds that the will is part of nature. To discover moral truths in nature is not to discover morality apart from the will. It is to discover the good natural to human beings, which is a good realized through acts of will. Perhaps the objections against perverted faculty reasoning are valid, but they are not objections against the natural law of Aquinas.

6.3

GOODS KNOWN *PER SE*

One matter remains before we proceed to discuss the next level of practical knowledge (that is, virtual practical knowledge), in which we make ought-judgments. We must consider the *per se nota* character of certain judgments concerning the good.

It is one thing to say that we know the good by way of inclinations; it is another to show that this knowledge is (sometimes) *per se nota*. In Aquinas's description of a *per se nota* proposition, the predicate term is included within the subject term. The discovery of this relation might prove difficult, however, as in Aquinas's example, "Those which are equal to one and the same thing are equal to one another," or even in Aquinas's formulation of the principle of noncontradiction.

It is difficult to see how our knowledge of particular goods fits Aquinas's description of *per se nota* propositions. Apparently, we are immediately aware that "knowledge of the truth is a good"; our awareness has no need of any argumentation or middle term. Yet surely being good does not fall within the very definition of knowledge.[13]

---

13. Brock raises this objection in "Natural Law," 692.

THE WILL

6.3.1: Nature Provides *Per Se* Knowledge of the Good

Our knowledge of the "good" of artifacts appears, sometimes, to be immediate. It takes no reasoning to see that writing is the good of a pen and cutting is the good of a knife. Other "goods" of the artifact may be recognized through reasoning — for instance, we may need to argue in order to see that it is good for a knife to be sharp or for a pen to have ink — but the very first good is recognized from the very nature of the artifact.

The link between an artifact and its end is not difficult to see, for we know artifacts through their ends. A knife is a tool for cutting, a pen is an instrument for writing, and so on. Similarly, we know the nature of bodily parts through their ends. The eye is an organ for seeing, the heart has the end of pumping, the lungs are organs for acquiring oxygen, and so on. If we do not understand these ends, then we do not understand the organs. At one time, we did not understand the purpose of tonsils or of the appendix; consequently, we did not really understand these organs. A knowledge of nature demands a knowledge of the ends of nature. In contrast, mathematical entities abstract from ends; we can understand the nature of a triangle without worrying whether triangles have ends.[14]

It does not surprise us, therefore, to find that writing is the good of a pen, for in knowing the nature of a pen we also know its end, which is its good. The link between nature and good is immediate. If we know the nature of a thing, which we know through its end, then we also know what completes it; we know what is its good.[15] It is good for a knife to cut, an eye to see, the heart to pump, and so on. If our understanding of the nature of a thing includes its end, and if the good has the *ratio* of an end, then it seems that our understanding of a thing implies an understanding of its good.

As we have seen, this strong statement concerning the link between nature and the good is not a claim that nature has, as Henry Veatch

---

14. See I, 5, 3, ad 4. In "Is-Ought Question," 301–2, Veatch emphasizes that human nature is dynamic, unlike mathematical natures.

15. In this manner, Foot ("Moral Beliefs," 216) shows that the word "good" has an objective meaning for functional terms. Similarly, Chappell ("Natural Law Revived: Natural Law Theory and Contemporary Moral Philosophy," in *The Revival of Natural Law: Philosophical, Theological and Ethical Responses to the Finnis-Grisez School*, ed. Nigel Biggar et al. [Sydney: Ashgate, 2000], 45) claims that an essential function allows us to move from an is to an ought.

THE WILL

says, "ought built right into it," at least not in any literal sense.[16] It is not a claim that our knowledge of nature is practical knowledge.[17] It is simply a recognition that nature is dynamic; it is heading somewhere. As such, it is completed by arriving.

6.3.2: The Fourth Mode of Per Seity

It is one thing to point out an immediate link between our knowledge of nature and our knowledge of the good; it is another to explain this link in terms of a *per se nota* proposition. If we have succeeded at the first, we might well fail at the second. We have already suggested that even Aquinas's formulation of the very first principle, the principle of noncontradiction, is difficult to explain as a *per se nota* proposition. A simpler version — being is not nonbeing — is rather straightforward, but Aquinas chooses to describe the principle in terms of the mental acts of affirming and denying. In what follows, therefore, it should be little surprise if we provide only suggestions and partial explanations concerning the *per se nota* character of our knowledge of the good.

The link between nature and the good is by way of final causality, for nature is understood through its end. We might expect this link, then, to be expressed in the fourth mode of per se, for this mode concerns external causality, including final causality. Aquinas's Aristotelian example — that which is killed dies — buttresses this expectation. The act of killing is itself directed to an end or object, namely, death; this object appears — in the temporal form of a verb — in the predicate. We cannot exactly say that the predicate is included within the subject term, for then we would be in the first mode of per seity. Nevertheless, the predicate term is intimately connected with the subject term; the subject term, we might say, points to the predicate term, even if it does not contain it formally as a part.

The key, here, is that the subject term is not self-contained. It concerns a reality that is directed beyond itself. Activity (such as killing) does not have much by way of an internal formal cause; its formal cause, that which makes it to be what it is, is something beyond itself, namely, its end or object.

---

16. Veatch, "Is-Ought Question," 303. See also Lisska, *Analytic Reconstruction*, 199.
17. Finnis speaks this way ("Is-Ought Question," 270–71).

THE WILL

The link between the subject term and the predicate term, then, will not be that of containment, as is the case with the first mode, involving formal causality. Rather, the link will be one of pointing or directedness. "Dying" does not belong as a formal part of "that which is killed." Nevertheless, it is a kind of part. "Killing," after all, might be defined as "the activity of bringing about death (or dying)." The *ratio* of "death" is not a specific difference or a genus of "killing," but it does enter into the *ratio* of "killing" as an object, as something external to which the activity is directed. By understanding the *ratio* of "killing" we also understand the *ratio* of "dying," which appears in the predicate term; we understand the two as linked not because one is part of the other but because one is inherently directed to the other.

In this manner, then, a proposition in the fourth mode of per seity might loosely fit Aquinas's description of a *per se nota* proposition. The predicate does belong to the *ratio* of the subject; it does not belong to it as a component part, but it does belong to it obliquely, as something essential to the understanding of the subject, as something to which the subject points.

6.3.3: The Good as *Per Se Nota*

The understanding of certain artifacts is also an understanding of that to which they are directed, for example, to understand a pen is to understand that it is directed to writing. Similarly, the understanding of certain powers is to understand that to which they are directed; it is to understand their inclination. To grasp the intellect is to grasp the intellect as directed to being or to truth.

If the intellect is understood as directed to a certain object, then it is also understood as inclined toward this object. To grasp the inclination is simply to grasp the movement toward the object. As we have seen, however, the good is simply the object of an inclination; it is that object insofar as it has what it takes to complete the inclination. Consequently, the proposition "Knowledge is the good of the intellect," is *per se nota*. The good of the intellect does not fall within the very definition of knowledge, as would be the case in the first mode of per seity. Rather, the *ratio* of "intellect" points toward knowledge, and to speak of the "good" is simply to speak of the object of this pointing. In short, our awareness of particular goods is in the fourth mode.

THE WILL

Our account of coming to know the good follows this pattern, although we used an example that was not *per se nota*. We come to understand that beavers are felling trees. Then we come to understand that beavers are moving toward, or are inclined toward, the felling of trees. This step corresponds to the understanding of a power being directed to its object. Finally, we recognize that the object (the felling of trees) completes the inclination of the beaver; we recognize that the felling of trees is good for beavers.

It does not belong to the very nature of the beaver to be inclined to felling trees; consequently, it is one thing to understand the beaver and another to understand its inclination, and our knowledge of this good will not be *per se nota*; it will be mediated by a middle term. In contrast, it is the same thing to understand the nature of a pen and to understand it as directed toward writing, so that we need no middle term to grasp that a pen is good through writing. Similarly, our very understanding of the intellect is an understanding of it as directed to truth, so that no middle term comes between our awareness of the intellect and our awareness of its object and of its good.

The dynamic character of nature, then, propels our minds to discover the good in things. When we strip nature of its teleological impetus, making it into a kind of mathematical nature, then we also strip nature of its good. Then it becomes a mystery how we come to know the good. Certainly not by way of nature. The very meaning of the good becomes a mystery.[18]

---

18. What are we to do with pseudosyllogisms of the following sort?
   The good is that toward which something is inclined.
   The intellect is inclined toward the truth.
   Therefore, the truth is good.
This question is no easy matter. Even when discussing various formulations of the principle of noncontradiction Aquinas seems to use syllogisms (*In Metaphysicorum*, lib. 4, lect. 6, n. 604–6; see McInerny, *Human Action*, 198–204).

We say, "the truth is good," "continued life is good," "society together is good," and so on. We use one word, namely, "good," but only because we elliptically include the inclination of which it is the good. Each good is in fact a distinctive notion of the good. There is not some universal good, except analogically, that is predicated of all of these subjects, for the *ratio* of the good includes the subject and its inclination within it (*Sententia Ethicorum*, lib. 1, lect. 7, n. 14).

Let me tentatively suggest, then, that before we can subsume the particular good under the analogical concepts included within the major premise, we have already perceived it as a particular good. The syllogism can be used, but it provides us no new information.

7

OUGHT

At the level of virtual practical knowledge the word "ought" is introduced, a word more emblematic of the naturalistic fallacy than anything found in materially practical knowledge. The term "good" is plausibly descriptive; at least it uses the descriptive copula "is." But when we begin to speak about what ought to be the case, then we no longer seem to be describing anything. We are now making plans, or we are dictating the way the world is to be. As Hume suggested, we have an entirely new kind of copula.

Unfortunately, the claim that ought-statements are not descriptive rarely gets beyond intuition; the precise meaning and nature of ought-statements is never clarified.[1] On the face of it, certain ought-statements seem descriptive. A waiter ought to bring food out to the customer; a builder ought to lay the foundation first. In these cases, no prescription is being given but only a description of these roles or professions. But if these instances are descriptions, then precisely what are they describing? What is being attributed to the waiter and the builder? Certainly nothing so straightforward as the color yellow.

Furthermore, sometimes ought-statements seem to be something other than descriptive. The statement, "You ought to take the food out to the customers," when addressed to the waiter himself, seems to be providing guidance or direction. The statement is not merely describing what is the case; it is recommending something that is not yet the case.

In the next chapter, we will examine the guiding or directive elements of ought-statements. The primary purpose of this chapter is to determine in what manner ought-statements are descriptive. Of first importance, then, will be a determination of the precise meaning of ought-statements. This meaning will be illumined, however, through

---

1. See Martin, "Distinction."

OUGHT

an investigation into the manner in which ought-statements are derived; consequently, after considering the general meaning of ought-statements, we will examine the reasoning processes of resolution and composition. We will close the chapter by addressing the question of whether ought-statements are practical or speculative, prescriptive or descriptive.

7.1
THE MEANING OF "OUGHT"
7.1.1: Hypothetical Ought-Statements

Given how much grief the move from is to ought has occasioned, it is surprising with what alacrity we make the move on a daily basis. "I am going to the opera, therefore I ought to turn right." "I want to lose weight, therefore I ought to go on a diet." These examples, it will be objected, smuggle in an ought-statement, because they include desires. The desire to lose weight and the desire to go to the opera include a movement toward what does not in fact exist, a movement toward what "ought" to be.

The desire need not be one's own. Knowing that somebody else desires to get to the opera, we can tell him to turn right. We can say of a murderer that he ought to give a double dosage of the poison. We do not want him to, and we are not recommending that he do it, but we recognize that he ought to. We are not saying that he *morally* ought to, but that he ought to, given his goal.

Such an "ought," one might object, is only a hypothetical "ought." Indeed, it is. But is there some alternative? Is there some categorical imperative, an "ought" that obliges apart from some end or goal? Aquinas does not think so. When discussing the obligatory force of a precept of the law he states that what ought to be done arises from an end.

> A precept of the law, since it is obligatory, concerns that which ought to be done. That something ought to be done, however, arises from the necessity of some end. Clearly, then, it belongs to the very notion of a precept that it implies an order to an end, insofar as that which is commanded is necessary or expedient for the end.[2]

---

2. I-II, 99, 1. "Praeceptum legis, cum sit obligatorium, est de aliquo quod fieri debet. Quod autem aliquid debeat fieri, hoc provenit ex necessitate alicuius finis. Unde manifes-

OUGHT

We use the word "ought" in this manner on a regular basis. The builder ought to lay the foundation first; the waiter ought to bring the food to the customers; the farmer ought to plant the seeds in the spring; to get to the opera, Louis ought to turn right on Louisiana Street. The examples can be multiplied indefinitely. Why should we suppose there is any other meaning for the word "ought"? We can even use the word in this manner — quite speculatively — for nonhumans. A bird ought to collect twigs for its nest; the beaver ought to drag the trees to the river. We can even use it for nonconscious things. A tree ought to put out roots; a knife ought to be sharp; and a bicycle ought to have a chain.

7.1.2: Modalities

Grammatically, the word "ought" is a modal helping verb; it is usually used in the present or future tense but is sometimes used in the past tense, as in "He ought to have turned right at Louisiana Street."[3] Originally, it derived from the past tense form of the verb "to owe," thereby implying some kind of necessity for the base verb it helps. If Kevin ought to go on a diet, then there is some necessity for him to do so; it is owed. If the cake ought to be done by now, then there is some necessity in it being done.

Ought-statements usually concern something that is not the case, or at least we are not certain that it is the case. Sometimes they concern the future, which is not yet but might come to be. When they concern the present, they have the uncertainty of a subjunctive: the cake ought to be done but it might not be. When they concern the past, they almost always concern what in fact was not the case: he ought to have turned right (but he didn't). Sometimes, however, they merely express subjunctive uncertainty of what was done: he ought to have paid his bill last month (but maybe he didn't).

We might suppose that this feature of ought-statements — that they concern what is not the case, at least not yet — distinguishes them from speculative statements, which are statements about the way the

---

tum est quod de ratione praecepti est quod importet ordinem ad finem, inquantum scilicet illud praecipitur quod est necessarium vel expediens ad finem."

3. For an investigation of the modal character of ought-statements, see Arthur N. Prior, "The Ethical Copula," *Australasian Journal of Philosophy* 29 (1951): 137–54.

world is.[4] Clearly, however, this feature cannot be the distinguishing mark of practical knowledge. As we have already seen in chapter 4, many speculative statements concern what is not the case, for instance, "Mars will align with Jupiter next year."

Aquinas says that our knowledge of the future concerns what is in fact the case, namely, present causal tendencies. Examining future statements, then, might help to illuminate our understanding of ought-statements. Take a simple example of a sphere hanging from the ceiling by a thread. Consider three statements we might make concerning the sphere.

If the thread breaks, then the sphere will fall.

If the thread were to break, then the sphere would fall.

If the thread breaks, then the sphere ought to fall.

All three statements concern the future. All involve a helping verb for the verb "fall." The first is a simple future tense; the latter two involve a modal future.

As we have already noted in chapter 4, Aquinas says that we know the future through the inclinations found in present causes. As such, it is more a knowledge of the present than of the future. We can predict a solar eclipse, for instance, by knowing the current positions of the sun, earth, and moon, together with the causes of gravity and momentum. Aquinas thought that this example, since it concerned heavenly bodies, was necessary. We know better now; something like the impact of a large asteroid could disturb the movement of the earth or moon.

Although Aquinas was mistaken about heavenly bodies, he was clearly aware that sublunary events are contingent (or not necessary). He argued, therefore, that our knowledge of future contingent events is uncertain, because something can interfere with the activity of the cause.[5] Aquinas speaks of something impeding the cause. If the thread breaks, for instance, the sphere still might not fall; perhaps someone

---

4. Lee, "Naturalist," 571. Surprisingly, Finnis (*Aquinas*, 86–87) claims that ought-statements are not in the indicative, since they concern what is-to-be done; he upholds this position even after acknowledging (102, endnote y) that Aquinas describes these ought-statements as indicative (I-II, 17, 1); according to Finnis, Aquinas is merely trying to emphasize that they are not imperative.

5. *De malo*, 16, 7.

OUGHT

holds his hand under the sphere and prevents the cause (gravity) from bringing about its effect (of falling); perhaps the sphere is also a magnet and a magnetic force in the ceiling holds it in midair.

Certain things exist in their causes not only according to possibility but also according to the character of an active cause that cannot be impeded from its effect, and these are said to happen from necessity. Other events exist in their causes according to possibility and according to an active cause, but they are able to be impeded from their effect, and these are said to happen for the most part....

Those things that exist in their causes as coming forth necessarily from them can be known in their causes with certainty by a human being.... Those things that happen for the most part cannot be known in their causes with entire certainty but only with a certain conjectural knowledge.[6]

The first statement, then — If the thread breaks, then the sphere will fall — includes the supposition, not stated in the antecedent, that there are no other interfering or impeding factors besides the thread. The second statement differs from the first only in supposing that the antecedent will not be met. It is a counterfactual statement concerning what will not happen. Both statements, then, presume a fair amount of certainty by presuming the absence of interfering causes. They look to a current cause (the weight of the sphere), projecting its efficacy to its effect (the sphere falling), while considering interfering causes to be absent.

The third statement — If the thread breaks, then the sphere ought to fall — includes a measure of uncertainty. It ought to fall, but it might not. Why not? Because there might be interfering causes. In the same way, the present tense use of ought in "The cake ought to be done by now" indicates that if there were no interfering causes, then the cake would be done, but perhaps something has interfered. "Ought," then, usually indicates a degree of uncertainty. Unlike simple future predic-

---

6. *De malo*, 16, 7 (Leonine ed., v. 23, 315–16, 228–47). "Quedam uero sunt in causis suis non solum secundum potentiam set secundum rationem cause actiue que non potest impediri a suo effectu, et hec dicuntur ex necessitate contingere ; quedam uero sunt in causis suis et secundum potentiam et secundum causam actiuam que tamen potest impediri a suo effectu, et ista dicuntur contingere ut in pluribus..... Ea uero que sunt in causis suis ut ex necessitate ab eis prouenientia possunt per certitudinem cognosci in causis suis ab homine.... Ea uero que contingunt ut in pluribus possunt cognosci in causis suis non per omnimodam certitudinem set per coniecturalem quandam cognitionem."

OUGHT

tions, it does not presume the absence of all interfering causes. Rather, "ought" focuses upon the necessity in the thing (or in the situation) and prescinds or abstracts from the presence or absence of interfering causes.[7] Indeed, most properly an ought-statement of this sort need not be a prediction at all. It merely states the sort of activity that belongs — or is owed — to the sphere in itself, or according to some attribute of it, such as its weight. By its nature, one might say, the sphere will drop, but there might be impediments that prevent it. Similarly, "being done" belongs to a cake in this situation, barring any interference.

7.1.3: Belonging by Necessity

The sense of belonging implied by "ought" includes the possibility of interference. We might say that having interior angles equal to two right angles belongs to a triangle, but it would be odd to say that a triangle ought to have interior angles equal to two right angles. The oddity arises because the necessity deriving from formal causality, as found in the triangle, does not allow the possibility of interference. The efficient causality of gravity might happen not to be realized for the sphere on account of some impediment. In contrast, the measure of the interior angles of the triangle will always be realized.

Occasionally, we do use "ought" for something that is (or was) the case, for example, as a chess player moves his queen we might say, "Yes, that is what he ought to do," or after the fact we might say that is what he ought to have done. This action can no longer be interfered with; nevertheless, we use the word "ought." The case is still different from the triangle, however, because we recognize that the action could have been interfered with, although it no longer can be.

The modal verb "ought," then, involves necessity, but not absolute necessity. It is concerned with a conditional necessity. What ought to be is necessary only by abstracting from impediments and focusing simply upon the feature that gives rise to the necessity, such as the weight of the sphere. The necessity of an ought-statement, then, can be clarified with a qualifier. "The sphere ought to fall" is better understood with the qualifier "Insofar as it is a heavy body, the sphere ought to fall." It might

---

7. By "abstract" I do not refer to a denial, which is what happens with predictions, but noncommitment, that is, an openness to either possibility, to either the presence or absence of interfering causes.

turn out that the sphere is something more than a heavy body; it might turn out that there are other, interfering causes. In contrast, the absolute necessity found in a triangle needs no qualification.

Since what ought to be can be interfered with (or at least could have been) an ought-statement generally concerns what is not yet; it concerns what is to be. The sense of "belonging," then, parallels a debt, in which the money belongs to someone, but he does not have it right now; at the moment, it is in the possession of another. Consequently, the money that belongs to him is "owed" to him. Likewise, if the sphere ought to fall, then falling belongs to the sphere. At the moment, however, the sphere is being suspended, so the sphere does not "have" the falling; it is "owed" to the sphere, like a debt. Similarly, if Louis ought to turn right on Louisiana Street, then turning right belongs to him, but he does not yet have it; it is in some sense owed to him.

What is essential to ought-statements is an assertion concerning what belongs to a thing in itself. In itself, the sphere falls; in itself, someone going to the opera (from a certain starting point) turns right on Louisiana Street. Regarding this assertion there need be no uncertainty whatsoever. I can be absolutely certain that someone going to the opera, just considered in itself, ought to turn right on Louisiana Street. The uncertainty concerns the presence or absence of impediments.

7.1.4: Ought-Statements Concerning an End

In general, then, ought-statements identify what belongs to a thing in itself, when that possession is not yet realized (it is to be), so that in some sense the possession is "owed." The particular kind of ought-statements with which we are concerned involve some necessity from an end. "Louis ought to turn right at Louisiana Street" expresses what belongs to him precisely insofar as he has an end of getting to the opera. Unlike Kant, Aquinas believes that moral precepts belong to this subset of ought-statements.

The "binding force" of a final cause, of which Aquinas speaks when discussing the obligation of precepts, is absent in the example of the hanging sphere, which involves necessity of an efficient cause rather than of a final cause. The thread acts as an interfering efficient cause, preventing the weight of the sphere, itself an efficient cause, from realizing its natural course.

OUGHT

Aquinas himself seems to express something like these two kinds of "oughts," one from an efficient cause and the other from a final cause, in the *Summa contra Gentiles*.[8] He goes on to identify these two ways of being owed with two kinds of necessity, absolute necessity, which is associated with an efficient cause, and conditional necessity, which is associated with an end or final cause.[9]

7.2

REASONING TO AN OUGHT-STATEMENT

7.2.1: Deliberation

The necessity of obligation from an end can be better understood by examining deliberation, which Aquinas says proceeds by resolution. A goal that is sought is reduced into its causes.[10] Suppose that Clare begins with the goal of getting across the sea. She considers the various causes that might bring about this goal. She might take an airplane or she might take a ship. If she decides to take the ship, then she must investigate the causes for getting on the ship. She considers various tickets that she might buy. Settling upon one, she looks for the causes of buying this ticket (credit card, etc.). When she reaches some initial cause that she herself institutes, then she chooses in reverse order. She pays for the ticket, she gets the ticket, she gets on the boat, she crosses the sea.

If that which is prior in knowledge is posterior in existence, then reasoning proceeds by resolution, for example, when we judge concerning perceived effects by resolving them into simple causes. Since the principle in the inquiry of deliberation is the end, which is prior in intention but posterior in existence, the inquiry of deliberation must be by way of resolution. It must begin from that which is intended in the future and come back to that which must be done right now.[11]

---

8. *Summa contra Gentiles*, II, cap. 28, n. 14.

9. See *Summa contra Gentiles,* II, cap. 28, nn. 15 and 16; *Summa contra Gentiles,* II, cap. 30, nn. 16 and 17.

10. I-II, 14, 5. For a detailed account of this deliberative process, see *In Metaphysicorum*, lib. 7, lect. 6, 1404–10.

11. I-II, 14, 5. "Si autem id quod est prius in cognitione, sit posterius in esse, est processus resolutorius, utpote cum de effectibus manifestis iudicamus, resolvendo in causas simplices. Principium autem in inquisitione consilii est finis, qui quidem est prior in intentione, posterior tamen in esse. Et secundum hoc, oportet quod inquisitio consilii sit resolutiva, incipiendo scilicet ab eo quod in futuro intenditur, quousque perveniatur ad id quod statim agendum est." See also *Sententia Ethicorum*, lib. 3, lect. 8.

OUGHT

If one of the causes is necessary to achieve the end, then we have conditional necessity. Aquinas gives the example of getting on a ship in order to cross the sea. Of course, in the current era a ship is no longer a conditional necessity. Without airplanes, however, the final cause of getting across the sea required the causal means of getting on a ship.

> Necessity can be said in many ways, for that which is necessary cannot not be.... which can happen on account of something extrinsic, either the end or the agent. It happens by the end when someone cannot attain an end without this [cause], or he cannot attain it well, as food is said to be necessary for life and a horse for a journey. This is called necessity of the end, which is also sometimes called utility ... from the will to cross the sea it becomes necessary to will a ship.[12]

We have seen that Aquinas thinks the obligation of precepts arises from this necessity of the end. The necessity, however, can sometimes be a qualified necessity. Clare might reason that "I ought to take an airplane," even though she knows that she could take a ship. The necessity here concerns not the *only* way to attain the end, but as Aquinas says, it concerns the way to attain it well.[13]

In addition, sometimes we consider other ends besides the immediate goal in view, for example, besides considering the end of getting across the sea, Clare might also consider the end of saving money. Taking the airplane, then, might be best because it is fastest, safest, least expensive, and so on. The necessity for taking the airplane, then, is qualified, but it is necessary for the end in some manner, namely, for attaining the end best of all.

7.2.2: Resolution and Composition in Speculative Reason

The resolution of an effect into its causes, with the search for what is necessary in those causes, is not peculiar to deliberation. Speculative

---

12. I, 82, 1. "Respondeo dicendum quod necessitas dicitur multipliciter. Necesse est enim quod non potest non esse. Alio modo convenit alicui quod non possit non esse, ex aliquo extrinseco, vel fine vel agente. Fine quidem, sicut cum aliquis non potest sine hoc consequi, aut bene consequi finem aliquem, ut cibus dicitur necessarius ad vitam, et equus ad iter. Et haec vocatur necessitas finis; quae interdum etiam utilitas dicitur. Necessitas autem finis non repugnat voluntati, quando ad finem non potest perveniri nisi uno modo, sicut ex voluntate transeundi mare, fit necessitas in voluntate ut velit navem." See also I, 19, 3.

13. See also II-II, 83, 13; III, 65, 4.

reasoning proceeds in the same manner.¹⁴ Indeed, Aquinas says that it is the proper manner of demonstration for contingent matters in natural philosophy.

> [Aristotle shows that] when something follows only for the most part, then demonstration ... should be taken from that which comes later in generation, insofar as one thing follows of necessity from another, just as the conclusion follows from the propositions of a demonstration. Then we proceed by demonstrating in the following manner: if this is going to come to be, then this and that are required, for example, if a human being is going to be generated, then it is necessary for human semen to act in the generation. If we proceed in the reverse manner, by beginning with human semen acting in generation, then it does not [necessarily] follow that a human being will be generated.¹⁵

When Le Verrier discovered Neptune he began with an effect, namely, the orbit of Uranus, in particular, the irregularities of that orbit. He reasoned back from this effect, searching for the cause. He determined that the cause had to exert such and such a force, thereby identifying some necessity. From this necessity, he worked out other details of what the cause must be like.

In speculative reasoning, the effect exists and is known first of all. The orbit of Uranus already existed and was already known. In contrast, for practical reasoning, the effect, such as getting across the sea, does not yet exist. Despite this difference, the reasoning in the two instances is similar. Both begin with the effect and look for causes; both search for something necessary in the causes. Both are trying to determine what the cause must be like.

Having completed the resolution of the effect into its cause, Le Verrier then discovers the cause, namely, Neptune. He can now reverse his procedure, reasoning not by resolution but by what Aquinas calls composition; rather than begin with the effect, he can begin with the

---

14. For a treatment of resolution and composition within reasoning, see S. Edmund Dolan, "Resolution and Composition in Speculative and Practical Discourse," *Laval théologique et philosophique* 6 (1950): 9–62; see also Flannery, *Acts amid Precepts*, 60–71.

15. *In Physic.*, lib. 2, lect. 11, n. 8. "Quando sequitur aliquid ut frequenter ... debet sumi demonstratio ab eo quod est posterius in generatione, ad hoc quod aliquid ex necessitate sequatur ex altero, sicut ex propositionibus demonstrationis sequitur conclusio; ut procedamus demonstrando sic: si hoc debet fieri, ista et ista requiruntur; sicut si debet generari homo, necesse est quod sit semen humanum agens in generatione. Si autem procedamus e converso: est semen humanum agens in generatione, non sequitur, ergo generabitur homo."

cause. Given that Neptune is of such and such a nature, it will act in such a way upon Uranus. He has not really introduced new information; he has simply reversed the order in which his mind approaches it.

This reversal is possible, in part, on account of Aristotle's teaching that action and passion (or undergoing) are one and the same change although considered in diverse ways.[16] The fire heating the water is not a different change from the water being heated by the fire. One change takes place, namely, the water increases in temperature. That change can be seen as residing in the water and coming from the fire, in which case it is an undergoing on the part of the water; it can also be seen as coming forth from the fire into the water, in which case it is the action of the fire upon the water.

Similarly, the movement of Uranus can be viewed as residing in Uranus but as arising from some cause, and hence we reason by resolution. The same movement can be viewed as coming from Neptune and affecting Uranus, and hence we reason by composition. The two are like correlatives, relating to one another as opposites. As we have already seen when looking at beavers, by knowing one term of the relation, we come to know the other, even as we know "double" in the very act of recognizing "half." This shift involves nonsyllogistic epistemological dependence. Our knowledge that six is double three depends upon our awareness that three is half of six, but no syllogism connects the two.

The same sort of movement occurs in the transition from resolution to composition. We begin from the effect and move to the cause, and then we reverse the procedure, composing the effect from its cause. The irregularities of the orbit of Uranus are caused by something with such and such features; that which has such and such features (Neptune) causes the irregularities in the orbit of Uranus. The latter knowledge depends upon the former, but we do not use a syllogism to move from one to the other.

Le Verrier, of course, uses syllogistic reasoning. I am suggesting only that the shift from resolution to composition is not reached by way of syllogism. This shift, which often introduces ought-terminology, involves nonsyllogistic dependence between propositions. Rather than move backwards from the effect, we move forward from its cause.

Le Verrier first reasons — probably with many syllogisms — that this

---

16. *In Physic.*, lib. 3, lectio 5.

effect (the irregularities of the orbit) requires such and such a force. He then judges — with no new syllogism — that the cause of the irregularities "ought to" exert such a force. He reasons that this force requires a mass of a certain quantity at a certain distance, again using syllogisms; he then judges, with a shift of perspective that involves no new syllogism, that the cause of the irregularities "ought to" have this mass and distance. As the reasoning continues, he eventually judges that the cause "ought to" be at a certain place in the night sky. He focuses a telescope on that place and discovers Neptune.

The shift to ought-terminology arises from a shift in the focus of the necessity.[17] The reasoning begins with the effect, determining what is necessary for this effect. It then shifts, focusing upon what is necessary in the cause for the effect. First, this effect requires such a force; second, this cause ought to exert such a force on this effect. First, such a force requires a certain mass; second, this cause ought to have such a mass.

7.2.3: Composition in Practical Reason

The same shift takes place in practical reasoning. When we have completed the resolution of deliberation, we transfer to composition, forming what Aquinas calls a judgment.

> The first task for knowledge of things composite is resolution, in order that we may divide the composite into its individual parts. Next, composition is required, in order that from the indivisible principles that we now know, we may judge of those things that are caused by the principles.[18]

Recall that virtual practical knowledge differs from materially practical knowledge in its mode. The contrast, first quoted in chapter 1, seems to fit the distinction between resolution and composition.

---

17. M. Zimmerman ("The 'Is-Ought': An Unnecessary Dualism," in *The Is-Ought Question: A Collection of Papers on the Central Problem in Moral Philosophy*, ed. W. D. Hudson [London: McMillan, 1969]) is partially correct, then, in claiming that the distinction between is and ought is unnecessary; we need speak only of what is needed for an end. He is not entirely correct, however, for the shift to composition does tell us what is necessary for the cause moving toward an end, while resolution focuses upon the necessity for the end.

18. *Sententia Politic.*, lib. 1, lect. 1 (Leonine ed., v. 48, 73, 142–47). "Ad cognitionem compositorum primo opus est uia resolutionis, ut scilicet diuidamus compositum usque ad individua; postmodum uero necessaria est uia compositionis, ut ex principiis indiuisibilibus iam notis diiudicemus de rebus que ex principiis causantur."

OUGHT

Second, knowledge is speculative with respect to the mode of knowing, for example, a builder might consider a house by defining and dividing and by considering what can be said of it in general. This manner of knowing considers what can be brought about through human activity in a speculative mode, and not precisely insofar as it can be brought about, for to bring something about through activity is achieved by applying form to matter, not by resolving a composite into formal universal principles.[19]

We first determine that crossing the sea requires a cause of such characteristics, for instance, getting on a ship. We then judge that someone crossing the sea ought to get on a ship. We begin with the effect, looking for what is necessary to bring it about; we shift to the cause, judging what it must have to bring about the effect. In the movement from the first to the second no syllogism is required; no new information is injected. The same knowledge is judged in two different ways.[20]

Deliberation considers the effect (the end sought) insofar as it is brought about by certain causes. Judgment considers the causes insofar as they bring about some end.[21] Deliberation views the operation from the perspective of passion or undergoing; the effect undergoes the change brought about by the causes. Judgment views the operation from the perspective of action; the causes introduce a change into the effect. By knowing undergoing, we also know action, since the two are like correlative relations; the same information is known in two different ways. The murderer begins by considering the desired endpoint, namely, the dead victim. He then considers the possible causes of this effect (strangling, poisoning ...), viewing the effect of death as a passion introduced by the causes; he then reverses the procedure, considering what kind of cause he must be (a strangler, a poisoner ...) to

---

19. I, 14, 16.

20. Finnis (*Natural Law*, 315) gives a good example of such a derivation of an ought-statement from an is-statement. He notes that when the law has specified a course of action, then it is the only way of satisfying the need to respect the common good (resolution). He then moves to composition, beginning with the inferential word "so": "So, in the case mentioned in step B, I must (ought to) act in the way specified as obligatory."

21. If judgment is viewed simply as the discernment of which means among many is best, without transferring to the active ought-mode, then, by my terminology, I would be placing it within deliberation. Clare, for instance, might recognize that taking an airplane is better than getting on a ship. This recognition still belongs to deliberation, until she judges that she ought to get on an airplane.

bring about the effect, now viewing the action as leading to the effect, rather than the effect as brought about by the action.

7.3
DESCRIPTIVISM OR PRESCRIPTIVISM?

The ought debate is sometimes posed as an opposition between descriptivism and prescriptivism. Do statements concerning the good describe the way the world is or do they prescribe how the world ought to be? We have seen that statements concerning the good do describe a certain state of affairs involving desire or inclination. The good is a kind of final cause; it is that which completes an inclination. We recognize this causality through its effect; therefore, we define the good in terms of its effect, so that the good is the object of desire.

What about ought-statements? Are they prescriptive or descriptive? They do not seem to describe what is now the case; rather, they point us to some future state, a state that may or may not be the case. On the other hand, they do not always seem to be prescriptive. The judgment that a waiter ought to take food to the customers might be made quite apart from any prescription. Indeed, it might enter into a kind of speculative examination of waiters.[22]

7.3.1: Future States or Present Existence?

Patrick Lee and others distinguish between speculative and practical knowledge based upon what is the case — which applies to speculative knowledge — and that which is not now but what is to come to be — which applies to practical knowledge.

Ought-statements do seem to apply to the future; they are a kind of future modal that applies rarely to the present or the past. More essential than the future state, however, is the element of uncertainty that accompanies the future state. An ought-statement always involves necessity, but the necessity is cloaked in uncertainty. The necessity is conditional, applying to some aspect of an agent, considered apart

---

22. Janice L. Schultz ("'Ought'-Judgments: A Descriptivist Analysis from a Thomistic Perspective," *New Scholasticism* 61 [1987]: 400–426) argues that ought-statements are descriptive; they describe what is fitting to something.

from possible impediments or interfering causes. The sphere ought to fall — just insofar as it is a heavy body — but it might not fall.

Future existence as such is not peculiar to ought-statements or to practical knowledge. We make predictions about the future based upon current causes. We can even predict based upon resolution from an end, for instance, we might predict that Clare will get on a ship. Our prediction depends upon a chain of reasoning that begins by knowing that she wants to cross the sea; we resolve this desired effect into its causes, and then we proceed, in composition, to make our prediction. Such reasoning is commonplace, and is exemplified clearly in a game of chess, as a player predicts what his opponent will do.

Ought-statements are not predictions. Unlike predictions, they abstract from possible impediments. In contrast, predictions include a judgment that no interfering cause will prevent the agent from its action. Both ought-statements and predictions, however, are based upon the current state of affairs. By knowing the present causes, with their inclinations, we project into the future. Ought-statements make no definitive projection, because they focus upon one aspect of the agent, setting aside the possibility of impediments.

Predictions can be true insofar as they are statements about what in fact is the case; it is the case that the current causes are moving toward this outcome. Similarly, ought-statements are statements about what is currently the case, even though they direct our attention to the future. The statement "The cake ought to be done in one hour" makes a claim about the current state of the cake; according to its current conditions, it is moving toward being done in one hour. Other conditions, however, might interfere, so that no definitive prediction is made. In this respect, ought-statements have a firmer claim to truth than do predictions. Predictions make strong assumptions about the way things actually are with respect to impediments. Ought-statements remain aloof from these concrete assumptions, leaving the truth at the level of abstraction from the presence or absence of impediments.

An ought-statement usually concerns what is not the case, typically because it is a future state, sometimes because it is contrary to a past state, and sometimes because we are uncertain of the present state. While an ought-statement concerns what is not the case, it nevertheless concerns that which belongs to an agent. The belonging is of some future state, but based upon some present condition of the agent. "Being done" belongs to the cake in one hour, based upon certain present conditions. "Getting on a ship" belongs to Clare, based upon her current end of crossing the sea.

Because the "belonging" concerns what is not yet the case, it gives rise to a sense of being "owed." If Chuck is owed $10, then the $10 belongs to Chuck, although he does not currently possess it. Similarly, if getting on a ship belongs to Clare, but she is not currently getting on a ship, then it is "owed" to her. A belonging that is not currently the case is an "owing"; it is something that ought to be. In contrast, the copula "is" typically expresses a belonging that is currently the case. "The cake is yellow" indicates that the quality yellow belongs to the cake as it is now, not awaiting any future state.

This sense of "owing" can be found in speculative knowledge as much as practical knowledge. "The sphere ought to fall" is a speculative judgment that indicates a future state as belonging to the sphere under a certain condition, namely, insofar as it is a heavy body. Even ought-statements that derive from an end need not be practical: when the guidance of practical knowledge is out of the question, we still make ought-judgments involving necessity of an end. We might say of a mouse working its way through a maze that it "ought to turn right." We are certainly not guiding the mouse, who can receive no guidance by words. Nor are we making a prediction; indeed, we might predict that the mouse will turn left even as we judge that it ought to turn right. What, then, are we saying about the mouse?

We are stating that "turning right" belongs to the mouse precisely insofar as the mouse is working its way through the maze. This is a simple observation — a speculative judgment — about what applies to such agents. The judgment has something of a practical character to it, for it is in the mode of composition, not in the mode of resolution. We are "putting together" what belongs to the mouse based upon its current state of working through the maze. Nevertheless, our judgment is — like the judgment that the sphere ought to fall — ultimately speculative. By composing certain elements we are passing judgment upon what is the case, upon what truly belongs to the mouse under this condition.[23]

---

23. In a similar manner, Aquinas says that angels have speculative knowledge of things in the mode of practical knowledge. See *Sent.*, II, 3, 3, 2, ad 1.

OUGHT

New natural law theorists have insisted that "practical truth" is true only by a kind of analogy. It does not express a conformity with what is the case, but rather it anticipates what is the case; the "is" of speculative knowledge cannot replace the "is-to-be" of practical knowledge.[24] It turns out, however, that speculative knowledge can also concern an "is-to-be." Turning right belongs to the mouse even though the mouse is not now actually turning right; the turning right "is-to-be." Nevertheless, we know this future state as belonging to the mouse by way of knowing a present state in the mouse, namely, that it is working toward a certain end.

The new natural law theory, then, does not err in supposing that virtual practical knowledge concerns what is yet to be; it errs in supposing that speculative knowledge does not. Furthermore, it errs in supposing that this knowledge of what is-to-be cannot also be a conformity with what is the case. It is the case, right now, that turning right belongs to the mouse (as a future state) insofar as the mouse is working through the maze. It is the case that turning right is "owed" to the mouse insofar as it has this end, that is, while turning right belongs to the mouse, it is not yet realized in the mouse. Turning right is a property of the mouse existing in its potential, waiting for realization.

7.3.2: Guidance and Direction

The distinction between what is the case and what "is-to-be," then, is not a promising avenue for separating practical knowledge from speculative. The guiding role of practical reason seems more hopeful. The judgment concerning the mouse is not practical, in part, because it provides no guidance. The mouse will not be affected by the judgment in any way whatsoever.

In contrast, practical judgments provide guidance for our actions. Unlike most other causes, rational agents require knowledge to act upon their inclinations. A tree seeks water and puts out roots; it does not need to know how to put out roots. Someone who wants to get to the opera, however, does not go there automatically, without knowing how. Practical knowledge provides this how-to knowledge. It does not predict; it shows the way.

---

24. Grisez, "Practical Principles," 116.

OUGHT

If guidance is the distinguishing mark of practical knowledge, then certainly not every ought-statement is practical. Even what Aquinas calls virtually practical knowledge is not necessarily practical in the sense of providing guidance. The judgment "The builder ought to lay the foundation first" can sometimes provide guidance, but it need not. When Kay makes the judgment, she neither plans on building a house — so she is not guiding her own behavior — nor is she guiding anyone else who is building a house. In contrast, when Clare judges that she ought to get on a ship, the judgment provides guidance for her.

Nevertheless, Kay's judgment concerning the builder is certainly more practical than the judgment concerning the mouse. The movement of the mouse is not even materially practical; it does not fall within the domain of human actions. Building a house is at least something that Kay could do, even though she currently has no interest in it. In the end, however, the judgment concerning the builder is similar to the judgment concerning the mouse. Both judge what an agent needs insofar as it is working toward some goal. Ultimately, both are judgments of the way the world is; they are descriptive.

Even when Clare says to herself "I ought to get on a ship," she is still describing what belongs to her insofar as she has the end of crossing the sea. In this case, her judgment does provide guidance. Such guidance, however, is not opposed to description. Indeed, the judgment provides guidance precisely because it describes; it shows the way to go; it describes the path. If someone gives directions to the opera, we think that the directions provide guidance precisely to the degree that they describe the correct path. If the directions did not describe, then their guidance would be useless.

Descriptions are fit for guidance insofar as they describe how to bring something about. As such, even Kay's judgment concerning the foundation of the house is fit for guidance, even though she is not using it for guidance. Even the judgment concerning the mouse has something of this character. If the mouse could be guided by knowledge, then this is the sort of knowledge it would need.

In this sense, ought-statements — at least those derived from an end — all have the practical character of guidance. They do not all actually provide guidance, but they are all the sort of knowledge that could provide guidance to a rational agent with this end. They describe how

OUGHT

the agent must be — or act — in order to achieve the end. As such, they describe something that really is the case, just as a description of what it means for somebody to sit — even when no one is sitting — is a true description of what is the case. Ought-statements describe what would be necessary for an agent, if it had this end. Only because these descriptions are true — that is, they reflect what belongs to agents with this end — can they actually provide guidance for those agents that do in fact have the end.

7.3.3: Is Judgment Fully Practical?

What is the status of ought-statements when the will is added? Do they become fully practical rather than virtually practical? It would seem so, since knowledge becomes fully practical based upon the end of the agent. As it turns out, however, matters are not so straightforward.

Consider first the judgment, made in Clare's practical reason, that she ought to get on a ship. Clare actually does have the end of crossing the sea. Does her judgment, then, become purely practical? Evidently not, at least not according to Aquinas. He identifies three acts of moral practical reason, namely, deliberation, judgment, and command. Both deliberation and judgment are speculative; only the last is practical.

> There are three acts of reason concerning moral deeds [agibilia]: the first is deliberation, the second judgment, and the third is command. The first two correspond to acts of the speculative intellect, namely, inquiry and judgment, for deliberation is a certain kind of inquiry. The third act properly belongs to the practical intellect, insofar as it has to do with operation, for reason commands only concerning those things that can be done by a man.[25]

Aquinas must mean that deliberation and judgment are not *purely* practical. Deliberation is practical in some sense or another, as Aquinas explicitly states.[26] In what way is it practical? It must be either materially practical or virtually practical. The same can be said of judgment,

---

25. I-II, 57, 6. "Circa agibilia autem humana tres actus rationis inveniuntur, quorum primus est consiliari, secundus iudicare, tertius est praecipere. Primi autem duo respondent actibus intellectus speculativi qui sunt inquirere et iudicare, nam consilium inquisitio quaedam est. Sed tertius actus proprius est practici intellectus, inquantum est operativus, non enim ratio habet praecipere ea quae per hominem fieri non possunt." See also I-II, 47, 8.
26. II-II, 47, 2.

OUGHT

which is our immediate concern. We will begin, however, by considering the status of deliberation.

As Thomas says, deliberation is a kind of inquiry that proceeds by resolution.[27] It seeks to discover the causes of the desired effect. Such an inquiry is indeed speculative. What are the various causes of getting across the sea? At this point, the inquiry is not providing guidance; it is working toward guidance, but at present it seeks only the truth about causes in the world.

Deliberation, then, appears to be materially practical. In chapter 1, when we first looked at Aquinas's division of speculative and practical knowledge, we saw that the speculative mode operates "by resolving a composite into formal universal principles."[28] We now see that deliberation also operates by resolution. As such, it focuses upon certain truths that apply to an agent and its end; it focuses upon the truth concerning human actions or human causes. It does not determine how something is to be done, although it is moving toward this conclusion; rather, it determines how certain causes behave, or rather, how certain effects can be brought about by certain causes.

From among the various causes, judgment must determine which is best. It determines, says Aquinas, what is to be chosen as a means to achieve the end sought (and, one might add, in conjunction with other ends).[29] The sort of judgment we are concerned with here is a judgment that precedes choice.[30] We will avoid getting embroiled in a dispute as to whether there is a judgment "of choice" that is distinct from the judgment preceding choice.[31]

At this point, "ought" is introduced. During the stage of inquiry, the individual seeks to know about causes. As she inquires into the means she does not determine what she ought to do, for instance, whether she ought to take an airplane or a ship. That determination occurs in judgment. The inquiry simply determines in what ways the various means are good or not good causes for attaining the end. De-

---

27. I-II, 14, 5. 28. I, 14, 16.
29. I-II, 14, 1; I-II, 13, 1, ad 2.
30. See Paul Morrisset, "Prudence et fin selon St. Thomas," *Sciences ecclésiastiques* 15 (1963): 73–98, 439–58. Aquinas clearly refers to a judgment concluding deliberation and preceding choice in *Sententia Ethicorum*, lib. 3, lect. 9 (Leonine ed., v. 47, 145, ln. 20–25.).
31. See McInerny, *Human Action*, 220–39.

OUGHT

liberation might even become aware that certain causes are necessary, whether strictly or loosely. Clare might recognize, for instance, that the only way to get across the sea is with a ship.

Judgment reverses this procedure of resolution and turns to composition. Thereby, it moves to the how-to knowledge of virtual practical knowledge. Clare judges not simply that the only way to get across the sea is with a ship; she judges that she ought to get on a ship. She judges that this action, of getting on a ship, belongs to her precisely insofar as she has the end of crossing the sea. As such, it provides guidance.

Nevertheless, says Aquinas, it is not purely practical. It is still a judgment about the way things are, a determination concerning what belongs, with a kind of necessity coming from the end, to agents such as this. Nothing has changed about the judgment itself. Only its use has changed; it is now used for guidance.

But is this not, someone may protest, precisely what makes knowledge to be purely practical, namely, its use? The builder who knows how to build a house, but does not want to, has virtually practical knowledge. But when he wills to build a house, and puts his knowledge to use, then it becomes purely practical. Why, then, would Aquinas say that judgment remains virtually practical? The answer to this question is best illuminated by examining the act that Aquinas does think falls in the category of purely practical, namely, command.

7.3.4: Why Is Command Fully Practical?

What happens in the act of command that brings us to purely practical knowledge? In order to answer this question, we should recognize that Aquinas is not using the word "command" restrictively, to refer to one person ordering another; we can command ourselves. What is essential to command is that we move someone to act. How does this happen when we command ourselves? Ultimately, we inject our wills into the knowledge. It is no longer merely knowledge; it is knowledge with the movement of the will.[32] Command, says Aquinas, is an act of reason

---

32. For an examination of the role of will in command, see Stephen L. Brock, "The Legal Character of Natural Law according to St Thomas Aquinas" (Ph.D. diss., University of Toronto, 1988), 110–15.

OUGHT

together with the movement of the will. Aquinas compares two ways in which reason can indicate the path to take. It seems that only the second is command proper; the first seems to be more what we have described as judgment. It is, says Aquinas, in the indicative mood.

> Reason is able to intimate or pronounce something in two ways. In one way, absolutely, which is expressed through a verb in the indicative mood, for example, when someone says to another, "This ought to be done by you." Reason intimates something to someone in another way by moving the person to this [act]; such intimation is expressed through a verb in the imperative mood, for example, when it is said to someone, "Do this." The will is the first mover in the powers of the soul for performing acts. Since a second mover moves only through the power of the first mover, it follows that reason moves by commanding only through the power of the will. Consequently, to command is an act of reason presupposing an act of the will, by which power reason moves, through command, to perform actions.[33]

According to Aquinas, then, the will as moving power enters only in the act of command; it is absent in the indicative act of judgment.

Someone might object that even at the stage of judgment, prior to command, the will of the agent is involved, for she seeks the end. Even before Clare commands herself to get on the ship, while she has only judged that she ought to get on the ship, she has, in her will, the end of crossing the sea. The knowledge that she ought to get on the ship is not a mere curiosity, like someone who might idly want to find out how houses are built. It is knowledge that she seeks in order to accomplish her end or goal.

We must distinguish between the end sought and the action sought. Clare does seek the end of crossing the sea. When she has made a judgment to get on the ship but before she has chosen, then she does not yet seek to get on a ship. Her knowledge is fully practical with regard to

---

33. I-II, 17, 1. "Sed ratio potest aliquid intimare vel denuntiare dupliciter. Uno modo, absolute, quae quidem intimatio exprimitur per verbum indicativi modi; sicut si aliquis alicui dicat, hoc est tibi faciendum. Aliquando autem ratio intimat aliquid alicui, movendo ipsum ad hoc, et talis intimatio exprimitur per verbum imperativi modi; puta cum alicui dicitur, fac hoc. Primum autem movens in viribus animae ad exercitium actus, est voluntas, ut supra dictum est. Cum ergo secundum movens non moveat nisi in virtute primi moventis, sequitur quod hoc ipsum quod ratio movet imperando, sit ei ex virtute voluntatis. Unde relinquitur quod imperare sit actus rationis, praesupposito actu voluntatis, in cuius virtute ratio movet per imperium ad exercitium actus."

crossing the sea; it is only virtually practical with regard to getting on the ship. She must move herself to get on the ship, and she still might fail to do so; perhaps in the end fear will dissuade her.

Judgment, then, is speculative, that is, not purely practical; the will of the agent is not yet behind the action. Of course, purely practical knowledge may underlie the judgment. The purely practical knowledge with regard to crossing the sea underlies the judgment that Clare ought to get on a ship. Nevertheless, the latter judgment is only virtually practical.

It follows that virtually practical knowledge can be further divided. On the one hand, some virtually practical knowledge provides guidance only potentially. Kay's knowledge of how to build a house does not now provide guidance (nor is it likely to provide guidance at any point in her life, since she is not likely to build a house). It is a mere curiosity; she finds it interesting to know how houses are built.

On the other hand, some virtually practical knowledge provides guidance actually. If Clare plans on crossing the sea, then the judgment "I ought to get on a ship" provides guidance to her right now. It is still virtually practical, and does not become purely practical until Clare actually chooses to get on a ship. Nevertheless, it seems more practical than Kay's knowledge of how to build a house.

7.3.5: Description

We are not surprised to find that the statement "If you want to get to the opera, then you ought to turn right on Louisiana Street" is simply a description of what is the case. Nor are we surprised to find that "One ought to turn right on Louisiana Street" is a description of how to get to the opera. What should surprise us is that anyone ever thought ought-statements are anything but descriptions of the way things are. Even the statement of H. L. A. Hart's frustrated poisoner — that he ought to have given his victim a second dose — is a description of the world; it expresses a necessity that applied to his action, insofar as it was directed to the end of killing his victim.[34]

The question of "deriving" an ought-statement from an is-statement

---

34. See H. L. A. Hart, "Positivism and the Separation of Law and Morals," *Harvard Law Review* 71 (1958): 593–629, at 613.

OUGHT

has proved to be a red herring. An ought-statement is in fact a certain kind of is-statement.[35] It describes a certain kind of necessity, a necessity that applies to an agent insofar as it has an end. This necessity is first recognized by way of resolution, at which stage it does not yet have the mode of an ought-statement. Clare judges that the end of getting across the sea requires the kind of cause that gets on a ship.

The ought-statement is "derived" in the stage of composition, when we recognize this necessity applying to agents insofar as they have this end. The same reality is perceived; all that has changed is our mode of approaching it. On the one hand, we consider the end insofar as it is caused by certain agents; on the other hand, we consider the agent insofar as it causes this end. The former does not contain an ought-statement; the latter does. Nothing mysterious has materialized in this new ought-statement. Only our manner of perceiving has changed.

---

35. Murphy, then, has misstated the case when he speaks of the "drastic difference" between practical and theoretical concepts (*Practical Rationality*, 13).

8

OBLIGATION

Even those who staunchly defend the naturalistic fallacy, asserting that we can never begin with an is-statement and reach an ought-statement, may be unperturbed by the last chapter's defense of descriptivism. After all, they might say, the argument concerns only hypothetical ought-statements, which are unproblematic; they are not *essentially* practical or prescriptive.

In contrast, so the argument goes, "moral" ought-statements are prescriptive and cannot be derived from mere description. They have binding force independently of any presupposed desire or endpoint. No amount of what-is-the-case will ever generate this moving and directive force of reason, which involves an entirely different meaning of "ought." The last chapter may have been of interest in its own right, but it was irrelevant with regard to the question that really matters.

Grisez asserts that a "moral ought," for Aquinas, is distinct from other ought-statements.[1] For evidence he provides only the inadequate argument, already addressed, that the first moral precepts are underived; the presumption is that all "hypothetical" ought-statements are derived syllogistically. He also adds that the very first principle of practical reason is not hypothetical, for it leaves no options; a "moral ought" must be categorical; it allows no escape clause because it is overriding or necessary.

Because Aquinas seems to have room only for hypothetical ought-statements, D. J. O'Connor accuses him of having "a very much diminished theory of natural law. It prescribes no unconditional moral imperatives.... It is uncontroversial only because the mainspring of morality has been extracted. We are given no reason why we ought to act in any particular way."[2]

---

1. Grisez, "First Principle," 194–95.
2. D. J. O'Connor, *Aquinas and Natural Law* (London: Macmillan, 1968), 83–84.

OBLIGATION

These are strong charges. Evidently, Aquinas's natural law theory is trivial. We might try to rescue Aquinas, as does Grisez, by claiming that he in fact does have a "moral" or "prescriptive" ought, distinct from the hypothetical ought-statements investigated in the last chapter. As we have seen, however, Aquinas explicitly states that the binding force of the natural law is a conditional necessity from an end.[3] Must we, then, accept O'Connor's verdict? Or can we discover the needed characteristics of a "moral ought" within Aquinas's account of hypothetical ought-statements?

Unfortunately, as Phillipa Foot has observed, these needed characteristics have never been clearly defined.[4] Evidently, a "moral ought" is distinct from a hypothetical ought; beyond this first requirement, the "moral ought" remains mysterious. Somehow it has a strong binding force; at the same time, it does not impose absolute necessity. Then what is the nature of the necessity it imposes?

8.1
THE NATURE OF THE MORAL OUGHT

Hypothetical ought-statements seem inadequate because they lack necessity. They have force only insofar as the agent desires the end. As such, an agent can opt out of them simply by abandoning the end. If Clare is truly averse to getting on a ship, then she can simply abandon the goal of crossing the sea; the statement "I ought to get on a ship" will dissipate and lose all force.

We should not so readily — so the intuition goes — be able to weasel out of moral ought-statements. If Louis is told that "He ought (morally) to give to the poor from his surplus," he should not be able to reply "But I do not really care about the good of the poor; I prefer the opera for myself." His preferences, so the argument goes, are irrelevant. The moral ought-statement has force whatever his desires happen to be.

As we have seen, ought-statements retain their guiding power even when they are not currently giving guidance. Insofar as someone is

---

3. For an analysis of Aquinas's notion of obligation, see Brock, "Legal Character," 194–204.

4. See Philippa Foot, "Morality as a System of Hypothetical Imperatives," in *Virtues and Vices and Other Essays in Moral Philosophy* (Berkeley and Los Angeles: University of California Press, 1978).

OBLIGATION

concerned with the good of the poor, he ought to give to the poor. This statement is still true, and it still shows the way to achieve the end, even for Louis who does not have this end. Likewise, the directions to the opera retain the ability to guide someone to the opera, even if he currently does not plan to go to the opera. In a sense, then, even hypothetical ought-statements retain a guiding force — the potential to provide guidance — despite an agent's particular preferences. We could say of Louis that he knows he ought to give to the poor — *if* he were seeking to attain the end of the welfare of the poor.

Evidently, this guiding force, which remains even for agents who do not have the end, is not sufficient for the categorical imperative. This guiding force is still conditional. It shows the way only for those who have the end. In contrast, a categorical imperative, or a moral ought, does not depend upon the condition of the agent desiring some end.

Categorical necessity, then, cannot be hypothetical. Neither can it be absolute. We do not want to say that Louis has no choice in the matter, as if he is determined to seek the welfare of the poor. A categorical ought-statement is meant to guide behavior, not to force behavior. A categorical ought is a moral ought, and a moral ought makes no sense if it forces behavior.

What remains? How does a categorical ought-statement make the end in some manner necessary? It does not do so hypothetically, nor does it do so absolutely. What kind of necessity remains? Unfortunately, the answer to this question never becomes clear. One is left with the uncomfortable feeling that Phillipa Foot is correct when she says "Perhaps it makes no sense to say that we 'have to' submit to the moral law, or that morality is 'inescapable' in some special way."[5]

In our attempt to find some meaning behind the necessity of the moral or natural law, we will consider three possibilities. First, the law might derive binding force from the command of some superior, a king or a parliament, or in the case of the natural law, God. Second, reason itself might have a special power of binding the will, separate from the conditional force of a hypothetical ought-statement, so that the force of the natural law derives from the nature of practical reason. Third, nature might impose a necessity upon the will, not the absolute neces-

---

5. Foot, "Hypothetical Imperatives," 163.

OBLIGATION

sity by which the will must desire the last end, but a necessity that the will can still reject.

8.2
THE ACT OF COMMAND AND THE BINDING FORCE OF LAW

Finnis and Grisez attribute to Suárez a view of the natural law in which our human good or perfection depends upon our nature.[6] The force of the natural law, however, depends upon a command from God to seek our good or our perfection. Without God, we would still have some kind of guidance from our nature, but it would not have the force of obligation; it would consist merely of hypothetical ought-statements. The force of obligation comes only from the command of God.

In this manner, the necessity of a moral ought — or a precept of the natural law — might be explained. The precept holds force even for the person who does not desire to follow it, because the necessity comes from the outside, from the divine lawgiver. Human beings can be held to the natural law under pain of punishment because the necessity of the law arises from something beyond their own desires.

This view is the primary nemesis for Finnis and Grisez. It is this misunderstanding of Aquinas, so they claim, that has led to naturalism and physicalism. Nevertheless, on the face of it, this Suárezian view has much going for it.[7] The natural law, it will turn out, looks a lot like a command of God. The very word "precept" seems to imply as much, for in the Latin it is a form of the word "command." We must begin, therefore, by examining the nature of a precept of law.

8.2.1: The Status of Precepts

What is typically translated as "command" is, in the Latin, two different words: *imperare* and *precipere*. Evidently, Aquinas does not use the two Latin words to refer to two distinct concepts.[8] Both describe

---

6. Grisez, "First Principle," 192–93; Finnis, *Natural Law,* 46–48.

7. I am not concerned with determining the view of Suárez himself; I wish only to address the perceived view of Suárez, as presented by Finnis and Grisez. For a defense of Suárez, see Di Blasi, *God*; see also Harris, "Naturalism," 123–24.

8. I-II, 92, 2. "Quidam actus sunt boni ex genere, qui sunt actus virtutum, et respectu

OBLIGATION

an act of reason ordering, together with an act of the will moving.[9]

As we have seen, the act of command, since it includes an act of will, belongs to fully practical knowledge. Unfortunately, the precepts of the natural law, as Aquinas describes them, seem to be virtually practical, like a judgment rather than a command. The will of the agent is not necessarily behind them, moving to act; rather, the precepts show the way to act, and the person must yet choose to follow them or not. The precept "Do harm to no one" guides the behavior of all human beings, but not all human beings act upon it. The precepts, then, seem like virtually practical knowledge. As Grisez insists, the first precepts of the natural law are not imperatives.[10] If Grisez is correct — and it seems he is — then why did Aquinas choose the word "precept"? Would it not have been better had he used the word "judgment"?

In fact, the word "precept" arises from the character of law as an external principle of human action; laws give rise to human actions but they are not within the person acting, as is clear for human laws.[11] The law to drive on the right side of the street is a principle of my doing so; the law itself, however, is something outside of me. Ultimately, the law is always given by one person to another: "The law directs acts of those who are properly subject to the government of another, so that no one, properly speaking, imposes a law on his own actions."[12]

Law most properly is found in the lawgiver, that is, in the person who directs by way of the law. As such, it is like giving a command. If an officer tells a private to scrub the floors, then by way of his command he is moving the private to act. The principle of movement is in the officer; the one who must act is the private. The officer, it seems, has reached purely practical knowledge. He does not merely judge that the private ought to scrub the floors; he proceeds to the final act of practical reason, directing to act with an impetus of his will. He does so by issuing an order.

The same order as it is received in the private, however, takes on the character of a judgment, which the private can follow or not follow.

---

horum, ponitur legis actus praecipere vel imperare." See also I-II, 92, 2 arg. 1; II-II, 47, 8 arg. 3.

9. II-II, 47, 8, ad 3 and I-II, 17, 1.   10. Grisez, "First Principle," 192.
11. I-II, 90, introduction.
12. I-II, 93, 5. "Lex est directiva actuum qui conveniunt subiectis gubernationi alicuius, unde nullus, proprie loquendo, suis actibus legem imponit."

OBLIGATION

He sees that he ought to scrub the floor; doing so is necessary for the sake of the military end. The command of the officer, then, becomes a judgment in the private. In the officer, it is purely practical; in the private, it is virtually practical.

Similarly, the precepts of the law are like commands — existing in the lawgiver — that move someone else to act.[13] Like the command of the superior officer, laws are purely practical in the one issuing them; in the one receiving the law, however, they become judgments at the level of virtual practical knowledge.

"Precept" is the past participle of *precipere,* and as such it refers to that which has been commanded; it is not itself the command, but it is the content of the command. Insofar as this content is received into the one commanded, it becomes a judgment.[14] Is a precept, then, fully practical or virtually practical? In itself, a precept is neither or it is both. In itself, a precept is simply the content of a command. That content can be found either in the command itself or it can be found in the one commanded, in which case it is realized in a judgment.

At the very least, then, human laws are commands in the lawgiver. All of the acts of the law, says Aquinas, can be described as "commands," taken in a broad sense.[15] In this sense, even to permit something might be considered a command. Even an officer permitting a private to take a trip into town is a kind of command. Insofar as this command is received in the private, however, it becomes a judgment; it is not fully practical but virtually practical, awaiting the full movement of the private's will.

What of the natural law? If we are looking at the precepts of the natural law as they exist in us, then it seems that Grisez is correct; they are not imperatives or commands; they are judgments.[16] The character of these judgments will be a matter of dispute, but for the moment we are concerned with the precepts in the lawgiver. If God is the lawgiver, then it seems that the precepts of the natural law are commands in God, which explains why Aquinas says that the natural law is simply our participation in the eternal law.[17]

13. Long defends the nature of law as command in "Looking-Glass," 268–73.
14. See Brock, "Legal Character," 136n30, and 137n45.
15. I-II, 92, 2, ad 1.
16. Schultz ("Ought-Judgments," 408) incorrectly claims that the precepts of the natural law are imperatives.
17. I-II, 91, 2.

OBLIGATION

8.2.2: Natural Law as an External Principle of Action

Like human law, the natural law is an external principle of action. Originally, it exists in the one who promulgates, which seems to be God. Aquinas says, "The promulgation of the law of nature arises because God has placed in the human mind the ability to know it naturally."[18] With God as the author of the natural law, the external character of the law is maintained.

At the same time, the natural law is internal to the person, since it is a work of reason.[19] How can it be both external and internal? In the same manner in which a command is both external and internal. The lieutenant commands the private to clean up the mess hall. In relation to the private, the command is something external, since it arises from the lieutenant. On the other hand, within the private himself the command becomes a kind of judgment. As such, it is internal to him.

The same kind of duality applies to the natural law. It originates as a precept of God, that is, an order of reason impelled by an act of will. The immediate effect of God's will is certain inclinations in nature. As human beings, however, we become aware of these inclinations and thereby become aware of the will of God. This awareness, in us, is a work of reason; it is a judgment about what ought to be done. In God, the precepts or commands are the same as the eternal law. In us, the awareness of the commands of God is our participation in the eternal law; this participation is also the natural law.

A precept, then, is the content of a command. In the one who commands, it is fully practical; in the one who is commanded, it is a judgment at the level of virtual practical knowledge. Even within this judgment, however, the content must be perceived as arising from outside. If the private thinks to himself "I ought to clean the mess hall," but does not perceive this ought-statement as arising from a superior, then

---

18. I-II, 90, 4, ad 1. "Promulgatio legis naturae est ex hoc ipso quod Deus eam mentibus hominum inseruit naturaliter cognoscendam."

19. Rhonheimer emphasizes the natural law as a work of reason; see Rhonheimer, "Work of Reason"; see also Rhonheimer, "Cognitive Structure," 175–77. Aquinas himself rarely uses the term *opus rationis* in reference to the natural law. More often, he uses the term to express the work of speculative reason (see esp. I-II, 90, 1, ad 2). A work of reason, then, might well be a received reflection of the way the world is.

OBLIGATION

it is not perceived as a command or precept but merely as an ought-statement. Even when a person commands himself, he has one part directing another part.

Similarly, law is an external principle of action; less properly, it is the individual's awareness of this principle. The individual must be aware that a precept comes from outside; otherwise, he does not perceive it as a precept; he does not perceive it as law. He may know a set of judgments about what ought to be done, but these judgments will have the character of law only insofar as they are perceived as arising from some external command. We might call these judgments moral principles, but we should not call them law.[20]

The natural law fits this pattern insofar as it is a participation in the eternal law. The natural law and the eternal law are distinct in scope; the natural law is only that part of the eternal law that applies to voluntary human actions. Within this narrower scope, the two are identical in content, for instance, both the eternal law and the natural law prescribe marriage. Precisely as a law, the content of the prescription must be perceived as arising from God; the natural law is our perception of God's commands as realized in nature. If we know that we should keep sexual relations within marriage, but we do not know that this rule arises from some authority, then we do not perceive it as a law.

Most properly, then, the natural law is a participation in the eternal law. It is the antecedent will of God for human beings, insofar as we have become aware of it.[21] As an act of knowledge — as opposed to the content of this act — the natural law resides in us; as such, it is a

---

20. See Dewan, "Natural Lights," 298, 303–4; see also Brock, "Legal Character," 82–84. Fortin goes so far as to say that the legal character of the natural law is perceived only with revelation, through which we become aware of the eternal law; see Fortin, "New Rights Theory," 607–11.

21. Long ("Autonomous Practical Reason") emphasizes the natural law as a participation in the eternal law. He pushes the effect of God's command farther than is suggested here, claiming that the natural law requires God's causality with regard to the determination of our free actions. This seems excessive. The natural law concerns God's antecedent will and is therefore perceived in the effect of inclinations rather than in the effect of actually chosen actions. Concerning the question of whether Bañez is correct with respect to the determination of freely chosen actions see Garrigou-Lagrange (*Providence* [St. Louis, Mo: Herder Book Co., 1937]), who favors Bañez, and Michael D. Torre (*Do Not Resist the Spirit's Call: Francisco Marín-Sola on Sufficient Grace* [Washington, D.C.: The Catholic University of America Press, 2013]), who favors Francisco Marín-Sola (which is also the view of Jacques Maritain).

OBLIGATION

work of reason. The content of this work of reason concerns the order of human actions; the origin of this content is found in God. Of course, someone might perceive the content without perceiving that it arises from God. Then this content would still be a law, since it does in fact arise from God, but it would not be perceived as a law; it would be perceived only as what is necessary for the agent directed to some end.

What we have called the classical picture, then, is reaffirmed. God's will brings about the effect, in creatures, of certain natural inclinations toward certain ends. The good of these creatures is determined by these ends. Human beings are distinctive in that they become aware of these inclinations and ends, thereby becoming aware of their own good. They also become aware of what is necessary to attain these ends, which awareness can be formulated by way of ought-statements. Only when human beings come to perceive these ought-statements as expressing the will of God do they perceive them as law.

8.3

POLITICAL AUTHORITY

At this point, it seems that the view attributed to Suárez has much in its favor. The natural law is indeed commanded by God. Furthermore, we perceive it as law only insofar as we perceive it as commanded. Nevertheless, it does not follow that this view has explained the force of the moral ought. It is unclear how the command of someone outside of ourselves makes an ought-statement to be especially necessary. What kind of necessity does a command introduce?

Aquinas does speak of a necessity that one person can impose upon the will of another, for example, the government can state that those who steal will be put in prison. On the face of it, however, this necessity seems to be nothing other than the force of a threat. Something more is needed to explain why this threat has moral force, why it is *authority* rather than simply brute power. Consequently, we will look at the role of the common good in political authority and the role of coordinated activity. In the end, however, these considerations will be inadequate to explain the force of a moral ought.

OBLIGATION

8.3.1 Binding the Will

Aquinas discusses a necessity that arises from another. First, he contrasts it to the necessity of nature, which is not properly called "binding" or "obliging," terms that imply some necessity from outside the thing.[22] We cannot say, then, that an individual is "bound" to pursue happiness, because he does so by nature. We are bound to do only what we must do by some external necessity. Aquinas next distinguishes between two kinds of externally imposed necessity:

> The first necessity is through coercion, when someone has an absolute necessity to act in the way determined through the action of the agent; otherwise it is not properly speaking called coercion but inducement. The second necessity is conditional, namely, from the supposition of an end, as when the necessity is imposed upon someone such that if he does not act in a certain way then he will not get his reward.[23]

Finally, Aquinas notes that only the second necessity applies to the will.

> The first necessity, which is coercion, does not apply to the movements of the will but only to bodily things, for the will is naturally free from coercion. But the second necessity can be imposed upon the will, such that it is necessary to choose something if it is required to attain a certain good or to avoid a certain evil, for in such cases to avoid an evil amounts to the same thing as attaining the good.[24]

When it comes to the will, then, Aquinas still grants only the necessity of nature and the necessity from an end. Sometimes, however, this necessity from an end comes from another agent. Unfortunately, as Aquinas has stated the case, it might well apply to thieves, bullies, and tyrants. "Your money or your life," effectively imposes this external ne-

---

22. *De veritate*, 17, 3.
23. Ibid, (Leonine ed., v. 22, 522, 41–49). "Una quidem coactionis per quam aliquis absolute necesse habet hoc facere ad quod determinatur ex actione cogentis, alias coactio non proprie diceretur sed magis induction; alia vero necessitas est conditionata, scilicet ex suppositione finis, sicut imponitur alicui necessitas ut si non fecerit hoc non consequatur suum praemium."
24. Ibid., 49–57. "Prima quidem necessitas, quae est coactionis, non cadit in motibus voluntatis sed solum in corporalibus rebus, eo quod voluntas naturaliter est a coactione libera; sed secunda necessitas voluntati imponi potest, ut scilicet necessarium sit ei hoc eligere si hoc bonum debeat consequi vel si hoc malum debeat evitare: carere enim malo in idem computatur cum habere bonum in talibus."

OBLIGATION

cessity as much as a proper authority laying down the law. Surely, however, we would not say that we are "bound" to follow the threats of a robber, or if we did we would not mean that there is any kind of moral necessity involved.

Nevertheless, there is no doubt that Aquinas has this conditional necessity in mind for command and for the law.

> Just as the necessity of coercion is imposed upon bodily things through some action, so conditional necessity is imposed upon the will through an action. The action by which the will is moved, however, is the command of a ruler or governor, for which reason Aristotle says that a king is the principle of movement through his command. Consequently, the command of the one commanding relates to obligation in voluntary matters — in the manner in which the will is able to be bound — just as the action of a body relates to the binding of a body through the necessity of coercion.[25]

Aquinas still has not distinguished a proper authority from a robber, but he clearly thinks the distinction can be made. This conditional binding, which he sometimes calls coercive power, applies only to the proper authorities.

> A private person is unable to lead someone efficaciously to virtue, for he can only advise and if his advice is not accepted then he does not have coercive power, which the law ought to have so that it can lead someone to virtue efficaciously. Either the multitude or a public authority, to whom it belongs to inflict punishments, has this coercive power.[26]

Why is the power to coerce limited to the proper authorities? Without an answer to this question, the position attributed to Suárez cannot explain the force of the moral ought. It can claim that law is a certain kind of command, and it can claim that command imposes an external

---

25. Ibid., 58–70. "Sicut autem necessitas coactionis imponitur rebus corporalibus per aliquam actionem ita etiam ista necessitas conditionata imponitur voluntati per aliquam actionem. Actio autem qua voluntas movetur est imperium regentis et gubernantis, unde Philosophus dicit in V Metaphysicae quod rex est principium motus per suum imperium. Ita igitur se habet imperium alicuius imperantis ad ligandum in rebus voluntariis, illo modo ligationis qui voluntati accidere potest, sicut se habet actio corporalis ad ligandum res corporales necessitate coactionis."

26. I-II, 90, 3, ad 2. "Persona privata non potest inducere efficaciter ad virtutem. Potest enim solum monere, sed si sua monitio non recipiatur, non habet vim coactivam; quam debet habere lex, ad hoc quod efficaciter inducat ad virtutem, ut philosophus dicit, in X Ethic. Hanc autem virtutem coactivam habet multitudo vel persona publica, ad quam pertinet poenas infligere."

OBLIGATION

necessity upon the will. It will be unable to explain, however, how this external necessity is any different from a bully or a robber.

Aquinas restricts coercive power to proper authorities because of the good involved; it is not merely a private good but a shared good of the community. Only the community itself, or its representatives, can order to this good.[27] If we are to make the case for Suárez, then, we must investigate how a shared good might give rise to moral obligation.

8.3.2: Political Authority and the Common Good

If a man says to himself that he must get a job for the sake of sustenance, then he has discovered a certain necessity from an end. But if that man happens to be a father, then the sustenance with which he is concerned is not merely his own; it is also the sustenance of his family. For this reason, the necessity seems stronger. If he is concerned only with his own sustenance, then it seems that he has something of a freedom to "opt out" of the end, or at least to pursue it with less priority.

In a similar manner, society and the political authority behind it concern some shared good. Indeed, the notion of a shared good is the very basis of authority; some individuals are given authority over others only because several individuals are working toward a shared good. John Finnis fills out this account of authority by focusing upon the need for coordinated activity.[28] This need is especially evident when multiple means are possible to achieve the shared end. The community must settle upon one of these means. Sometimes one means stands above the others, as being best or most fitting. At other times, multiple means seem equal in relation to the end, or at least nearly equal, such that it is difficult to determine which is best.

When a shared good requires coordinated activity, such that the multiple individuals who share the good must work together to achieve it, then there must be some manner of determining which means will be used. If each individual is left to decide for himself, then multiple means will be chosen (except in the happy chance of unanimity), and coordination will be lost. If the community is sufficiently large, then pure democracy becomes unmanageable. As such, some individuals

---

27. I-II, 90, 3.
28. See Finnis, *Natural Law*, 231–33.

OBLIGATION

must be given the role of directing and coordinating the activity of the whole.[29] These individuals are in some manner "superiors," that is, they can give direction to others in the community.

It becomes necessary — with a necessity deriving from the end — for an individual in the community to follow the directives of the superior.[30] When coordinated activity is required, an individual within the community can direct himself to the shared end, as Finnis emphasizes, only by following the directives of those in charge of ordering the community.[31]

This reasoning operates by resolution. Beginning with the shared end of the community, we work backwards and look for the cause. We recognize that sometimes coordination is required. What is the cause of coordination? Some individuals (perhaps the majority) must determine the means to be taken. With a necessity that derives from the end, then, it is necessary, insofar as one is pursuing the shared good, to follow the directives of these individuals. To divert from this direction is to divert from the order to the end, which belongs not only to oneself but to others. By diverting from these directions, then, one takes away from others what belongs to them, namely, the shared good.

Aquinas applies this form of reasoning to laws concerning marriage.

> The act of generation is ordered to the good of the species, which is a common good. While the private good is subject to the directive of each person, the common good must be ordered by law. Therefore, in an act of the nutritive power, which is ordered to the preservation of the individual, anyone can determine for himself what food is appropriate. But to determine in what way the act of generation is to be performed does not pertain to just anyone, but to the legislator, whose care it is to direct the begetting of children.[32]

---

29. See I, 96, 4.

30. Obviously, there will be exceptions, when the superiors fail in their tasks so egregiously that they fail entirely to direct to the shared good, and even oppose the shared good.

31. Finnis's account of the obligation to follow the law is essentially the same as that given here; see Finnis, *Natural Law*, 314–20.

32. *De Malo*, 15, 2, ad 12 (Leonine ed., v. 23, 276, 320–37). "Actus generationis ordinatur ad bonum speciei, quod est bonum commune; bonum autem commune est ordinabile lege: set bonum priuatum subiacet ordinationi uniuscuiusque: et ideo quamuis in actu nutritiue uirtutis que ordinatur ad conseruationem indiuidui unusquisque possit sibi determinare cibum conuenientem sibi, tamen determinare qualis debeat esse generationis actus non pertinet ad unumquemque set ad legislatorem, cuius est ordinare de procreatione filiorum, et etiam Philosophus dicit in II Polit."

OBLIGATION

We are trying to determine whether the command of some authority can bind the human will in a special way, in a manner akin to the moral ought. Aquinas claims that an authority binds the will through its command by way of a conditional necessity, that is, by the coercive power of removing the good from the individual.

We can now see that this coercive power differs from the threat of a robber in three significant ways. First, it concerns a shared good. As such, the necessity for the end involves what is owed to others, and not just to the individual. Second, the good removed is the very shared good. Third, coercive power concerns coordinated activity toward the end; as such, an authority is needed to direct to the end. Can these three features transform the coercive power of authority into a moral ought, which binds an individual despite his personal desires? As we will see in the next section, Finnis and Grisez do not think so.

8.4
PRESCRIPTIVE REASON

Finnis argues that the commands of another person, whether human or divine, can never generate a new necessity for our actions.[33] As we have seen, commands can impose conditional necessity, but they cannot—Finnis argues—impose the necessity of moral obligation. Any attempt to justify obligation in terms of command places the necessity of obligation in an efficient cause of our actions, for the individual who commands us to act plays the role of an efficient cause.

Efficient causality, however, imposes no necessity upon the will. The will, Aquinas recognizes, has only natural necessity and conditional necessity; he explicitly rejects necessity from efficient causality.

> Sometimes necessity arises from something extrinsic.... which happens from an agent cause when someone is coerced by some agent, so that he cannot do the opposite. This is called necessity of coercion, and it is always repugnant to the will, for something is called violent when it is contrary to the inclination of a thing, but the very movement of the will is a certain inclination toward something.... Therefore, just as it is impossible that something should be both violent and natural at the same time, so it is impossible that something should be coerced or violent and also voluntary.[34]

---

33. Finnis, *Natural Law*, 342–43.
34. I, 82, 1. "Alio modo convenit alicui quod non possit non esse, ex aliquo extrinseco,

OBLIGATION

Finnis concedes that the command of human law can impose a conditional necessity. The law is a needed tool to pursue the human good; consequently, it is binding upon those subject to it.[35] The position attributed to Suárez, however, claims that the natural law imposes necessity upon our actions by a kind of efficient causality, namely, by the command of God. Suárez, then, makes moral necessity into a kind of natural necessity. Consequently, moral obligation is severed from the human good. We are not obliged to do something because it is good; rather, we are obliged to do it because it is commanded. Aquinas claims, however, that one individual can move the will of another only by presenting him with some good.[36]

The new natural law theory, then, rejects hypothetical necessity as the basis of the moral ought; it now also rejects the necessity of the efficient causality derived from command. While hypothetical necessity can explain many of our obligations (as with Finnis's explanation of our obligation to follow human law), it can never explain the ultimate source of obligation. A means can be necessary for some end, and that end can, in turn, be necessary for some further end. At some point, however, we must come to some last end or ends, which will have no further end to provide hypothetical necessity. Without hypothetical necessity as an option for these last ends, we might turn to a necessity of command, but this option, as well, has been rejected by the new natural law theory. What then remains?

Grisez claims that the necessity comes from practical reason itself. By its nature, practical reason is prescriptive; it moves us to act. In what way do the first precepts of the natural law move us to act? Not by force of will, for Grisez argues that the first precepts are not imperative; they do not include the force of will behind them.[37] The first precepts, then, do not presuppose an act of will; to the contrary, Grisez insists that the

---

vel fine vel agente.... Ex agente autem hoc alicui convenit, sicut cum aliquis cogitur ab aliquo agente, ita quod non possit contrarium agere. Et haec vocatur necessitas coactionis. Haec igitur coactionis necessitas omnino repugnat voluntati. Nam hoc dicimus esse violentum, quod est contra inclinationem rei. Ipse autem motus voluntatis est inclinatio quaedam in aliquid.... Sicut ergo impossibile est quod aliquid simul sit violentum et naturale; ita impossibile est quod aliquid simpliciter sit coactum sive violentum, et voluntarium."

35. Finnis, *Natural Law*, 45–46.   36. See I-II, 9, 1 and 2 and 3; I-II, 80, 1.
37. Grisez, "First Principle," 191–94.

desires of the will follow upon these first precepts; the precepts themselves are the necessary condition for any act of will.

How are we, on this view, to characterize the first precepts? Are they fully speculative, materially practical, virtually practical, or fully practical? Clearly, they are not speculative, since speculative knowledge describes the way the world is and does not move to change the world. Equally clear, they are not fully practical, since the fully practical act of command has the force of will behind it. Materially practical knowledge also seems inadequate to capture these first precepts of Grisez, since materially practical knowledge examines the nature of the good and does not move to act.[38]

Can we say, then, that Grisez's prescriptive knowledge is virtually practical? It does seem to be a fairly good fit. Both Grisez's precepts and virtual practical knowledge can be expressed in terms of ought-statements. Both provide guidance for action. Nevertheless, the fit is not perfect. Virtually practical knowledge is too passive; it moves to action only through an act of will. In contrast, the precepts of Grisez initiate the first acts of will.

What, then, is the status of these precepts? The short answer is that they are not any kind of knowledge identified by Aquinas; they are what Grisez calls prescriptive knowledge.[39] Prescriptive knowledge seems to be knowledge with a moving force to it, but not the moving force of the will; rather, the knowledge by its very nature has a moving force. Indeed, this knowledge is prior to the act of will and causes the act of will. This prescriptive knowledge in no way depends upon some prior end; rather, it determines the end. Since this prescriptive knowledge is practical, it does not simply reflect the way the world is, but rather precedes the world and ultimately shapes the world. Practical propositions, on this view, are true by preceding their realization.[40]

---

38. The new natural law theorists, as well as Martin Rhonheimer, typically blur the difference between materially practical knowledge and virtually practical knowledge. Indeed, it is not clear that, for them, there is any difference. Knowledge of the good is simply knowledge of what ought to be. Sometimes they will speak of a kind of theoretical knowledge of the good, but this knowledge does not enter into natural law precepts. It is, rather, knowledge of what is in fact the case, from which — so they claim — knowledge of what ought to be the case cannot arise.

39. Grisez, "First Principle," 194. In contrast, Rhonheimer ("Cognitive Structure," 178) insists that practical and prescriptive knowledge is a command.

40. Grisez, "Practical Principles," 116.

OBLIGATION

This state, says Grisez, is expressed in the Latin by the gerundive, translated as "is to be." In contrast, Aquinas claims that the gerundive is in the indicative mood.[41]

Unfortunately, Grisez never clearly defines what this is-to-be status means, nor does Finnis or Lee, nor any other new natural law theorist. As is usually the case when "ought" is left undefined, we get nothing more definite than the hint of a categorical imperative, a mysterious knowledge that binds by its very nature. Practical reason itself becomes the lawgiver.

Prescriptive knowledge imposes a kind of odd necessity. It is not the necessity of commanded efficient causality. Nor is it a hypothetical necessity depending upon the desires of the individual, for it precedes the desires of the individual. Prescriptive knowledge attempts to walk a fine line. Its necessity does not arise internally from the individual's desires, but neither does it arise externally from someone else's command. Rather, it arises internal to the individual — from his knowledge — but external to his desires.

This balancing act, however, still does not explain the necessity found in a moral ought. It is neither the necessity of efficient cause, formal cause, nor hypothetical final cause. Once again, the moral ought escapes our grasp. As Foot says concerning those who use an "emphatic use of 'ought'," it seems "they are relying on an illusion, as if trying to give the moral 'ought' a magic force."[42]

In the end, we are left with no explanation of the necessity behind a moral ought. Suárez substituted the desires of the individual for the command of God; Grisez substituted the command of God with prescriptive reason. In both cases a special power of binding is asserted but not explained. Should we follow Philippa Foot, then, and simply abandon the "moral ought," affirming that all ought-statements are hypothetical?[43] Is the will bound by nothing beyond itself and its own ends? Perhaps the moral ought is, as G. E. M. Anscombe says, "A word

---

41. Finnis (*Aquinas,* 102, endnote y) claims that Aquinas is merely emphasizing that the gerundive is not imperative. Surely, Aquinas could have denied the imperative character of the gerundive without asserting, falsely, that it is indicative.

42. Foot, "Hypothetical Imperatives," 167.

43. Later, Foot claims to have abandoned this position, but her later view does not seem essentially different; see Foot, *Natural Goodness,* 60–61.

OBLIGATION

containing no intelligible thought."[44] We have yet to consider a final possibility. Can nature provide a source for the necessity of the moral ought?

8.5
NATURE AND THE MORAL OUGHT

8.5.1: Two Kinds of Hypothetical Ought-Statements

The question before us is whether the natural law can give rise to a "moral ought" rather than simply to a hypothetical ought. Let us return to a position that we raised and rejected earlier, a position that emphasizes ought-statements that are true independent of personal desire.

Some hypothetical ought-statements refer to a particular person's desire. "You (who are building) ought to lay the foundation first," or "You (who are going to the opera) ought to turn right on Louisiana Street." The truth of these statements depends upon the individual's desire. If he no longer wants to build, then it is no longer true that he must lay the foundation. If Louis no longer wishes to go to the opera, then it is no longer true that he must turn right.

Other hypothetical ought-statements retain their truth independently of an individual's desires: "A builder ought to lay the foundation first" or "Someone going to the opera (from this starting point) ought to turn right at Louisiana Street." These statements are true even if someone does not intend to build a house or even for someone not going to the opera.

We have, then, two kinds of hypothetical ought-statements. Some ought-statements are derived solely from the end of a conscious desire, such as Clare's desire to cross the sea. Other ought-statements are derived from an end defined by a nature or a certain kind of thing. "Nature" is taken broadly here, to include such things as the "nature of a builder" or even "the nature of someone going to the opera." What it means to be a builder implies a certain end, and we can derive ought-statements from this end. Similarly, the power of reproduction has its own end, from which we can derive ought-statements, such as the need for marriage.

The two kinds of ought-statements can apply to the exact same

---

44. See Anscombe, "Modern Moral," 32.

thing. If we say "Louis (who is going to the opera) ought to turn right on Louisiana Street," then we are basing the ought-statement on a conscious desire. If we say "One who is going to the opera (from such and such a starting point) ought to turn right on Louisiana Street," then we are basing the ought-statement on the definition, or nature, of someone going to the opera.

If Louis should say, "Oh, but I really wanted to go to the homeless shelter," then we recognize that the first ought-statement does not apply to him; perhaps he ought to turn *left* at Louisiana Street. In contrast, the second ought-statement — that based on the nature of someone going to the opera — remains true for Louis wherever he wants to go; his particular desires do not change the nature of the ought-statement.

When we say that hypothetical ought-statements are optional, we have the first kind in mind. They apply to a particular individual, given his desires; if his desires change, then they no longer apply to him. The second kind of ought-statements are still hypothetical, in that they are derived from some end. Nevertheless, they are not hypothetical in the sense that worried Kant. They are based upon an end, but they are not based upon some individual's desire.[45]

These "nature"-based ought-statements, then, have one characteristic of a categorical ought-statement but lack another. On the one hand, they do not depend upon individual desires; on the other hand, they impose no necessity upon the will. One can acknowledge that those going to the opera should turn right on Louisiana Street, but that implies nothing at all about one's own behavior. Similarly, while acknowledging that the natural end of procreation requires marriage, one's own desires can remain untouched.

8.5.2: An Analogy with Ownership

Is there any way in which a nature-based ought-statement can impose necessity on the will? Philippa Foot gives the example of a club mem-

---

45. Foot (*Natural Goodness*, 53–80) abandons her view of ethics as a system of hypothetical imperatives only because she takes "hypothetical imperative" to be restricted to those conditional ought-statements that concern desire. She allows for conditional ought-statements that do not arise from desires but from what she calls "reasons." She does not classify such conditional statements as hypothetical imperatives, but they seem to be similar to the hypothetical ought-statements we are here describing. In effect, Foot may be making a similar move as we are.

OBLIGATION

ber who flaunts the rule that no females are allowed.[46] The rule barring females is based upon the function or nature of the club facilities. Their purpose, evidently, is fellowship between males; from this end — and not from the end of any particular person's desire — the hypothetical ought-statement concerning females is derived. Nevertheless, it seems to impose a necessity upon the members; indeed, it imposes necessity upon all who use the facilities. These facilities belong to the club, and their use is not open to anyone for any purpose.

Foot observes that we treat the rules of the club like a categorical ought-statement, for we do not suppose that the member's change of heart, such that he no longer desires the shared good of the club, allows him to break the club rules. Foot does not bother to explain why we think these various rules have an overriding character; rather, she supposes it is simply a matter of training.

Is it really merely a matter of our upbringing? What strikes us is that the member wants to use the facilities of the club (since he is going there with a female) and yet he does not want to abide by the rules of the club. He does not sufficiently recognize the ownership of the club. He himself does not own the facilities; others do, so that he cannot use them any way he pleases. His change of desire cannot change the facts of ownership. He cannot say "As far as I'm concerned, these facilities belong to me." Or rather, he can say it, but his saying it does not change the facts. His change of heart does change his desires, but his change of attitude does not change the ownership of the club.

The member can change the ends that he pursues in his own desires, but he cannot change the end toward which the facilities are directed. That end is determined by the club owners, which may be the members united together. The rule excluding females is a rule concerning the use of the facilities. It is derived hypothetically from the end of these facilities. Furthermore, it applies to all who use the facilities, because whatever further ends they desire, they desire at least to use the facilities.

The whole practice of ownership, of course, is based upon human convention. Nevertheless, ownership might be used as a tool to understand how a nature-based ought-statement can impose necessity upon a will. The use of an item that is owned, whether it be the club facilities

---

46. Foot, "Hypothetical Imperatives," 160.

OBLIGATION

or a car, is itself the good of the owner. The club members use the club for their own good, and Mike uses his car for his good. If the use of the item is taken by another and twisted away from the good of the owner, then the owner has reason to take it back and restore it to his good. Doing so involves taking the use of the item, and the good that goes with it, away from the "offender."

This "penalty" can impose a certain hypothetical necessity upon the will of the offender. The club member, for instance, enjoys using the facilities, so that the threat of their removal (when he breaks the rules) imposes a necessity upon his will. Is this necessity like the case of the robber? It would seem not. The robber threatens to take away a good that is not his own (the life of his victim), and he seeks to acquire a good that is not his own (the money of his victim). In contrast, the club seeks to restore its own good (the use of the facilities) and to take from the offender what is not his own.

This account reflects — better than Foot's account of training during youth — why the club rules have some characteristics of a categorical ought-statement. First, the rules do not depend upon the particular desires of an individual; they depend on the "nature" of the club facilities, and are true for anyone, whatever his desires, because they reflect how the facilities must be used to attain the end of the facilities. Second, the club can legitimately (unlike the robber) impose a hypothetical necessity upon the will of those who use the facilities.

This reasoning can be applied to our previous account of human society, which makes certain hypothetical rules based upon a shared good. These rules are true for anyone who has the shared good, for anyone who has the "nature" of belonging to this society; they are "nature"-based ought-statements. At the same time, society can legitimately take away the shared good from an individual who "opts out." They are not taking away his private good but the good that belongs to society. Again, we find two aspects of a categorical imperative: (1) these ought-statements do not depend upon an individual's desire and (2) these rules can be tied to a hypothetical necessity, through the threat of removing a good that belongs to the community and not to the individual.

OBLIGATION

8.5.3: Nature Binding the Will

Unfortunately, the account given above depends upon the notion of ownership, which involves human convention. The force of a categorical imperative, it seems, requires more than this human convention. It requires a stronger sense of ownership. When the robber says "Your money or your life," we recognize that the money belongs to the victim, rather than to the robber, only by human convention; at the same time, however, we see that the life of the victim belongs to her by nature and not by convention. The robber cannot claim that his victim's life belongs to him. Can this stronger sense of ownership, which is independent of convention, provide the basis of some hypothetical necessity imposed upon the will?[47]

An artifact does not really have the purposes attributed to it; the metal we call a knife does not really have the purpose of cutting. In contrast, the things of nature are truly directed to some end or good. This good, then, properly belongs to the nature. The "good" of a knife does not truly belong to the knife, which has no real purpose or function on its own. In contrast, the good of an individual's intellect truly does belong to that individual, since he is ordered to this good through the inclination of his intellect.

As we have seen, however, all natural inclinations are ordered to a common or shared good. The good of the individual, then, is not simply his own; it is a good to be shared. His good belongs not only to himself but also to the whole species. Nature (or the author of nature), then, can legitimately impose a penalty upon those who abuse nature, those who use it for their own private good while twisting it away from the shared good. The nature can be restored to its proper use, and thereby taken away from the offender.

Through convention, the use of the club facilities is directed to male fellowship. Through nature, the use of the power of reproduction is directed toward the good of offspring. When somebody commits adultery he twists the use toward his own purposes. Nature, however, can restore

---

47. In this manner, Robert Sokolowski ("Discovery and Obligation in Natural Law," in *Natural Moral Law in Contemporary Society*, ed. Holger Zaborowski [Washington, D.C.: The Catholic University of America Press, 2010]) explains the obligation of the natural law on the basis of natural ends, rather than on the basis of human purposes.

OBLIGATION

the good that belongs to it. The individual's nature can be coerced back to the order of the common good, back to the proper order. The private good that the individual has taken for himself can be taken away. This penalty is not like the threat of the robber but like the demands of the club. It has, however, something more than the club. It has a true link with the good, a link that goes beyond human convention.

The hypothetical necessity imposed upon the will by nature, then, is unlike the threat of the robber. Nature is simply restoring what belongs to it, and thereby removing the private good that the individual has taken for himself. Indeed, the contrast between nature and the robber can be deepened. The very will of the individual is part of his nature and has an order to the common good. In other words, the will has an end of its own — independent of the desires of the individual — from which hypothetical ought-statements can be derived; the individual, for instance, should love the good of others.[48] If he contradicts these ought-statements, then he takes his will away from nature, using it for his own private purposes.

This will must be restored to its true good, to the good of nature or to the common good; it must come under the use of nature rather than under the private use of this individual; it must be directed by those who have care of the common good, to the shared good rather than to the private good of the individual. This hypothetical necessity imposed upon the will is simply a matter of using the will for its true good.

The hypothetical necessities imposed by society (discussed above) can be given a firmer foundation if human beings are naturally social, that is, if by their nature they belong to society. The end of the intellect, we have seen, is not simply knowing the truth; it is knowing the truth as a shared good. This sharing, however, is ultimately realized through cooperation with others. The natural inclination of the intellect, then, involves a natural inclination to civil society. The good of civil society is not a mere human convention but is part of nature.

8.5.4: The Hypothetical Moral Ought

We are suggesting, then, that the force of a "moral ought" depends upon two elements. First, a "moral ought" is a hypothetical ought-statement

---

48. See Steven J. Jensen, *Good and Evil Actions: A Journey through St. Thomas Aquinas* (Washington, D.C.: The Catholic University of America Press, 2010), 257–64.

OBLIGATION

derived from an end that is not (solely) the end of the individual. The rules of the club are not derived simply from the desires of this particular individual; they are derived from the purposes set by the whole club. As such, they do not concern a singular good but a shared good. Similarly, the rules of society are indeed hypothetical, but they are derived from a shared good, and not just from the goals of this or that particular individual. Again, the ought-statements of nature, such as the rules concerning procreation, are not derived from the desires of the individual; they are derived from the ends associated with natural inclinations. As with the previous two examples, the ends of nature also concern shared goods.

Second, a "moral ought" imposes hypothetical necessity upon an individual through the threat of removing its good from the individual. The club threatens to remove the use of the facilities from those who break the rules. Society threatens to remove the sharing or participation in society. Aquinas provides other examples of removing some shared good: nature can take away the peace of conscience, and the author of nature can take away the sharing or participation in the goods of nature.

If an individual wishes to use the club facilities, then the threat of their removal imposes a kind of hypothetical necessity upon him. Likewise, if an individual wants to share in the goods of society, then the rules of society impose a hypothetical necessity upon him. Since everyone wants some of the basic goods of society, such as freedom, social intercourse, and his own life, the rules of society impose a universal hypothetical necessity. Likewise, since everyone wants some of the goods of nature, nature can impose a universal hypothetical necessity.

These hypothetical necessities are unlike the robber. They threaten to remove not simply a good that belongs to the individual; rather, they threaten to remove a shared good, a good that ultimately belongs to others beyond the individual; they threaten to remove the shared good that initially gives rise to the hypothetical ought-statement.

In the case of the club, the good belongs to others — and not just to the individual — by way of human convention. In the case of nature, however, the good is truly good only on account of the natural inclination, which natural inclination is directed to a shared good. The basis of the natural good, then, reveals that it belongs not simply to the individual. Even the goods of material possessions, which we have emphasized as being based upon human convention, can find a firmer

OBLIGATION

foundation than mere human convention, if in fact civil society (and therefore its rules of ownership) is itself founded in nature.

Any individual can "opt out" of the shared goods that give rise to these hypothetical ought-statements. He can decide that he no longer wishes the fellowship of the club, he can decide that he does not want the cooperative good of society, and he can decide that he does not care for the ends of nature, at least not insofar as they are shared. The hypothetical necessity imposed upon the will simply states, "If you want this good, then you must follow these rules." It does not force you to want the good. Opting out of the good is a choice open to everyone, and it is a choice taken by sinners.

Even the sinner wants some of the shared goods; he simply wants them as his own private good, and not as shared. It follows that the removal of the shared good will involve the removal of some of his private goods. The hypothetical necessity that threatens to remove a shared good, then, influences even the private goods of individuals. This universal application is to be expected, since the sinner takes a good that is not his own. He has opted for a personal good, but he has done so by taking a shared good.

Finally, because the will itself is naturally ordered to a shared good, those who opt out of the shared good ultimately opt out of a good that they naturally desire, a good that they can never fully cease to desire. The loss of this good, removed as a consequence of the hypothetical necessity, will inevitably leave an emptiness in the individual.

I do not claim that these hypothetical ought-statements are in fact the same as the moral ought, for Philippa Foot correctly observes that the moral ought has never been clearly defined. I claim only that these statements seem to correspond with much of what is expected from the moral ought. In the end, then, natural teleology is not the enemy of the moral ought, as is sometimes supposed, but rather its support and foundation. Attempts to base the moral ought simply upon command, without a foundation in nature, or upon some imaginary prescriptive reason, are ultimately inadequate. Only nature can rescue the moral ought.

9

PRINCIPLES

We have been trying to unravel the flow of thought in the following passage:

The good has the *ratio* of an end while evil has the *ratio* of its contrary, *for which reason* all those things to which man has a natural inclination, reason naturally grasps as goods and *consequently* as to be pursued through activity, and their contraries as evil and to be avoided.

In the last two chapters, we have seen how the mind moves from materially practical knowledge of what is good to virtually practical knowledge of how we ought to behave. Chapter 7 first revealed this "derivation" as involving a hypothetical ought-statement. Chapter 8 showed how some hypothetical ought-statements can carry more of a "moral" force. It remains to consider how some ought-statements, namely, the first precepts of the natural law, can be known immediately, without syllogistic derivation.

Aquinas indicates that our knowledge of how we ought to behave is natural, that is, our awareness of the most fundamental ought-statements is *per se nota*. But in what way are these precepts *per se nota*? Does the subject term of such statements include the predicate term? Consider the statement "Knowledge ought to be pursued." Does "knowledge" include within its definition some necessity to be pursued? Clearly not. Once again, it seems, we will have to move in the direction of the fourth mode of per seity.

In order to understand the *per se nota* character of the first precepts of the natural law, we will do four things. First, we will consider the manner in which these precepts can be *per se nota*. Second, we will investigate the very first precept of the natural law, which poses special difficulties. Third, since this first precept of practical reason serves to unify the natural law, we will examine the manner of this unity. Finally, we will consider in what manner the first precepts of the natural law, which are discovered through nature, still allow for an active role of reason.

9.1
THE FIRST PRECEPTS OF THE NATURAL LAW
9.1.1: Snow Falls in Winter

The very first principle of practical reason, that the good ought to be done and pursued, seems like it might possibly conform to the first mode of per se. Desire falls in the very definition of the subject term, and it seems reasonable to suppose that pursuit is the same thing as desire. Then we have desire both in the subject term and in the predicate term, which looks something like a *per se nota* proposition.

McInerny worries that this approach seems to endorse whatever desires we happen to have. "The good is desired, therefore it ought to be desired" is akin to claiming that "Snow falls in winter, therefore snow ought to fall in winter."[1] Whatever is the case ought to be the case. Someone desires adultery, therefore he ought to desire adultery.

McInerny attempts to avoid this difficulty by distinguishing between the beginning desire, which defines the good, and the ending desire, which is enjoined by the precept.[2] The good is more properly defined, he notes, as the "desirable," which is that which is perfective, rather than that which happens to be desired, for we sometimes desire what is in fact not good (or desirable), and we sometimes fail to desire that which is truly good. In short, McInerny modifies the proposition to read, "The good (that which is *desirable,* or perfective) ought to be desired."

If McInerny's account solves his difficulty, it still does not get beyond the very first principle of practical reason. The more particular precepts, which are still *per se nota,* do not follow this pattern. The proposition "Knowledge is to be pursued" does not contain desire in the subject term, whether that be "desirable" or some other sense of

---

1. McInerny, "Naturalism," 238. Hayden ("Natural Inclinations," 135–37) also has this concern.
2. Ralph McInerny, *Ethica Thomistica: The Moral Philosophy of Thomas Aquinas* (Washington, D.C.: The Catholic University of America Press, 1997), 37–38.

PRINCIPLES

desire. Rather than attempt to discover desire where it is not, let us reconsider what it means to "pursue."

9.1.2: Desiring the Good or Doing the Good

Aquinas does not say that the good ought to be desired; he says that the good ought to be done and pursued. Pursuit might possibly be the same as desire, or at least include desire, but "doing the good" is another matter; it implies activity beyond desire; to do the good is to carry out desire. For the more particular precepts Aquinas says that the particular goods are "to be pursued *through activity*." The Latin for "through activity" is *opere*, which has more the sense of external activity of some sort, often the sort that has a product. I wish to suggest, therefore, that the first precepts of the natural law do not command desire; they command activity; they command the doing of the good.[3]

Concerning a doctor, we first know that he ought to heal (that is, pursue health through activity), not that he ought to desire to heal. Concerning a teacher, we know first that he ought to teach, not that he ought to desire to teach. In each case, we know that he ought to do the good. Consequently, Aquinas says, "It is owed per se to the doctor that he heal but on account of something else that he gives medicine for the sake of healing."[4]

Likewise, when we understand the particular good of knowledge, we then see that we ought to know the truth, which is to pursue knowledge through activity. The first precepts, then, do not have, as McInerny says, "The unfortunate result of commanding a natural inclination to have the end it has."[5] Rather, the precepts command the realization of this end.

Aquinas gives a double predicate for the (first half) of the first principle of practical reason: the good is to be *done and pursued*. We are claiming that these two are simply different ways of expressing the same thing. Pursuit, or more precisely, pursuit through activity, is

---

3. Grisez ("First Principle," 181–86) is concerned to argue that the first precepts involve pursuit of an end rather than an activity. It is not clear to me that these two are distinct. To pursue the end is precisely to do the activity that either is the end or attains the end.
4. II-II, 44, 1. "Medico per se debitum est ut sanet; propter aliud autem, ut det medicinam ad sanandum."
5. McInerny, "Grisez and Thomism," 68.

PRINCIPLES

simply the initial step of doing. Indeed, if the doing is easily achieved, then we do not distinguish between doing and pursuing. In this regard, pursuing is like trying. We do not say that we are trying to eat, if eating is easily achieved, but we might say that we are trying to write, if the writing is proving difficult. Trying to write really is just the initial stage of writing, when the ultimate accomplishment is in doubt.

That this double predicate should in fact be a single predicate conforms with the standard of *per se nota* propositions. If the two predicates were actually distinct, then we would need two *per se nota* propositions, and two first principles of practical reason. With a single predicate — doing and pursuing being two ways of expressing the same thing — we have but a single first principle.

9.1.3: *Per Se Nota*

In our examination of the per se character of the first precepts we will proceed in the same manner as we did with the good in chapter 6. We will begin by observing instances of immediate knowledge of what ought to be, knowledge that is linked with the awareness of a nature and its end. We will then try to discover in what manner these propositions are immediate.

Just as we have immediate knowledge of the good because certain things have an end built into them, so also we know what things ought to do insofar as those things essentially have some end. We know that the good of a doctor is to heal, because a doctor is someone directed toward healing; likewise, we also know that a doctor ought to heal, insofar as healing is the completion of a doctor. Similarly, we know what is good for a teacher and what a teacher ought to do; we know what is good for an eye and what an eye ought to do. Since human beings have certain ends essentially belonging to them, that is, since they have natural inclinations, we also immediately grasp what is good for human beings and what they ought to do.

This knowledge of what a nature ought to do appears to be immediate. This appearance is confirmed when we retrace our knowledge of the good and then move one step further, to our knowledge of what ought to be. We begin by observing some change (for example, felled trees). The change cannot come from itself, so it must come from something else. This something else (the cause) must be directed

PRINCIPLES

beyond itself, toward the change, that is, it must be inclined to bring about the change. At this point, we recognize the good. We recognize that the end toward which the cause is working is the completion of the cause; it is working to achieve this goal.

After we have recognized that the end completes the cause, we then perceive that the cause must achieve the activity of the end — or bring about the end — for its completion. This step is a simple reversal of the previous step. The end completes the cause (or, in the manner of resolution expressed in chapter 7, the completion of the agent requires this end); conversely, the cause must achieve the end for its completion. We have reached knowledge of what ought to be through our knowledge of what is good. Aquinas's "and consequently" is fully justified: "All those things to which man has a natural inclination reason naturally grasps as goods *and consequently* as to be pursued through activity."

In what manner are these propositions *per se nota*? Is the predicate term included within the subject term? Or, as seems more likely, are these propositions in the fourth mode of per seity? Are the terms connected not through containment but through one pointing to the other?

Aquinas rarely gives an explicit statement of a precept. When he does, it is often negative, and it is typically in the passive voice (gerundive) with the agent of the activity only implied. He says, for instance, "Harm ought to be done to no one [by you, or by human beings]."[6] At times, however, he phrases precepts in the active voice, for instance, "Human beings should avoid ignorance."[7] The precept concerning knowledge, then, which Aquinas does not explicitly state, might be phrased in two ways, either "Knowledge ought to be pursued [by human beings]" or "Human beings ought to pursue knowledge." In neither form is it immediately evident how the terms relate to one another.

Let us take the example of the doctor, and see whether we can uncover some connection between the terms. Then perhaps we can find a similar connection for the precepts of the natural law. The immediate proposition "A doctor ought to heal" can be rephrased as "That which is ordered to healing as toward an end (that is, a doctor) ought

---

6. I-II, 95, 2. "Est nulli esse malum faciendum."
7. I-II, 94, 2. "Homo ignorantiam vitet."

to heal."[8] The subject term and predicate term are now more obviously linked, although one is not contained within the other.

Further modification more clearly reveals the link. We have seen that "ought" indicates a certain necessity belonging to an agent insofar as it has a certain end. The proposition, then, may be rephrased as "That which is ordered to healing as toward an end has a (conditional) necessity to heal, insofar as it has the end of healing." Once again, one term is not contained within the other. Nevertheless, the two terms are intimately linked. One term points to the other.

These ought-statements can be easily rephrased into Aquinas's preferred passive voice. Rather than "A doctor ought to heal," we have "Healing ought to be done by a doctor." Filling in the details, we get "Healing is owed (belongs by a conditional necessity) to that which is ordered to healing as toward an end." In this case, the predicate term points to the subject term; once again, one is not contained in the other as a part.

A precept concerning knowledge can readily be rephrased in a similar manner. "Human beings ought to pursue knowledge" becomes "That which is ordered to knowledge as toward an end ought to pursue knowledge."[9] Because pursuing is simply the first stage of doing, the proposition can be further modified: "That which is ordered to knowledge as toward an end ought to know (or do the act of knowing)." We can eliminate the word "ought" and rephrase the proposition simply in terms of future necessity: "That which is ordered to knowledge as toward an end has a necessity to know, insofar as it has the end of knowing."

When the precept is put passively we get "Knowledge is to be pursued by human beings," and when we fill in the details we get "Knowing (or the doing of knowledge) is owed (belongs by a conditional necessity) to that which is ordered toward knowing as toward an end." As with the previous examples, we do not find the predicate term as a component part of the subject term; we do find, however, that the predicate term points to the subject term.

My claims here are fairly limited. First, it is obvious that certain

---

8. One might insist that this proposition is the truly *per se nota* proposition and that "doctor" is substituted in the subject term by way of a simple syllogism. I have no problem with this position.

9. It may well be that this rephrasing is the original grasp of the human mind and that filling in "human being" in the subject term is reached by a simple syllogism.

PRINCIPLES

propositions, such as "A doctor ought to heal" are immediate. Second, these propositions are not per se in the first mode or in the second mode, for although "healing" appears in the subject term and in the predicate term, it does not appear as a component part in the subject term. Third, the predicate term does appear in the subject term as the terminus of an order. Fourth, it seems plausible from examples such as "That which is killed dies" that in the fourth mode the connection between subject term and predicate term is by way of one pointing to the other. Consequently, it seems plausible that these propositions are *per se nota* in the fourth mode.[10]

9.2
THE FIRST PRINCIPLE OF PRACTICAL REASON

The first principle of practical reason poses a special difficulty. When it enjoins us to do good, to what good does it refer? Two possibilities present themselves. Either the good of the first principle is some particular good or it is the formality of good under which particular goods are desired, that is, it is the good in general. Both views have been defended. We will see, however, that the former view holds the better case.

---

10. In chapter 2 we saw that Aquinas apparently lays out a syllogism by which the particular precepts of the natural law can be derived from the very first precept:

> The good ought to be pursued.
> Knowledge is good.
> Therefore, knowledge ought to be pursued.

This syllogism was the primary target of Grisez's groundbreaking article that launched the new natural law theory. And indeed, Grisez must be right. Whatever the appearances, Aquinas cannot be making this syllogism, if he is to remain consistent with what he says at the beginning of the article, namely, that the first precepts of the natural law are *per se nota*. Once again, however, dispelling a pseudo-syllogism is no easy task. I put forward the following suggestion as a possibility.

What is meant by "pursuit" could not possibly be the same in the major premise and in the conclusion. "Pursuit" in the conclusion refers to knowing the truth, so that the conclusion would have to read something like "knowledge ought to be known by that which is inclined to know." The "pursuit" of the major premise is an analogical concept, as is the "good." Once again, I am suggesting that before we can subsume the particular "pursuit," such as knowing the truth, under the major premise, we have already perceived it as linked with the subject term. All the syllogism really does is help us to see that the particular activity can be placed under an analogical general rule, as a single instance under a quasi-universal; it does not help us to see anything new in the particular.

PRINCIPLES

9.2.1: The Good as the Ultimate End

For Germain Grisez and the new natural law theorists, the good refers to a formality, a formality that characterizes all human actions, whether sinful or virtuous.[11] Even the adulterer pursues the good, for he hopes to gain the good of pleasure through his action. As such, the first principle of practical reason is premoral; it does not direct us to any moral good. Indeed, even the more particular precepts, on this reading, are used in sinful reasoning. Someone who kills one innocent person in order to save another commits the sin of murder. Nevertheless, he uses the precept of the natural law that urges him to seek human life (for he does seek to save one human life, even if it is at the expense of another). The moral good arises only from the *manner* in which we pursue various individual goods.

Giuseppe Butera argues against this premoral, formalistic account of the first principle of practical reason.[12] He emphasizes that Aquinas also calls this principle the first law, presumably referring to the natural law. It would be rather odd if the natural law recommended sin as well as virtue. As a principle of law, it necessarily directs to the common good, a defining feature of all law. Since sin is opposed to the common good, the first principle cannot direct toward sin.

Furthermore, argues Butera, the natural law directs everyone to beatitude, or the last and final end. The new natural law theory excludes this interpretation from the outset, since it rejects the very notion of a single final end. Aquinas says, however, that the eternal law, of which the natural law is a participation, directs all things to their final ends. All law seeks to make men good, and God's law seeks to make men simply good. In no way, then, can the natural law direct toward sin.

For Butera, then, the first principle is not the first principle of any and all reasoning; it is the first principle of *right* reason. It directs us to the true good. For Grisez, it directs us to the formality of the good; as such, it is the principle both of right reasoning and of faulty or sinful reasoning. For Butera, the sinner is not using practical reason; he is

---

11. Grisez, "First Principle," 175, 181–90.
12. See Giuseppe Butera, "The Moral Status of the First Principle of Practical Reason in Thomas's Natural-law Theory," *Thomist* 71 (2007): 609–31. See also Paterson, "Non-Naturalism," 180.

abusing practical reason. In contrast, Grisez claims that the first principle must concern all reasoning, even sinful reasoning; otherwise, he asserts, someone who sins would be irrational or insane.[13] Surely, however, Grisez is mistaken. To claim that someone has faulty reasoning is not the same as claiming that he is insane.

The difference between Grisez and Butera might be expressed through a single article, an article that is unavailable in Aquinas's Latin. Grisez claims that the first principle says "A good ought to be pursued." Any of diverse goods should be pursued. According to Butera, the first principle reads "The good ought to be pursued." *The good* is a very definite identifiable good, namely, beatitude; even more precisely, it is beatitude as a common good. Grisez presents us with a common notion of the good, under which many goods might be subsumed; Butera presents us with one singular good, which is common by causality rather than by predication.[14]

9.2.2: The Good as the Object of the Will

For Butera, then, the first principle corresponds to the object of the will, namely, the highest good of the whole person.[15] The other precepts concern particular goods, which enter into the good of the whole person; the first precept concerns the unified good of the whole person, including all these other goods as parts.

We began this consideration of the first principle by asking what it means "to do the good." We can say that a doctor ought to heal or that we ought to know the truth because these are particular goods involving particular actions. But what does it mean to do the good in general? If the first principle refers simply to some common notion of the good, then there is nothing separate that it recommends. To do the good is always to do this or that particular realization of the good.

On the other hand, if Butera is correct, then to do the good is to do something definite; it is to pursue a good distinct from the other goods, distinct from those goods enjoined by the more particular pre-

---

13. Germain Grisez, "The Structures of Practical Reason," *Thomist* 52 (1988): 269–91, at 285.

14. McInerny sees this difference as the chief difference between Aquinas and Grisez; see McInerny, "Grisez and Thomism."

15. See also Brock, "Natural Law," 693–99.

cepts. The first principle does not enjoin us to do the good in general; it enjoins us to do the good of beatitude or to seek the whole good of the person (which might be described as "the good in general" but this would not refer to an abstract notion; rather, it would refer to the overall good). As Brock says, "The first precept is referring to and directing toward the specifically human good. But it is directing toward the human good as a whole."[16]

This conclusion draws support from Aquinas's repeated affirmation that the end—most especially, the ultimate end—serves as the principle of human action, just as the first indemonstrable principles of speculative reason serve as the principles of conclusions.[17] The very first principle of practical reason will concern the very first end, that is, the ultimate end:

> Insofar as it is a rule and measure, the law pertains to that which is the principle of human actions. Just as reason is the principle of human actions, so also in reason itself there is something that is a principle with respect to all the others, to which the law will belong principally and chiefly. The first principle of things to be done, however, upon which practical reason bears, is the ultimate end. Since the ultimate end of human life is happiness or beatitude, law will chiefly concern the order toward beatitude.[18]

The first principle of practical reason (which is also the first law), then, must concern the ultimate end of beatitude. It cannot be simply a logically general principle, directing to goods of any sort, including sinful goods.

This account corresponds with Kevin Flannery's analysis of what he takes to be the first principle of practical reason for Aristotle, which is none other than the Socratic principle to do what reason judges as best.[19] According to Flannery, the first principle directs us to what is

---

16. Ibid., 695.
17. II-II, 47, 6.
18. I-II, 90, 2. "Lex pertinet ad id quod est principium humanorum actuum, ex eo quod est regula et mensura. Sicut autem ratio est principium humanorum actuum, ita etiam in ipsa ratione est aliquid quod est principium respectu omnium aliorum. Unde ad hoc oportet quod principaliter et maxime pertineat lex. Primum autem principium in operativis, quorum est ratio practica, est finis ultimus. Est autem ultimus finis humanae vitae felicitas vel beatitudo, ut supra habitum est. Unde oportet quod lex maxime respiciat ordinem qui est in beatitudinem."
19. See Kevin L. Flannery, "The Aristotelian First Principle of Practical Reason," *Thomist* 59 (1995): 441–64.

PRINCIPLES

best, which is an overall good; it does not direct us to any and every good. As such, it is the principle of *right* reason; in contrast, the reasoning of the weak-willed individual is defective reasoning and involves a kind of internal divide within the person.

9.3
THE UNITY OF THE NATURAL LAW

This last point indicates another strength of the view of Butera and Flannery; it explains the main purpose of question 94, article 2. Given all that has been written about our knowledge of the natural law, we can easily lose sight of this purpose. Aquinas simply wants to determine whether there are many precepts of the natural law or only one. He seems worried that if he affirms a multiplicity of precepts, then he will lose the unity of the natural law; he will end up with many natural laws rather than one natural law. His answer, therefore, is nuanced. Yes, there are many precepts of the natural law, but they are all united by one single precept, namely, by the very first precept of the natural law. Any account of the first principle of practical reason, then, must explain how the first principle unifies the many precepts into a single natural law.

9.3.1: Unity of the Natural Law in Aquinas

Flannery is concerned with Aristotle, but the principle he provides — to follow reason concerning the overall good — also seems to be a variation of the first principle for Thomas Aquinas. Consider the reply to the second objection, which we have already discussed at length in chapter 3. Aquinas attributes the unity of the natural law to the rule of reason being applied to diverse inclinations, which rule he seems to think is equivalent to the first precept.

> All the inclinations of any part of human nature, for example, the concupiscible and irascible powers, pertain to the natural law insofar as they are ruled by reason and they are reduced to the one first precept, as was said. In this manner, there are many precepts of the natural law in themselves, which nevertheless share in a single foundation.[20]

---

20. I-II, 94, 2, ad 2. "Omnes inclinationes quarumcumque partium humanae naturae, puta concupiscibilis et irascibilis, secundum quod regulantur ratione, pertinent ad legem

PRINCIPLES

This text need not be read, then, as claiming that we discover the goods in our inclinations only insofar as reason orders them, which would make the ordering of practical knowledge precede our grasp of the good.[21] Rather, we can discover the goods associated with diverse inclinations, but these become part of the natural law only insofar as they are ordered to the ultimate end, that is, insofar as they are ordered and measured by reason.

Two articles later, in another reply that we have also discussed at length, Aquinas is again concerned with the unity of the natural law, namely, whether the natural law is the same for all people. Once again Aquinas finds unity in the order of reason.

> Since a man's reason rules and commands the other powers, so every natural inclination belonging to the other powers must be ordered according to reason, so that the same thing is right for all men in common, namely, that all their inclinations be directed by reason.[22]

The same line of thought appears in question 94, article 3, in which Aquinas asks whether all virtue belongs to the natural law. This question, also, focuses upon a certain unity of the natural law, namely, one natural law includes a multiplicity of virtues. Not surprisingly, then, Aquinas bases his conclusion upon the same principle, that is, the ordering of reason.

> As was said, all those things to which man has an inclination according to his nature belong to the natural law. Everything, however, is naturally inclined to that operation fitting to it according to its form, for example, fire is naturally inclined to heat. Since the rational soul is the proper form of human beings, every human being has a natural inclination to act according to nature, which is to act according to virtue. In this manner, all acts of virtue belong to the natural law, for each person's reason naturally dictates to him that he act virtuously.[23]

---

naturalem, et reducuntur ad unum primum praeceptum, ut dictum est. Et secundum hoc, sunt multa praecepta legis naturae in seipsis, quae tamen communicant in una radice. "

21. See Rhonheimer, "Cognitive Structure," 179–80.

22. I-II, 94, 4, ad 3. "Sicut ratio in homine dominatur et imperat aliis potentiis, ita oportet quod omnes inclinationes naturales ad alias potentias pertinentes ordinentur secundum rationem. Unde hoc est apud omnes communiter rectum, ut secundum rationem dirigantur omnes hominum inclinationes."

23. I-II, 94, 3. "Dictum est enim quod ad legem naturae pertinet omne illud ad quod homo inclinatur secundum suam naturam. Inclinatur autem unumquodque naturaliter ad

PRINCIPLES

In the next article, in which Aquinas is trying to show the unity of the natural law for all men, he begins, "To the natural law belong all those things to which man is naturally inclined, among which it is proper to man that he is inclined to act according to reason."[24]

Consistently, Aquinas attributes the unity of the natural law to the order of reason. By ordering diverse goods, diverse inclinations, or diverse actions, reason unifies the natural law. As Philippa Foot says, "Practical rationality has the status of a kind of master virtue."[25] Does any ordering of reason whatsoever, made by any deliberations, even the deliberations of a sinner, serve to unify the natural law? Clearly not. Reason unifies all virtues, not all human actions whatsoever. The order of reason, then, must refer to *right* reason, which for Aquinas is reason ordering to the ultimate end.

The same unifying power is attributed to the first precept of the natural law, to do good and avoid evil. The good done, then, must be the same as the order of reason, which is the order to the ultimate end. To seek the good, then, means to seek the complete good, the ultimate end. This pursuit unifies all our actions; it unifies the pursuit of all other goods. Evidently, then, the precept that we should act according to reason is not one precept among many; it is another way of expressing the very first precept.[26]

To come full circle, we find that the ultimate end also serves as a unifying force in human actions. The virtue of charity, for instance, is called the form of all the virtues, because it orders all of them to the ultimate end. This order to the end, then, seems to play the same role as reason, which unifies all the virtues under the natural law.

---

operationem sibi convenientem secundum suam formam, sicut ignis ad calefaciendum. Unde cum anima rationalis sit propria forma hominis, naturalis inclinatio inest cuilibet homini ad hoc quod agat secundum rationem. Et hoc est agere secundum virtutem. Unde secundum hoc, omnes actus virtutum sunt de lege naturali, dictat enim hoc naturaliter unicuique propria ratio, ut virtuose agat."

24. I-II, 94, 4. "Ad legem naturae pertinent ea ad quae homo naturaliter inclinatur; inter quae homini proprium est ut inclinetur ad agendum secundum rationem."

25. Foot, *Natural Goodness*, 62.

26. Grisez objects to this interpretation, insisting that the precept to follow reason is a particular precept, because the good that it enjoins is distinct from other goods, such as self-preservation ("First Principle," 198). The very claim we are making, however, is precisely that, namely, the very first principle of practical reason does direct to a distinctive good, namely, to the ultimate end.

PRINCIPLES

In moral matters, the form of actions is taken primarily from the end, since the principle of moral actions is the will, whose object and form is the end. But the form of an action always follows the form of the agent. Consequently, in morals, that which gives to the action the order to the end also gives to it its form. From what has been said, however, it is plain that the acts of all the other virtues are ordered by charity to the ultimate end, and as such charity gives form to the acts of all the other virtues.[27]

9.3.2: Unity according to the New Natural Law Theory

Grisez's account does provide a kind of unity, namely, a logical unity. The first precept is a kind of general law under which all others fall. "The first principle of practical reason gives practical thought its form."[28] Grisez's first principle, however, provides no other unity. It does not even provide enough unity to exclude sin. The individual precepts direct us to diverse goods, among which no priority can be given; they are all incommensurable. There is no unifying principle by which we can decide between them.

The incommensurability of the basic goods of diverse categories does imply that one cannot organize one's entire life in view of some prospective realization of a substantive good, such as life or knowledge of truth. No commitment to such a purpose can be relevant to every other choice one might make. Moreover, no upright person supposes that any instantiation or set of instantiations of any substantive good deserves to be given the priority required to organize the whole of life.[29]

As Finnis understands the foundations of the natural law:

It amounts to no more than saying that any sane person is capable of seeing that life, knowledge, fellowship, offspring and a few other such basic aspects

---

27. II-II, 23, 8. "In moralibus forma actus attenditur principaliter ex parte finis, cuius ratio est quia principium moralium actuum est voluntas, cuius obiectum et quasi forma est finis. Semper autem forma actus consequitur formam agentis. Unde oportet quod in moralibus id quod dat actui ordinem ad finem, det ei et formam. Manifestum est autem secundum praedicta quod per caritatem ordinantur actus omnium aliarum virtutum ad ultimum finem. Et secundum hoc ipsa dat formam actibus omnium aliarum virtutum."

28. Finnis, *Aquinas*, 86.

29. Germain Grisez, "Natural Law, God, Religion, and Human Fulfillment," *American Journal of Jurisprudence* 46 (2001): 3–36, at 15–16. Notice that Aquinas and a host of other philosophers or theologians in the classical tradition are not "upright."

PRINCIPLES

of human experience are, as such good, i.e. worth having, leaving to one side all particular predicaments and implications, all assessments of relative importance, all moral demands, and in short, all questions of whether and how one is to devote oneself to these goods.[30]

In contrast, Flannery and Butera provide a unity in which various goods can be ordered to one another. When an individual is faced with the choice between diverse basic goods, the first principle can provide the tools to prioritize these goods.

Consider someone who is pursuing a degree in philosophy. He takes various classes, pursuing different aspects of the truth. Not all of his classes are philosophy classes. He takes mathematics, science, literature, and so on; he takes these courses not simply because they fulfill some core requirement, but because they contribute to his goal of philosophical knowledge. When he must decide between courses, he can rank them based upon the manner in which they contribute to his goal.

Another individual has no definite goal as he takes classes. Each subject matter provides its own independent value, which can in no way be compared with the value of any other subject matter. All subject matters are unified in that they are "knowledge," but we must not suppose any grand unity to this knowledge, as was supposed, for instance, in classical education. In making choices, the individual must not choose against any subject matter, that is, he must not choose a course that would teach falsehood. Beyond that, however, he has no principle of choice between various courses. Or rather, whatever principle he uses is based upon his own preference.[31] It is not based upon a first principle (such as philosophical knowledge), nor does it belong to the nature of the goods.

The analogy falters, no doubt, but it furnishes a good feel for the different approaches. Flannery and Butera provide the unity of an end, through which all goods can be ordered and evaluated. Grisez provides a logical unity of universality and a negative unity of nonexclusion. Even this nonexclusion seems to be absent from the first principle of

---

30. Finnis, *Natural Law*, 30.

31. Finnis, *Natural Law*, 93. The preference can be constrained by moral grounds (see Grisez, "God, Religion," 15). Grisez et al. ("Practical Principles," 137) claim that it is not merely a matter of preference but depends upon a harmony among the goods. Unfortunately, this move will not work, since the only harmony provided is negative, namely, that the goods not conflict with one another.

PRINCIPLES

practical reason, although it is present in the first moral principle as expounded by Grisez.

As we saw in chapter 2, when Aquinas discusses the order of the more particular precepts, he says nothing indicating the nature of this order, whether it is merely logical or hierarchical. His manner of proceeding, from the more general to the more particular, does seem to favor a logical order.

It is a mistake, however, to place too much emphasis upon the ordering of these particular precepts. Ultimately, they are all united by the first precept. This unity is precisely a unity of ordering. Whatever order the particular precepts might have apart from the first precept — whether it be logical or hierarchical — the first precept itself provides a hierarchical ordering.

9.4
REASON AS AN ACTIVE PRINCIPLE

Before we move on to the final level of practical knowledge, to the fully practical knowledge embedded within action, one more problem must be addressed, namely, a discussion of Rhonheimer's emphasis upon reason as the rule and measure of human actions.

9.4.1: A Diminished Role of Reason?

More than any other, Rhonheimer has objected to arguments from nature on the grounds that such arguments diminish the role of reason.[32] Aquinas teaches that reason is the rule and measure of human actions. We determine the good and evil of actions by comparing them to the order of reason, not to the order of speculatively discovered nature.

This concern of Rhonheimer can be seen as an element of the objection concerning physicalism. When we use nature to determine moral good and evil, we end up with an inadequate morality, a physicalism that ignores the role of will and reason. To a large extent, we have already addressed this objection. We have shown that Aquinas views nature and will as intertwined, so that deriving our knowledge of the good from observations of nature does not in fact leave out the

---

32. See especially Rhonheimer, "Pre-Rational Nature."

PRINCIPLES

will. Even if this point should be granted, however, Rhonheimer might pursue the objection, arguing that emphasizing nature diminishes the proper role of reason.

Of course, reason has an obvious role to play within descriptivism or naturalism. It discovers the good and evil of nature and presents it to the will. As such, it becomes a kind of conduit or messenger between nature and will. Nature is the true standard of human actions; reason is a standard only to the degree that it discovers the standard of nature. Aquinas himself says that reason is the rule of the will but reason itself is measured by a higher standard, namely, by the eternal law.[33] Since the natural law is the rational participation in the eternal law, and since we have seen that the natural law is discovered through the inclinations in nature, might we also conclude that reason is measured by nature? These diverse layers by which human actions are measured do not detract from the role of reason. Reason is still the measure of human actions, even though it is measured by nature, which is in turn measured by the eternal law.

Rhonheimer, however, is not satisfied with this role for reason. He insists that the role ascribed to nature by the classical view does detract from the role of reason, for the classical view makes reason merely passive, discovering a standard that is out there. In contrast, Rhonheimer insists that reason is active, constructing the moral order of our actions. Reason institutes an order that does not yet exist. Consequently, the order cannot simply be "read off" from what already exists in nature; it must be constructed by reason.[34] Only as such does reason truly play the role of a measure of human actions.

One might well wonder how the eternal law, which Aquinas explicitly states is a measure of reason, can be reconciled with this active role of reason. Why can the eternal law serve as a measure of reason — giving reason the passive role of being a measured measure — but nature cannot serve as a measure? Such matters of consistency within Rhonheimer's own thought, however, will not be our concern. We are concerned only to show in what way descriptivism is consistent with a robust role of reason.

---

33. I-II, 19, 4.
34. See Rhonheimer, "Naturally Rational," 102.

PRINCIPLES

9.4.2: An Important Text

In support of his position Rhonheimer quotes the numerous texts in which Aquinas says that the good and evil of human actions depend upon reason; reason is the measure of human actions, so that an action is good when it conforms with reason and evil when in discordance with reason.[35] Strictly speaking, however, these texts do not distinguish Rhonheimer's view from the view he opposes. Both reason and nature can be the measure of human actions.

It will be helpful, therefore, to examine what might be the strongest text in favor of Rhonheimer's view. The text appears to posit an active role of reason within ethics, in stark contrast to the passive role of reason within natural philosophy. In his proemium to the *Ethics,* Aquinas says that ethics concerns an order that human reason places in the acts of the will; in contrast, the study of nature concerns an order that reason considers in things but does not make.[36] One might conclude — following the lead of Rhonheimer — that practical knowledge does not depend upon our knowledge of nature, for practical knowledge does not concern what is discovered in things.

Aquinas begins by noting two orders in things.

> There is found a twofold order in things. One is the order of the parts of a whole or of a multitude to one another, just as the parts of a house are ordered to one another. The other order is the order of things toward an end. The latter is more fundamental than the former, for as Aristotle says in book 11 of the *Metaphysics,* the order of the parts of an army to one another is on account of the order of the whole army to the general.[37]

Aquinas's examples — the house and the army — are both from the practical domain. In both instances, Rhonheimer's claim seems to be

---

35. See *De malo,* 2, 2; *De malo,* 2, 4; I-II, 18, 5; I-II, 24, 4; I-II, 59, 1; I-II, 71, 2; I-II, 71, 6; II-II, 47, 7; II-II, 123, 1.

36. Rhonheimer cites the proemium for his argument in *Natural Law,* 32–34; see also Rhonheimer, *Perspective of Morality,* 184.

37. *Sententia Ethicorum,* lib. 1, lect. 1, n. 1 (Leonine ed., v. 47, 3–4, 7–14). "Invenitur autem duplex ordo in rebus: unus quidem partium alicuius totius seu alicuius multitudinis ad invicem, sicut partes domus ad invicem ordinantur; alius autem est ordo rerum in finem, et hic ordo est principalior quam primus, nam, ut Philosophus dicit in XI Metaphysicae, ordo partium exercitus ad invicem est propter ordinem totius exercitus ad ducem."

PRINCIPLES

borne out: we do not discover the order of the house but make that order; similarly, we make the order of an army.

Aquinas proceeds to discuss how order relates to reason.

> Order relates to reason in four ways. There is an order that reason does not make but only considers, for example, the order of natural things. Another order reason makes, by considering, in its own actions, for example, when it orders its concepts to one another, as well as the signs of its concepts, which are meaningful words. A third order reason makes, by considering, in the activities of the will. The fourth order reason makes, by considering, in exterior things that reason itself causes, for example, a chest or a house.[38]

Aquinas goes on to say that natural philosophy concerns the first order, logic the second, ethics the third, and art concerns the fourth. Then he says, "Moral philosophy, which is our present concern, properly considers human actions insofar as they are ordered to one another and to the end,"[39] thereby referring back to the two orders with which he began.

The crucial claim concerns the orders that reason makes, especially the order that reason makes in the will, which is the order of morality. Aquinas says that reason considers, but does not make, the order in nature; the remaining three orders are made by reason. Reason makes these orders, however, *by considering*. What is the nature of this consideration? Is it a discovery? Or is it some sort of active constructive role?[40] Aquinas does not tell us. Nothing Aquinas says prohibits this consideration from being speculative, at least in its beginnings. The order we put into a chest or a house certainly might involve some discovery from nature. Furthermore, McInerny has shown that the order reason places into its own actions, that is, the order of logic, is itself founded

---

38. Ibid., 14–24 "Ordo autem quadrupliciter ad rationem comparatur: est enim quidam ordo quem ratio non facit, sed solum considerat, sicut est ordo rerum naturalium; alius autem est ordo quem ratio considerando facit in proprio actu, puta cum ordinat conceptus suos adinvicem et signa conceptuum, quae sunt voces significativae; tertius autem est ordo quem ratio considerando facit in operationibus voluntatis; quartus autem est ordo quem ratio considerando facit in exterioribus rebus quarum ipsa est causa, sicut in arca et domo."

39. *Sententia Ethicorum,* lib. 1, lect. 1, n. 2 (Leonine ed., v. 47, 4, 40–43). "Moralis philosophiae, circa quam versatur praesens intentio, proprium est considerare operationes humanas secundum quod sunt ordinatae ad invicem et ad finem."

40. Grisez et al. ("Practical Principles," 118) say that the difference between discovering and making is a false alternative. They then state that reason "makes" (but does not discover) through the first practical principles.

upon speculative knowledge of nature.[41] Perhaps the order that reason places in the will also depends upon a speculative consideration.

9.4.3: Two Active Roles

Aquinas's four practical examples — the house, the army, the chest, and the house — clearly involve reason making an order in things. In each case, however, there also seems to be a level of discovery. We are not dealing with entirely fictitious entities like a unicorn. We cannot devise a chest or a house any way we please.

To clarify matters we can distinguish between the very nature of an order and the institution of this order in things. Suppose we have a blueprint for a house. With our reason we can consider the order present within this blueprint; indeed, the blueprint need not be actually upon paper; it might be merely in the mind of the builder. We can consider this order even if we do not actually build the house. If we do choose to build a house, then we take this order that we have considered and we place it into actual bricks, stones, and lumber; we institute the order considered. The fact that these bricks, stones, and lumber are all ordered to one another in a precise way comes to be through reason. The house would not form by nature; it is definitely an order instituted by reason.

This distinction between the institution of the order and the nature of the order provides two possible active roles of reason: reason might be active in the institution and it might be active in forming the order. The first active role, the institution of the order, sufficiently accounts for what Aquinas says in the Latin: reason makes an order by considering. Even if the consideration is entirely passive — a simple matter of discovery — the verb "makes" (*facit*) would still be justified. Suppose that someone is given the blueprints of a house, and all he must do is construct the house. It would still be fair to say that the reason of the builder makes the order in the house, even though his reason is itself entirely measured by the blueprint. In short, the text, in which Aquinas says that reason makes by considering, allows for a completely passive consideration; the "making" might be simply the institution of the order that has been passively considered.

---

41. McInerny, *Human Action*, 194–204.

PRINCIPLES

Nevertheless, Aquinas probably had something more like the architect in mind, who is not simply given a blueprint; he constructs the blueprint; he determines the very nature of the order that must be instituted. Is this activity of reason, then, creative or does it involve passive reception?

There is reason to suppose that Aquinas would consider this activity of reason to be at least partly passive, a receiving from nature. In another proemium Aquinas emphasizes the importance of a passive role, in which art imitates nature. Since it is the proemium to the *Politics*, the imitation applies not only to the making of houses but also to the human institution of a political community, which is a moral endeavor.

> It is necessary that the operations of art imitate the operations of nature and that those things that are made by art imitate those things that are in nature. For if the teacher of an art makes a work of the art, then the student who learns the art from the teacher must examine his work, so that he himself can make similar work. Therefore, the human intellect, for whom the light of the intellect is derived from the divine intellect, must be informed in its actions by the examination of those things that are naturally made, and it must act in a similar way.[42]

Furthermore, in the *Commentary on the Metaphysics* Aquinas presents a detailed account of deliberation, at the end of which he indicates that the principle of all such practical knowledge is an awareness of things in nature; it all begins by knowing what certain things are.

> As a doctor, in order to bring about health, begins by considering what health is, so also in order to bring about a balance [of humors], he must know what the balance is, namely, that a balance is the proportion of humors with respect to human nature.... Clearly, then, the principle of bringing about health, from whence the movement toward healing begins, is the likenesses in the soul, either of health itself, or of any other intermediary, through which health is acquired.[43]

---

42. *Sententia Politic.*, pr. 1 (Leonine ed., v. 48, 69, 8–19). "Unde necesse est quod et operationes artis imitentur operationes nature, et ea que sunt secundum artem imitentur ea que sunt in natura. Si enim aliquis instructor alicuius artis opus artis efficeret, oporteret discipulum qui ab eo artem suscepisset, ad opus illius attendere ut ad eius similitudinem et ipse operaretur. Et ideo intellectus humanus, ad quem intelligibile lumen ab intellectu diuino deriuatur, necesse habet in hiis que facit informari ex inspectione eorum que sunt naturaliter facta, ut similiter operetur."

43. *In Metaphysicorum*, lib. 7, lect. 6, 1409–10. "Sicut medicus, ad hoc quod faceret sanitatem, incipiebat considerando quid est sanitas: ita, ad hoc quod faciat adaequationem,

PRINCIPLES

9.4.4: A Determination of a General Form

The example of the house also appears in Aquinas's discussion of the formulation of human laws from the natural law. The human law, he says, can be derived from the natural law in two ways, either by way of conclusion or by way of determination. Concerning the second, which touches our topic, Aquinas says,

> The second way is similar to the way that, in art, common forms are determined to something specific, just as an architect must determine the common form of a house to this or that structure of the house.... Certain [human laws are derived] by way of determination, for example, the natural law requires that those who sin be punished, but which particular punishment is given is a certain determination of the natural law.[44]

The example seems to allow leeway for reason. The architect begins with some common form of a house. Is this discovered or made up by reason? Aquinas does not say. In the next step, however, reason seems to have the liberty to make some things up. Reason can determine whether to place a door here or there, a bedroom in this location or in that location, and so on. Similarly, reason has some liberty with punishments. Should a certain crime receive a fine, an imprisonment, or both? Reason does not discover the answer to this question but creates it.

While reason has some liberty in these cases, there is also restraint, a restraint that seems to arise from discovery. The architect cannot do whatever he wishes with the house. At the very least, he needs walls, a roof, and an entryway. These characteristics might constitute the common form of a house, of which Aquinas speaks. This form, it seems, is discovered in the manner that we have discussed, that is, by reasoning back from the end.[45]

---

oportet quod sciat quid est adaequatio; videlicet quod adaequatio est hoc, scilicet debita proportio humorum in respectu ad naturam humanam.... Sic igitur patet, quod principium faciens sanitatem, unde incipit motus ad sanandum, est species, quae est in anima, vel ipsius sanitatis, vel aliorum intermediorum, per quae acquiritur sanitas."

44. I-II, 95, 2. "Secundo vero modo simile est quod in artibus formae communes determinantur ad aliquid speciale, sicut artifex formam communem domus necesse est quod determinet ad hanc vel illam domus figuram.... Quaedam vero per modum determinationis, sicut lex naturae habet quod ille qui peccat, puniatur; sed quod tali poena puniatur, hoc est quaedam determinatio legis naturae."

45. In the *Commentary on the Posterior Analytics* Aquinas does not argue from the end

PRINCIPLES

Aquinas says that the order of the whole to the end is more important than the order of the parts to one another. For a house, this order seems to be the purpose of providing protection from the environment. The second order, the order of the parts of the house to one another, is on account of this purpose. By reasoning backwards we discover what is needed for this goal of protection. A roof will be needed to protect from things coming from above, such as the sun and rain, and walls will be needed to protect from things entering from the sides (and to support the roof); an entry will be needed to come and go. When we switch to composition, we begin to say that the house ought to have a roof and ought to have walls, and so on.

These basic elements are discovered from the necessity of an end. Even the elements where reason has liberty have some constraints from the end, perhaps not the constraint of necessity but at least the constraint of fittingness. The architect does not want to design the door in any random fashion. The end of protection, and perhaps some secondary ends, such as convenience and beauty, limit the design. In a cold environment, for instance, the entryway is better if it has a covering.[46] Once again, these limitations are discovered from the end.

The same can be said concerning the human law of punishment, or any other determination made by the human law. The offense of trespassing upon someone's property deserves a punishment, but the death penalty is unreasonable. Why? Simply because of a preference of reason? Rather, it is on account of some necessity deriving from the end or purpose of the punishment.

In two ways, then, reason makes the order that we put into our own actions. First, reason institutes the order, just as it places the structure of the house into these bricks. Second, the very nature of order instituted, such as the blueprints of the house, might be made up by reason. Indeed, we have seen that this order is in some manner discovered and in some manner made up. First, it is discovered through the other more primary order, namely, the order of the whole to the end; by resolution from this end, the order of the parts to one another is discovered, at least in general form. Second, the order of the parts is made up by

---

to the general structure of a house, but he does explicitly argue from the end to the material components of a house. See *Expositio Posteriorum Analyticorum*, lib. 1, lect. 16.

46. Unless the entryway is the only effective means of air circulation, such as in an igloo.

reason (rather than discovered) when specific details are determined. Even then, however, the determination of reason has limits, limits that arise from discovery.

Clearly, reason plays the same roles in morals. Beginning from the end of providing for his family, for instance, Scott might discover that he must get a job, but whether it be this or that job might be a matter of determination, leaving some liberty to reason. Once he makes the determination, then he must institute this order in his actions and actually do the job. In short, the active role of reason expressed in the proemium of the *Ethics* — the making of the order of the acts of will — is sufficiently explained by determinations of reason that come after the discovery of the very first principles, a discovery that ultimately arises from an understanding of nature.

9.4.5: Active and Passive

A passive role of reason, then, is perfectly consistent with an active role. Reason can passively discover the ends to be pursued, as revealed through the inclinations of nature, and it can passively discover, by way of resolution, both what is necessary and what is possible in order to achieve these ends. Nevertheless, the determination of the means needed leaves room for an active constructive role. Reason begins with nature but then actively disposes other things: "The principles of reason are those that are according to nature, for reason, presupposing what is determined by nature, disposes other things insofar as they are fitting."[47] When multiple means are available for an end, reason can determine among these means. This determination often involves considering the relation of the various means to multiple ends, not only to the primary end being sought.

Even with regard to the first precepts of the natural law, reason can play an active role. Since there are many precepts, corresponding to diverse goods, and since we determine which goods to pursue based upon the ultimate end, it can happen that reason must determine between these most basic goods. Should Mary Catherine, at the moment, read Aristotle or have lunch with a friend? Both actions correspond to a first

---

47. II-II, 154, 12. "Principia autem rationis sunt ea quae sunt secundum naturam, nam ratio, praesuppositis his quae sunt a natura determinata, disponit alia secundum quod convenit."

PRINCIPLES

precept. In many situations, both will be consistent with the ultimate end. Mary Catherine has liberty, then, to determine which good to pursue.

9.4.6: The Principle and Source of Human Actions

No doubt this active role of reason would not satisfy Rhonheimer, but then no textual reasons indicate that it would not satisfy Aquinas.[48] Nevertheless, there is something more to Rhonheimer's claim. When Aquinas says that reason is the measure of human actions, he does not mean merely that nature is the true measure, for which reason is merely a conduit.

John is out for a drink with some friends. Should he have a third beer? He cannot simply "read off" the answer from nature. As we have seen, he must make a determination. That determination is constrained by the end sought; in this case, it is most forcefully constrained by the end of trying to maintain clarity of mind. Nevertheless, other ends come into play as well, such as sociability. The determination, like the determination of the architect concerning the location of the bedroom, can involve both liberty and constraint.

The constraint comes from nature, from the ends set by nature, and from the causal relations with regard to these ends. The liberty also comes from nature, which has a lack of determination. The determination itself comes from reason as it interplays with will. When the determination is made, however, then it serves as the measure of human actions. If John judges that he should not have a third beer but chooses to have one nevertheless, then he chooses poorly, even though there was some liberty allowing for the possibility of a third beer.

This rather strong role of reason indicates why reason is not merely a conduit of nature; it is not even a conduit with some variations. Reason is central to the moral good and evil of human actions because reason, together with the will, is the principle of human actions. We have seen that human actions, if they are to be good, must arise from the will. Likewise, human actions must arise from reason; indeed, if they do not, then they do not fully arise from the will.

---

48. Rhonheimer (*Perspective of Morality*, 289–301) acknowledges these active roles of reason as something separate from the active role of forming principles.

PRINCIPLES

Reason is not simply a conduit; reason is the principle and source of human actions. When we want to know whether an action was human, we do not ask whether it arose from nature; we ask whether it arose from reason. We have noted that the will is the inclination of the whole person, so that nothing is done by the person except through his will. Likewise, nothing is done by the person except through his reason. Reason is not the inclination or motive force of the whole person. It is, however, the form of that inclination. We cannot move to anything without the force of will; at the same time, the will does not move to anything definite without the guidance of reason. None of this prevents the guidance of reason from finding its original source in an understanding of nature.

It remains, then, to see how reason and will together finally bring about human action.

10

ACTION

We have seen that reason progresses from purely speculative knowledge to materially practical knowledge and from there to virtually practical knowledge. Even this last step still provides a description of the way things are; it describes what is necessary for an agent insofar as it has a certain end. We have yet to move to purely practical knowledge, a knowledge not expressed in the indicative mood but in the imperative. In this final chapter, we will examine the final move from knowledge to action.

10.1
THE SEPARATION OF SPECULATIVE KNOWLEDGE AND ACTION

Proponents of the new natural law theory sometimes argue that if practical reason begins with speculative considerations, then it can never possibly lead to action. The precise nature of this argument remains obscure; indeed, it seems to be an assertion rather than an argument. It is certainly not self-evident that speculative truth can never lead to action. The force of the objection seems to depend upon the notion that knowledge by itself, without desire, cannot move to act. After all, Aristotle says, "Intellect itself moves nothing, but only intellect that aims at an end and is practical."[1] Furthermore, David Hume argues that "reason alone can never produce any action, or give rise to volition."[2]

Lee presents the argument as follows:

Suppose one could determine by theoretical reasoning, anterior to practical reasoning, what the natural end or natural perfection of the human being is.

---

1. *Nicomachean Ethics,* book 6, chapter 2, 1139a35.
2. David Hume, *Treatise on Human Nature,* part 3, section 3.

ACTION

Then, we would know that the perfection of a human being consists in knowledge, friendship, health, and so on. What would follow from that fact? How does the fact that my perfection consists in this or that make a demand on my action? That is, how does it provide a reason which can motivate me? The answer is, nothing follows from that fact alone; just of itself, it does not make a demand on my action at all.[3]

What are we to make of this argument or assertion? If it means simply that knowledge without desire does not move to act, then it is uncontroversial. Aquinas is clear on the matter.

Knowledge insofar as it is knowledge does not designate an active cause.... Therefore, an effect never arises from knowledge except by way of an act of will, which of its very *ratio* implies a certain movement toward what is willed.[4]

Furthermore, Aquinas argues that

Just as the imagination of some image without the judgment that it is fitting or harmful does not move the sensitive appetite, so neither does the apprehension of the truth move the will without the *ratio* of the good and desirable. Consequently, the speculative intellect does not move the will but rather the practical intellect.[5]

This text, however, hardly settles the matter. What level of practical knowledge is needed to move the will? Is fully practical knowledge needed or does virtual or materially practical knowledge suffice? Even if fully practical knowledge is needed, it still might happen that our speculative knowledge of nature might underlie this fully practical knowledge.

In short, the current objection is befuddled. It asserts, with some plausibility but without justification, that speculative knowledge can never motivate, and concludes, without justification, that speculative knowledge can never lead to knowledge that does motivate.

The objection does, however, raise an interesting question. How

---

3. Lee, "Naturalist," 570.

4. *De veritate*, 2, 14 (Leonine ed., v. 22, 92–109). "Scientia inquantum scientia non dicit causam activam.... Et ideo a scientia nunquam procedit effectus nisi mediante voluntate quae de sui ratione importat influxum quendam ad volita."

5. I-II, 9, 1, ad 2. "Sicut imaginatio formae sine aestimatione convenientis vel nocivi, non movet appetitum sensitivum; ita nec apprehensio veri sine ratione boni et appetibilis. Unde intellectus speculativus non movet, sed intellectus practicus, ut dicitur in III de anima."

ACTION

do we move to action? From where does fully practical knowledge arise? The question may be narrowed to greater precision. From where does the very first fully practical knowledge arise? Some fully practical knowledge, no doubt, is derived from other fully practical knowledge. Such derived knowledge poses no great mystery or trouble. The difficulty is locating the initial fully practical knowledge. What are its origins?

In order to answer this question it will be helpful to examine the easier case, in which some fully practical knowledge gives rise to other fully practical knowledge. From this analysis we can work our way back to the initial practical knowledge.

10.2
FROM PRACTICAL KNOWLEDGE TO PRACTICAL KNOWLEDGE

10.2.1: The Desire for the End and the Means

Purely practical knowledge is united with desire, which moves to act. The desire is not in the background; rather, it is part and parcel with the practical knowledge itself. Clare's judgment that she ought to get on a ship is purely practical insofar as she actually desires to get on a ship. As such, it is better expressed by the imperative, "Get on a ship," than by the indicative, "I ought to get on a ship."

Before she actually chooses, while she has only judged (in the indicative), "I ought to get on a ship," Clare has virtual practical knowledge. Desire is present, but it is in the background, not yet joined to her judgment. The desire is to cross the sea, for which she has fully practical knowledge. Her desire is for the end; she wavers concerning the desire to get on a ship, since she fears travel by sea. Her virtual practical knowledge does provide guidance, but it does not yet move to act. It shows the way to go, but it does not yet direct the action.

Aquinas says that by the desire of an end, we can move ourselves to desire the means.[6] By desiring to cross the sea, Clare can move herself to get on a ship. In this manner, her virtual practical knowledge becomes fully practical. The judgment that she ought to get on a ship

6. I-II, 9, 3.

ACTION

transforms into the imperative "Get on a ship." Because she has some fully practical knowledge — the fully practical knowledge to cross the sea — she can move herself to other fully practical knowledge — the fully practical knowledge to get on a ship. The fully practical knowledge spreads itself, changing virtually practical knowledge into itself, into another instance of fully practical knowledge.

10.2.2: Practical Truth

Virtual practical knowledge is a judgment concerning the way the world is; it is a judgment of what an agent needs to attain some end. If the person making the judgment desires the end, then it is a judgment concerning himself, and the virtual practical knowledge actually provides guidance. Nevertheless, it is still a judgment upon, and reflection of, the world around him. Louis's judgment that he ought to turn right at Louisiana Street is a judgment of what he must be like in order to get to the opera. Since the judgment concerns the world, it is true or false in comparison to the world. If turning right actually does get Louis to the opera, then it is true; otherwise, it is false.

When Louis actually chooses to turn right, his knowledge takes on a new role. It no longer merely reflects the way the world is; it now shapes and forms his desire and his action. Acts of will take their form from reason, which knows the good. Insofar as acts of will direct other (external) activity to an end, they must have the form of order, a form that comes from reason.

Does this mean that fully practical knowledge is "merely theoretical knowledge plus force of will."[7] No. Rather, it is virtual practical knowledge united to force of will. Of course, virtual practical knowledge is still in some sense theoretical, for it is a description of what is the case, a description of what belongs to the agent insofar as it has a certain end. The act of will is not merely some external addition; rather, the role of the knowledge itself changes. The role of fully practical knowledge is not simply to reflect the world; in addition, it is to be the form of our actions. Fully practical knowledge does not simply add force of will; rather, the knowledge itself has now become the form of the will.

---

7. Grisez, "First Principle," 193. See also Rhonheimer, *Natural Law*, 26.

ACTION

As the form of action (and not simply as a reflection of the world) reason is "true" insofar as it correctly forms the action. Even the poisoner's judgment that he ought to give a double dose has a measure of this "truth," if indeed the double dose is needed to achieve the murder. The judgment correctly forms the act of murder. Ultimately, however, the judgment of the poisoner (expressed in the imperative "Give a double dose") lacks the complete practical truth of forming desire and action. Aristotle says that practical knowledge is true through comparison with right desire.[8] Since the desire to murder is itself disordered, the judgment of the poisoner does not conform with right desire but with wrong desire. As such, his judgment is false.

Fully practical truth, then, has two requirements. First, it must reflect the way the world really is. Turning right at Louisiana Street must truly be the way that gets Louis to the opera. Second, it must conform with right desire. Given the ultimate end of his nature, it must be proper for Louis to go to the opera, rather than to the homeless shelter. Only by meeting these two requirements can Louis's knowledge properly form his desire and action.

10.2.3: The First Fully Practical Knowledge

At the moment, our concern is the shift from virtual practical knowledge — which is still speculative with regard to the end — to fully practical knowledge. Virtual practical knowledge is simply a reflection of the world and does not yet shape action. It becomes the form of desire when the agent chooses. Having become the form of action, the knowledge has also become fully practical. The shift occurs by way of the background desire. Louis desires to go to the opera and thereby moves himself to desire to turn right at Louisiana Street. The initial desire moves to the second desire only by way of knowledge, that is, Louis must know the way to go; he must have virtual practical knowledge of what he ought to do.[9] Because desire follows upon knowledge, the will can then desire the means to the previously desired end.

Because someone wills one thing in act, he moves himself to will another in act, for example, because someone wills health he begins to deliberate on those

---

8. *Nicomachean Ethics*, book 6, chapter 2, 1139a30.
9. See *De malo*, 6, 1.

ACTION

things that will bring health, and when he has completed his deliberations, he takes medicine.[10]

In short, knowledge can progress in practicality, that is, it can move from less practical to more practical. This transformation takes place only by way of some prior purely practical knowledge. Because Clare is committed to cross the sea — that is, Clare has purely practical knowledge with regard to crossing the sea — she can move herself to get on a ship. In this manner, what was merely virtually practical knowledge (her judgment that she should get on a ship) becomes purely practical knowledge, for now she is moving herself to get on the ship. Purely practical knowledge can, so to speak, spread itself upon less practical knowledge, transforming it into purely practical knowledge.

By itself, this account will run afoul of an infinite regress. If knowledge becomes practical by some prior fully practical knowledge, then we can trace practical knowledge back in a series. Suppose that "Get on this ship" is fully practical knowledge that depends upon the prior knowledge "Cross the sea," which depends upon "Get to Casablanca," which depends upon "Save my brother," which depends upon "Protect human life." This chain cannot go on forever. At some point, Clare must reach fully practical knowledge that does not depend upon any prior fully practical knowledge.[11]

Not all fully practical knowledge, then, can be explained by prior practical knowledge. The initial practical knowledge must have some other source. No account can entirely explain how knowledge leads to action unless it explains this initial practical knowledge. Can this knowledge arise from speculative knowledge? Or must it be independent of speculative knowledge? Must it be practical by its very nature, with no reliance upon any speculative awareness of the good in the world around us?

We will consider three possibilities. First, the initial fully practical knowledge might be sui generis; it is a given of human nature, with no antecedent in any other form of knowledge. Just as speculative knowl-

---

10. *De malo*, 6, 1 (Leonine ed., v. 23, 149, 369–75). "Per hoc quod homo aliquid uult in actu, mouet se ad uolendum aliquid aliud in actu. Sicut per hoc quod uult sanitatem, mouet se ad uolendum sumere potionem: ex hoc quod uult sanitatem, incipit consiliari de his que conferunt ad sanitatem, et tandem determinato consilio uult accipere potionem."

11. See I-II, 14, 6.

ACTION

edge must start with some first principles, so fully practical knowledge must start with some original fully practical knowledge. Second, the initial fully practical knowledge might depend upon other independent practical knowledge, namely, Grisez's prescriptive knowledge. Third, the initial fully practical knowledge might depend in some manner upon speculative knowledge. The first view seems to correspond with that of Rhonheimer, and the second is advanced by Finnis and Grisez. We will argue that the third view is that of Aquinas.

10.3
THE FIRST PRECEPTS AS FULLY PRACTICAL
10.3.1: Fully Practical Precepts

The first view relies upon the observation, already made, that knowledge becomes fully practical by way of other fully practical knowledge. It follows, one might suppose, that no other sort of knowledge can give rise to purely practical knowledge. Neither speculative knowledge nor some lesser form of practical knowledge will ever give rise to fully practical knowledge. The very first purely practical knowledge, then, cannot be derived from any other form of knowledge; it must already be purely practical. From the very beginning, by its very nature, some knowledge is purely practical.

This original purely practical knowledge is found in the first precepts of the natural law. Our *per se nota* knowledge of the good, on this reading, is knowledge of what we are currently desiring. Our knowledge of precepts is knowledge of what we are currently moving ourselves toward. If this original knowledge were not fully practical, so the argument goes, it could never lead us to act. Rhonheimer sometimes seems to speak of the precepts in this manner, although he may do so simply because he has failed to make any distinctions within practical reason.[12]

Rhonheimer insists that the starting points of practical reason have inclination built into them.[13] He claims that "practical principles are consequently not really 'norms' to which practical knowledge must

---
12. Rhonheimer, *Perspective of Morality*, 116–21, 261–2.
13. Ibid., 121, 261.

ACTION

attend, but genuine achievements of practical knowing by the acting subject."[14] Sometimes new natural law theorists seem to hold this position, but we will see that ultimately they reject it for another position.[15]

We have already argued that the precepts of the natural law are not — in us — fully practical. They are not commands but the content of commands, received in us as judgments at the level of virtual practical knowledge. Nevertheless, this view of Rhonheimer has a certain plausibility to it. After all, Aquinas says that we have a natural inclination for the goods to which the precepts refer, and that this desire precedes our knowledge of the precepts. Practical knowledge united with desire, however, is fully practical knowledge.

10.3.2: Imperfect Desire

This view, however, cannot stand. For one thing, while it is true that our knowledge of the precepts is linked to inclinations, we have seen that these inclinations need not be conscious inclinations of the will, at least not initially. Someone might press the point, however, for we have also seen that the will has natural inclinations to the goods of all the other powers. Could these natural inclinations in the will give rise to fully practical knowledge in the first precepts of the natural law? We will argue, however, that even these desires in the will are inadequate; they are, ultimately, the wrong sorts of desire. They do not have the complete force of desire, which is found in the act of command. They might better go by the name of "want" or "wish."

Aquinas distinguishes between a full-fledged desire and an imperfect or incomplete desire.[16] The difference is clearly exemplified in the case of the sea captain caught in a storm, who must choose to lighten his load by throwing over his cargo. Does he want to jettison his cargo or not? He might well say "I really don't want to do it," but of course he does do it. In a way, then, he wishes to jettison his cargo, for he indeed chooses to do it, and in a way he does not, for he would prefer not to.

---

14. Ibid., 272.
15. Lee seems to maintain that the first precepts are fully practical, although he is not clear ("Naturalist," 570). Finnis (*Natural Law*, 45) says, "One is already beginning to direct oneself in this very act of practical understanding." On the other hand, Grisez insists ("First Principle," 192) that the first precepts are not imperatives, although they are prescriptive.
16. I-II, 6, 6.

ACTION

He has a full-fledged desire to jettison the cargo, while he has an incomplete desire, or a velleity, to keep his cargo; he "wishes" he could keep it.

The desire for something considered in itself is an imperfect willing, sometimes called a velleity; ultimately, it does not move us to act, as is clear with the captain. The captain wants to keep his cargo, but decides not to. Only the desire for something considered as it actually exists, all things considered, is truly a full-fledged or complete desire.[17]

In other places, Aquinas makes the distinction slightly differently. He calls the velleity a "will-as-natural" and the full-fledged will a "reasoned-will." The will-as-natural desires a good apart from the consideration of how it relates to the ultimate end, while the reasoned-will desires the good together with its ordering to the end.[18]

The two distinctions are not exactly parallel, but some apparent differences will turn out to be irrelevant. As the terminology implies, the will-as-natural refers to natural inclinations; in contrast, the desire for something considered in itself can be natural or derived; the desire to keep the cargo, for instance, is not a natural inclination. Apparently, then, the will-as-natural is a specific instance of a desire for something considered in itself, apart from the concrete details.

Human beings cannot possibly consider every single detail of an action. What does it mean, then, to consider something in its concrete details? Aquinas provides his answer in the account of the reasoned-will, which considers an action insofar as it is ordered to the end. The sea captain need not consider the color of every item he throws overboard, since color will typically be irrelevant for the ends that he pursues. As he decides which items to jettison, their value might enter into his decision, since the value relates to the profit he pursues; the weight of each item might also enter into his decision, since weight relates to

---

17. The terminology "all out" is used by Donald Davidson ("How Is Weakness of Will Possible," in *Essays on Actions and Events* [Oxford: Clarendon Press, 1980]); Joseph Boyle (in "Practical Reasoning and Moral Judgment," *Proceedings of the American Catholic Philosophical Association* 58 [1984]: 37–49, at 40) says that we must consider all of the features of an action that might make a difference; Philippa Foot ("Moral Beliefs," 208) speaks of "a reason" for acting as opposed to "an overriding reason" for acting, and later (*Natural Goodness*, 57) uses the terminology of "all things considered." I apply Davidson's terminology to Aquinas in "The Error of the Passions," *Thomist* 73 (2009): 349–79.

18. *Sent.*, III, 17, 1, 2, qc. 1; III, 18, 3.

ACTION

the end of saving the ship and his life. To consider an action in the here and now, then, is to consider it insofar as it relates to the end; to consider something in itself is to consider it, at least partially, in separation from its order to the end.

The desire for something considered apart from its relation to the ultimate end, says Aquinas, is conditional, that is, we desire it on the condition that it turns out to be ordered to the ultimate end, or the end in which the will rests entirely.

If the will considers something [that is not the end but rather] is directed to the end, but it considers this thing apart from the order to the end, then the will can be moved toward this object according to some good or evil found in it considered absolutely. But because the will does not rest in its movement concerning these objects, since it is not drawn to them as into the end, it does not ultimately adhere to this movement until it considers the end toward which it orders it. Consequently, the will does not will these things simply speaking; rather, it wills them under the condition that it does not find anything repugnant in them.[19]

Christine might say, for instance, that she desires the pleasure of eating chocolate, on the condition that it is ordered to the ultimate end, or alternatively, on the condition that it poses no obstacle to the ultimate end. How does this conditional desire become unconditional? How does Christine move from her tentative desire for chocolates to a full-fledged desire by which she moves to act? The good must be traced to the ultimate end, for which she has perfect desire. When the condition is removed, that is, when the good is indeed ordered to the ultimate end, then the desire becomes full-fledged. The will-as-natural has become a reasoned-will.

The natural will moves toward some object absolutely, as was said.... But if [reason] orders this object toward the end, then the will does not adhere to it completely until [reason] reaches a consideration of the end, at which point

---

19. *Sent.*, III, 17, 1, 2, qc. 1 (Mandonnet, v. 3, 537). "Sed si consideretur hoc quod est ad finem sine ordine ad finem, movetur voluntas in ipsum secundum bonitatem vel malitiam quam in eo absolute inveniet. Sed quia voluntas non sistit in motu quem habet circa hujusmodi, cum non feratur in ipsum sicut in finem; ideo non sententiat finaliter secundum praedictum suum motum de illo, quousque finem in quem ordinat illud, consideret; unde voluntas non simpliciter vult illud, sed vellet, si nihil repugnans inveniretur." The text in Mandonnet says "non consideret" rather than "consideret." I can make no sense of the text with the "non."

reasoned-will adheres to it. Plainly, then, the natural will wills an object imperfectly, under a condition.... On the other hand, those things that are ordered toward the end, the reasoned-will adheres to as if by an ultimate and complete judgment.[20]

This process involves both reason and will. Reason perceives the order, in the concrete, of the action to the ultimate end. Only with the will, and the choice to act, however, is this order realized in the concrete. This process, then, is no different from that which we analyzed earlier, in which virtually practical knowledge becomes fully practical by way of other fully practical knowledge.

The first precepts of the natural law, then, are indeed associated with desire; nevertheless, they are not fully practical, for they are associated with imperfect desires. As we argued in chapter 8, the first precepts are not commands, which are fully practical and therefore linked with full-fledged desire; rather, they are judgments that happen to be associated with imperfect desire.[21]

We do naturally desire knowledge, life, and other basic goods, but we desire them on a condition, that is, only insofar as they are ordered to the ultimate end. As we have seen earlier, all things are desired only insofar as they are ordered to the ultimate end. In the concrete, a basic good may turn out not to be ordered to the end. Anna desires — just considered in itself — to study about the natural law, but right here and now the house is on fire, and her concrete act of knowing cannot be ordered to the ultimate end.

10.3.3: The General and Concrete

Earlier, we suggested that the will desires all things insofar as they fit into the good of the whole person. When the intellect perceives, fol-

---

20. *Sent.,* III, 17, 1, 2, qc. 1 (Mandonnet, v. 3, 537). "Voluntas autem ut natura movetur in aliquid absolute, ut dictum est.... Si autem ordinet in finem, non acceptabit aliquid absolute circa hoc, quousque perveniat ad considerationem finis quod facit voluntas ut ratio. Patet igitur quod voluntas ut natura imperfecte vult aliquid, et sub conditione.... sed eorum quae ordinantur ad finem, habet voluntas ut ratio ultimum judicium et perfectum." Both ellipses contain important content, but I wish to address it later rather than at the moment.

21. See Lawrence Feingold (*The Natural Desire to See God according to St. Thomas Aquinas and His Interpreters* [Ave Maria, Fla.: Sapientia Press of Ave Maria University, 2010], 20–6); see also Sullivan, "Natural Necessitation," 388–93.

ACTION

lowing upon a recognition of its own inclination, that knowing the truth is good, the will desires this good because it is a good of the person. This account fits with Aquinas's own description of the natural inclinations, for he says that the will desires these things insofar as they fall under the ultimate end of happiness.

We are now claiming that the natural inclinations of the will toward knowledge, life, and so on, are imperfect desires, which do not include an order to the ultimate end. This new claim appears to contradict the earlier account, which emphasized that individual goods are desired precisely insofar as they are ordered to the ultimate end, that is, the good of the whole person. A reconciliation of these two claims is possible with a better understanding of imperfect desires.

Recall that the will-as-natural is a particular case of desiring something considered in itself. Knowledge, life, the continuation of the species, and so on, are desired naturally, apart from their order to the ultimate end. But the preservation of cargo, for which the captain has no natural desire, is also desired just considered in itself. The captain desires, with an imperfect desire, both the preservation of his own life and the preservation of the cargo. In the concrete situation only the former can be ordered to the ultimate end, so only the former desire is transformed into a perfect desire. At present, however, we wish to emphasize that initially both the desire for life, which is a natural inclination, and the desire for cargo, which is not natural, are imperfect; both concern a good apart from its order to the end.

The derived desire for cargo, then, seems something of an anomaly. It is desired in itself, apart from the order to the end; at the same time, however, it is desired as ordered to the end. Why? Because derived desires, by definition, depend upon an order to an end. These goods are not good in and of themselves; they are good only insofar as they are ordered to some other good. Cargo is ordered to profit which is ordered to power or self-preservation or to a multitude of other goods. Even when it is desired just as considered in itself — and not in the here and now — it is still desired as ordered to some end. To be considered in itself, then, cannot mean to be considered in isolation from everything else. When cargo is considered in isolation from all possible ends, then it is not desired at all, even with an imperfect desire.

In what way, then, is the cargo considered in itself? From what is it

ACTION

abstracted? It is abstracted from the concrete order to the end, from the order as it exists here and now. I am suggesting that an action can be ordered to the end in two ways, in general and in the concrete. In general, certain characteristics of an action order it to an end, for example, in general transporting cargo to port is ordered to profit. These characteristics, just by themselves, if there were nothing else to the action, would direct to the end.

In the concrete, however, an action is much more than this or that characteristic. In the concrete situation of this storm, transporting cargo to port is a danger to the ship and to the captain's life. Real life is a messy business, and that which is cargo, in the concrete, is many other things besides. It is, in this instance, a deadly weight, threatening to sink the ship. If the captain considers the cargo just as cargo, then he considers it insofar as it is ordered to making money. But the same thing is not only cargo but a deadly weight as well; in this latter respect, it is opposed to the end of life.

Aquinas says that we desire imperfectly on the condition that the good is not repugnant to the end. In this concrete situation, however, the cargo does become repugnant to the end. In itself, cargo has an order to the end, but in the concrete this order can be destroyed, because the cargo is more than cargo. One aspect of the cargo orders it to the end of profit; another presents an obstacle to this order.

This same sort of reasoning can be transferred to our natural desires for particular goods. Upon becoming aware of his inclination to know the truth, an individual recognizes that the truth is a good of his person, that is, it is a partial good within the complete good of his person. Only as such does he desire it with his will, for the will has as its object the complete good of the person. An individual desires truth, then, insofar as it is part of the complete good.

Man naturally wills not only the object of the will but also those that are fitting for the other powers, for example, knowledge of the truth, which is fitting to the intellect, and to be and to live and other things of this sort, which belong to natural welfare, all of which are contained under the object of the will as certain particular goods.[22]

22. I-II, 10, 1. "Unde naturaliter homo vult non solum obiectum voluntatis, sed etiam alia quae conveniunt aliis potentiis, ut cognitionem veri, quae convenit intellectui; et esse et vivere et alia huiusmodi, quae respiciunt consistentiam naturalem; quae omnia compre-

ACTION

We know these basic goods as good, then, precisely insofar as they are ordered to the complete good of the individual.[23]

Nevertheless, in the concrete situation they might prove to be something more; they might prove to be an obstacle to the complete good. As Mary Catherine is reading her Aristotle, the house catches on fire. Does she continue reading her Aristotle? The truth is a basic good, ordered to her complete good. In this situation, however, it is also a danger. Contemplating the truth is, right here and now, placing herself at risk from the fire. The same individual action — knowing the truth — is both a basic good, desired with a natural inclination, and an evil, opposed to the natural inclination to the good of life.[24]

When we say, then, that the basic goods are desired as considered in themselves, apart from their order to the ultimate end, we do not mean that they are considered in isolation from the end.[25] Rather, they are considered in abstraction from the concrete situation, in which they might prove to be more than a basic good. Just considered as such, these goods are ordered to the ultimate end; considered as something more, they might prove to be in opposition to the end; they might prove, as Aquinas says, to be repugnant to the end.

All things, then, are desired in relation to the ultimate end. Even our imperfect desires, our desires for something considered in itself, are directed to the complete good of the person. The order to the ultimate end is there, but it is there in the abstract. In reality, that which is good can have many other orders associated with it, some of them not so good. To consider a particular good as good is to consider it just insofar as it has an order to the end. In the concrete, however, it may have other orders that ultimately destroy this order to the end.

Someone may well protest that if all goods, even the basic goods of the natural law, are good only through an order to the ultimate end, then all goods, except the ultimate end, are merely derivative. Only incommensurable goods, which receive their goodness from themselves

---

henduntur sub obiecto voluntatis, sicut quadam particularia bona." See also *De virtutibus*, I, 5, ad 2.

23. See Sullivan, "Natural Necessitation," 396–97.

24. For this reason Flannery (*Acts amid Precepts*, 10–11) says that practical reasoning is "defeasible," that is, it might not hold in the concrete.

25. Hayden ("Natural Inclinations," 140–49) also emphasizes the need for the goods of the precepts to be ordered to the ultimate end.

ACTION

and not from some external end, can be inherently good. The monism of an ultimate end destroys all other goods.

Something may still be called "a good," however, insofar as it is some partial completion of the individual. Knowledge is a good because it completes the power of the intellect. This particular knowledge, right here and now, may not be good, even though it does provide some completion for the individual, because it is not ordered to the overall completion of the individual. Something is inherently good, then, insofar as it provides some completion. Not every instance of an inherent good, however, is good; it might be only apparently good.

The difference between full-fledged desire and imperfect desire, then, concerns the concrete order to the end. Does this instance of the good, here and now, realize the order to the end? In the abstract, this sort of thing (such as knowledge) is part of my complete good. In the concrete, this instance of knowing, on account of other attributes it has, might not be ordered to my end.

We have been trying to determine the origin of the first fully practical knowledge, knowledge wedded with desire. In particular, we have been trying to determine whether the first precepts of the natural law are originating instances of fully practical knowledge. Our knowledge of the basic goods as realized in the first precepts does seem to be joined with desires in the will. We have now seen, however, that these desires do not lead to fully practical knowledge, because they are imperfect. The good is considered insofar as it is ordered to the ultimate end of happiness. At the same time, the good is considered apart from other details that it might take on in a concrete situation, details that might pose an obstacle to the ultimate end. In no way, then, do our natural inclinations make the first precepts to be fully practical. The very first fully practical knowledge must arise from some other source.

10.4

PRESCRIPTIVE KNOWLEDGE

If the precepts of the natural law are not, of themselves, fully practical, then how do they become fully practical? Grisez suggests that the original source of all practical knowledge is what he calls prescriptive knowledge, knowledge of that which is-to-be. As we have seen, this

ACTION

knowledge is unlike speculative knowledge because it does not reflect the way the world is but rather shapes the world. On the other hand, it is unlike fully practical knowledge because it does not have desire behind it; to the contrary, it is the source and origin of desire in the will.

Grisez correctly notes that desire follows upon knowledge.[26] Prior to fully practical knowledge, then, there must be some other knowledge that gives rise to desire. This prior knowledge, Grisez argues, cannot be speculative, since speculative knowledge does not move to act but rather reflects the way the world is. What is the nature, then, of this prior knowledge? It is prescriptive; it is a middle ground between speculative knowledge and fully practical knowledge. Unlike fully practical knowledge it does not have the will behind it; unlike speculative knowledge, it nevertheless moves us to act. It is knowledge that has a moving force built into it. In this manner, Grisez hopes to account for the origin of desire and action.

We have already argued against this view. It is certainly not that of Aquinas; furthermore, it is a rather odd position. Knowledge takes in the world; it is a likeness of the way things are. In contrast, appetite, such as the will, is an efficient cause, moving to act. When the two are wedded, in the act of command, then knowledge moves to act. Short of this purely practical knowledge, however, our knowledge is descriptive. As we have seen, even future statements and subjunctive statements in some manner express what is the case. Grisez's prescriptive knowledge is a hybrid, a mysterious knowledge that seems to warrant an entirely new faculty, a faculty of practical reason, separate and distinct from our faculty of grasping the world around us.[27]

Has Grisez explained the origin of desire? No more than the view he criticizes. No more than does speculative knowledge, which Grisez supposes cannot lead to action. If it is mysterious how speculative knowledge leads to action, then it seems equally mysterious how "prescriptive knowledge" could lead to action. It just does, by definition, but that is hardly an explanation.

---

26. Grisez, "First Principle," 192.

27. Paterson ("Non-Naturalism," 177) claims that Finnis gives verbal assent to Aquinas's assertion that practical intellect and speculative intellect are a single faculty, but in fact Finnis's view separates them into two faculties. A similar accusation is made by Douglas Flippen in "Natural Inclinations," 306.

ACTION

Prescriptive knowledge — realized in the precepts — gives rise to desire, but what kind of desire? If it gives rise to full-fledged desire, then it is unclear how the precepts can be such that we are still free not to act upon them. The precepts would be, in this case, something like fully practical knowledge, a conclusion that Grisez rightly wishes to avoid. If the precepts become fully practical, then there is no hesitation or wavering with regard to them. We automatically act upon them.

On the other hand, if prescriptive precepts give rise to a conditional or imperfect desire, then what compels them to become, at times, fully practical? Perhaps Grisez has explained imperfect desire, but full-fledged desire remains unexplained; consequently, so does action.

A series of imperfect desires will never lead to action. Someone may desire knowledge considered in itself, life considered in itself, procreation considered in itself, friendship considered in itself, and so on. No matter how lengthy the list becomes, whether it stops at seven or goes to one hundred, no desire will be efficacious. Considered in itself, knowledge is good and worth pursuing. Is it worth pursuing in the concrete, right here and now?

This question remains unanswered. The answer cannot be derived from an examination of other goods that are likewise good only considered in themselves. As Aquinas says, the will must reduce the conditional good into something in which it rests completely, which is the ultimate end. Unfortunately, the new natural law theory has no ultimate end to provide efficacious desire.

The new natural law theory provides no way of reconciling conflicting desires for basic goods. Anna now desires knowledge and she also desires play, both of which have been described as basic goods within the new natural law theory. Which does she choose, since she cannot do both at once? If she has an ultimate end to which she can compare them, then she has a means of determining which is better to do right now. But if they are both incommensurable basic goods — having no higher standard by which they can be evaluated — then she must simply choose. Her preference is all that matters. She moves from something like an imperfect desire (since she has not yet chosen between these basic goods) to a full-fledged desire. How? She has no natural desire that is full-fledged, no desire more complete then her desire for the basic goods. Only her own uncaused preference, then, can decide between basic goods, moving her desire for these goods from imperfect to perfect.

On Aquinas's view, it seems, the precepts can become fully practical by pushing back beyond the first precepts to the very first principle of practical knowledge, that is, to do good and avoid evil. We cannot stop at the first precepts, because they are virtually practical, lacking the full force of will needed for the act of command. We must go one step further, to the ultimate end, to the whole good of the person. All purely practical knowledge must be traced back to this first practical knowledge. Everything is desired insofar as it is ordered to the ultimate end.

How does this very first principle become linked with efficacious desire? Is it purely practical by its nature, as Rhonheimer seems to claim concerning all the precepts? Grisez's criticism excludes this possibility. All desire must ultimately arise from some knowledge. The very first knowledge that gives rise to desire, then, must precede desire; consequently, it cannot be fully practical.

The very first practical knowledge, then, can be neither fully practical nor "prescriptive." Fully practical knowledge still needs explaining: what gives rise to the desire to which it is wedded? Prescriptive knowledge explains nothing. It claims to account for our first desires, but if it is unclear how speculative knowledge can give rise to desire, then it is equally unclear how prescriptive knowledge can. To where, then, can we turn in our search for the origin of desire? It remains to consider speculative knowledge.

10.5

SPECULATIVE KNOWLEDGE

10.5.1: Knowledge of the Object of the Will

We are trying to rebut the objection that if we start with speculative knowledge we can never arrive at action. Peter Geach faced a similar objection against his descriptivism. According to prescriptivism all statements concerning the good are prescriptive, urging action in some way; none are merely descriptive, or if they are, then they involve a special usage.[28] In contrast (so claims prescriptivism), what is descriptive cannot identify the good, and so it can never move us to action.

---

28. See Geach, "Good and Evil," 36.

ACTION

How can descriptivism cross the gulf from knowledge of the world to action? Geach suggested that some knowledge just does propel us to action, such as the knowledge that ants are crawling up our pants.[29] The example is inadequate, since it undoubtedly involves derived knowledge that has become second nature by way of habituation. Nevertheless, the fundamental idea is sound.

The objection under consideration insists that knowledge by itself, without desire, does not lead to action. Consequently, it looks to knowledge that is backed by desire, that is, to purely practical knowledge. But what if some knowledge has desire not behind it, so to speak, but in front of it? That is, what if some knowledge has desire as a necessary consequence?[30] Such is Aquinas's claim concerning our knowledge of the ultimate end. If we think upon the ultimate end, then necessarily we desire it.

When we think about the ultimate end, necessarily we desire it, just as we necessarily see color when we look at a colored object.[31] Desire is a necessary consequence of the knowledge of the ultimate end; it follows from the very nature of the will. The will is like any other power; it has its own proper object, to which it responds with necessity. The intellect is necessarily directed to knowledge; the power of reproduction is necessarily directed to new life. Likewise, the will is necessarily directed to the good of the person. Of necessity, then, the will seeks happiness, and some knowledge necessarily gives rise to desire, namely, the knowledge of the ultimate end.

What is the nature of this knowledge? According to Grisez, it is "prescriptive" knowledge. Aquinas affirms, he says, that practical knowledge sets the ends that move the will.[32] That is true enough. Unfortunately,

---

29. Ibid., 37.

30. See Dewan, "Philosophy of Cooperation," 113. Philippa Foot uses the example of hands and eyes, which are always useful for attaining whatever our desires might be. Likewise, she says that the virtues are always useful. Necessarily, then, everyone desires healthy hands and eyes and everyone desires the virtues (see Foot, "Moral Beliefs," 206–13). Since these desires, however, are for what is useful, they must presume some prior desire. Foot, then, does not explain the very origin of desire itself. In *Natural Goodness,* however, she suggests that we can have intentions not based upon desires but based upon "reasons."

31. *De malo,* 6, 1; I-II, 9, 1; I-II, 10, 2. Aquinas allows that we can choose not to think about the ultimate end and thereby cease desiring it (a decision we make often, for example, whenever we choose to go to sleep). Nevertheless, given that we are thinking about it, we will desire it.

32. Grisez, "First Principle," 193.

ACTION

Aquinas has no such thing as "prescriptive" practical knowledge. He has only materially, virtually, and purely practical knowledge. Which of these gives rise to the necessary desire in the will? Grisez rightly rejects purely practical knowledge as an originating source for the act of will, for purely practical knowledge does not give rise to an act of will but presupposes an act of will. Two kinds of practical knowledge remain, material and virtual. Which gives rise to desire? The obvious candidate is our knowledge of the good, which is materially practical, for the object of the will is the good, not "that which ought to be done."

The will, like any power, moves to act in the presence of its object. This object, which is the good, is made present to the will by way of knowledge. When we know the good of the whole person, then we also desire this human good. From where does the desire arise? Not from any magical power in the knowledge. Rather, it arises from the nature of the will, which moves to act in the presence of its object. All action must begin with nature, which is an internal principle of movement and rest. Human action begins with the nature of the will, which is a power inclined to the human good. By its nature the will moves to the human good, which is presented to it by way of materially practical knowledge.

Desire arises by nature.[33] At some point we must come to nature; we must come to something that follows upon what things are. Aquinas clearly indicates a simple nature to the will; its object is the good of the person.

> The principle of voluntary motion must be something naturally willed, which is the good in common, toward which the will naturally tends, as does any power toward its object, and also the ultimate end, which, for things desirable, is like the first principles of demonstration in things that may be known, and also universally all those things that are fitting to the will according to its nature.[34]

The will is moved naturally by the good as known. We must first know the good before we desire it. That knowledge, of course, is practical,

---

33. Schultz-Aldrich ("Revisiting Aquinas," 124–29) also traces the prescriptive force of reason back to nature.

34. I-II, 10, 1. "Similiter etiam principium motuum voluntariorum oportet esse aliquid naturaliter volitum. Hoc autem est bonum in communi, in quod voluntas naturaliter tendit, sicut etiam quaelibet potentia in suum obiectum, et etiam ipse finis ultimus, qui hoc modo se habet in appetibilibus, sicut prima principia demonstrationum in intelligibilibus, et universaliter omnia illa quae conveniunt volenti secundum suam naturam."

ACTION

but it is not purely practical, which is a knowledge with desire behind it; rather, it is materially practical.

The very first fully practical knowledge, then, arises from a natural desire of the will, the desire of the will for its own proper object, the whole good of the human person. When this good is known, then desire follows. Given this desire, fully practical knowledge arises.

The will has a natural desire for the good of the whole person. As we have seen, however, it also has a natural desire for various particular goods.[35] When we come to understand that knowing the truth is good, we naturally desire to know the truth; when we come to understand that union with others is good, we naturally desire friendship. As we have seen, these desires are not full-fledged but imperfect. Nevertheless, they arise from materially practical knowledge, from the knowledge that something is a part of the overall good of the whole.

10.5.2: From Speculative Knowledge to Action

It is now possible to trace our knowledge from its purely speculative beginnings to its fully practical upshot. We begin with the purely speculative knowledge of certain inclinations. We observe ourselves spontaneously acting in certain ways, for example, we know being. We recognize that this activity arises from ourselves, so that we ourselves must be directed toward this activity, that is, we recognize that we are inclined to this activity.

At this point, we see that we ourselves are incomplete; we are directed to something beyond ourselves. We will become complete only by attaining the end to which we are directed. We have now reached materially practical knowledge, for the awareness of an end as completing ourselves is an awareness of the good. This awareness is practical only insofar as it concerns an object about which we might act. In other regards, this knowledge is speculative. It is an observation of the way things are.[36]

Now desire in the will is stirred. The will is a power with its own

---

35. Philippa Foot's account of reasons for acting that are not desires (*Natural Goodness*, 62–65) seems to be her way of having action (and intention, which is a kind of desire, in a broad sense) follow upon knowledge. Her reasons for action include our human good, teleologically determined. In short, Foot's account may not be that distant from Aquinas's.

36. Long (*Teleological Grammar*, 7) simply calls it speculative knowledge, without acknowledging its practical character.

ACTION

proper object, and when presented with its object, it moves to act. What is that object? The good of the person. When we perceive, then, that knowing the truth is a good — that we are completed through it — desire follows. We desire knowledge conditionally, insofar as it is part of our complete good. In the very same action, as in all acts of the will, we desire our complete good. We may not yet understand precisely what that good is, but we can seek it nevertheless, even as we can seek knowledge without knowing what precise knowledge we will find.

Having recognized some good, we then come to see that doing this good, or attaining this good, is required for our completion. We perceive, then, that our completion requires this good. We have resolved our completion into its causes.

We now reverse the procedure, composing the cause, judging what is necessary for this cause to attain its completion. We ought to do the good, that is, insofar as we are inclined to our completion, it is necessary that we do the good. We have reached virtual practical knowledge.

This judgment can be at two levels, either considered in itself or all things considered.[37] After Clare recognizes that getting on a ship is necessary to cross the sea, she judges that she ought to get on a ship. In the concrete, however, getting on a ship is more than a means of crossing the sea. It is something that costs money; it is a danger; it is time-consuming; and so on. Clare must consider how these concrete factors relate to her end. Some of them may prove to be obstacles to the end.

Only when Clare has considered all the details concerning the action, that is, when all things are considered, can she judge without qualification that she should get on the ship. Realistically, no such judgment can ever be reached, for the concrete situation includes an indefinite number of details that might impinge upon the end. Nevertheless, many of the details can readily be discounted as insignificant, for example, the ship is blue, has a statue of the Queen at its helm, and so on. It may turn out that during the journey the statue of the Queen cracks and falls upon Clare, thereby killing her. She will never be able to consider all the possibilities. Therefore, Clare eliminates those that are unlikely and judges that all things considered she ought to get on the ship.

When she reaches the all things considered judgment, then her de-

---

37. For discussion of all things considered judgments see Jensen, "Error."

ACTION

sire moves to act. Or, what may amount to the same thing, when her desire moves her to act, she reaches the all things considered judgment. Prior to the all things considered judgment, her desire is only imperfect; she *wants* to get on the ship — insofar as it is a means to cross the sea — but she does not efficaciously will to get on the ship.

The same distinctions apply at the highest level, at the level of the very first precepts perceived by reason. Anna understands that insofar as we are completed through knowledge, she ought to know. This awareness, however, is still at an abstract level. What about this concrete act of knowing the truth? It may turn out to be more than just an act of knowing the truth; if the house is on fire, it may turn out to be an act of staying in a burning house. Anna must move, therefore, from the imperfect want, associated with her knowledge that a basic good ought to be pursued, to a full-fledged desire, associated with an all-out judgment that the good ought to be pursued.

When all is said and done Anna has moved from an awareness of her nonconscious inclination to an efficacious willing for knowledge. She has moved from purely speculative knowledge to purely practical knowledge. Desire had to arise along the way. It did so at the level of materially practical knowledge, when she became aware that life and the truth are goods. This desire is not behind the knowledge but in front of the knowledge. Following upon the awareness, the desire arises naturally.

We are contesting the claim that if someone begins with speculative knowledge he will never reach activity. The claim was never much more than an assertion; at best, it was a claim about how knowledge becomes practical — with the backing of desire — by way of other practical knowledge. It turns out, however, that some knowledge has knowledge follow upon it. Ultimately, materially practical knowledge gives rise to desire.[38]

---

38. One final objection to this account should be noted. According to the new natural law, the account we have given cannot explain sin; see, for instance, John Finnis et al., "The Basic Principles of Natural Law: A Reply to Ralph Mcinerny," *American Journal of Jurisprudence* 26 (1981): 21–31, at 27; Lee, "Naturalist," 576–79. Mortal sin is a matter of turning away from the ultimate end, but on the account of Aquinas, we desire the ultimate end necessarily. How, then, can we divert from it? Any reply to this broad attack should begin by noting that an account of sin is not, strictly speaking, an account of practical reason; it is an account of the breakdown of practical reason. It is not an account of how someone moves from is to ought; rather, it is an account of how someone has failed to move from is

ACTION

10.6

CONCLUSION

10.6.1: Knowledge and Action

Reason becomes practical in the service of desire. Consequently, fully practical knowledge is the standard of true practical knowledge; all other knowledge is called practical only in comparison to it. Only fully practical knowledge moves us to act; all other knowledge takes in and reflects the world around us, and it is true or false as measured by that world. Yet even the moving force of fully practical knowledge is borrowed; it moves by force of the will.

The will itself moves only consequent upon knowledge. Reason, then, precedes the will. Nevertheless, it does not precede the will as a moving force; it simply knows the good and thereby presents it to the will. The movement in the will follows not on account of the nature of the knowledge; rather, it follows on account of the nature of the will. By itself, the knowledge that something is a human good is just that, knowledge. In relation to the will, however, it is knowledge – and presentation – of the proper object. This materially practical knowledge, then, does not move by efficient causality; it moves by a kind of final causality.

Practical knowledge, then, is practical precisely as derivative upon the will. Even when the will is absent, we do call some knowledge practical, but we do so only because it shares some features with truly practical knowledge. Some knowledge, for instance, concerns the same sorts of things as does fully practical knowledge; we call this knowledge materially practical. In essence, however, it is simply knowledge. The fact that its object relates in a certain way to the will is incidental to the knowledge itself. In itself, it is simply an awareness of some object in the world.

Other knowledge shows what belongs to an agent insofar as it has an end. We might know, for instance, that insofar as a mouse is working through a maze, it ought to turn right. The presence or absence of

---

to ought. The sinner either does not use the precepts of the natural law, or he uses them incorrectly. Aquinas maintained that every sin involves some ignorance; the ignorance itself, however, must be in some manner voluntary (see *De malo*, 1, 3).

ACTION

the end — in the will — is incidental to this knowledge.[39] Such knowledge can apply to a mouse or a tree, concerning objects that do not even come into the domain of the will; equally, it can concern knowledge that does pertain to the will.

Once again, the relation of the object to the will is incidental to the knowledge itself. In itself, the knowledge is an awareness of a modal reality; it is an awareness of what belongs to a thing by a certain necessity, that necessity coming from the end. Whether the will has or does not have this end is irrelevant to the essential nature of the knowledge. This knowledge is essentially descriptive, reflecting the way things are. Such knowledge can be very useful to the will, but that usefulness does not make the knowledge to be prescriptive.

If knowledge concerns an object that falls within the domain of the will, and if that knowledge is also modal knowledge about what is required of an agent for an end, then we call the knowledge virtually practical. Nevertheless, as long as the will itself is not yet engaged, that is, as long as we do not have fully practical knowledge, then the knowledge remains essentially speculative, an awareness of the way things are; indeed, it can be a kind of curiosity that the knowing individual seeks to fulfill, since the knowledge has no impact on his ends. Still, we call the knowledge "practical" because it shares two features with practical knowledge. First, it shares the same sort of object; second, it shares the same modal characteristic, that is, it is how-to knowledge.

The will itself can be engaged at two levels. It can be fully engaged, such that we actually will what is presented. With her reason, Clare judges that she ought to get on a ship (insofar as she wants to cross the sea), and she actually wills to get on the ship. Such knowledge is fully practical. The judgment that she ought to get on the ship transforms into the imperative "Get on the ship," a command directing her body to act through the impulse provided by the will.

On the other hand, the will can desire the end but only imperfectly desire the immediate object presented, which is the means. Clare does want to cross the sea, but she has not yet committed herself to getting on a ship because she is afraid of shipwreck. She wants to get on the ship, considered in itself, just insofar as it gets her across the sea, but

---

39. I, 79, 11.

ACTION

she is not sure that she wants to get on the ship as it actually exists, for it is not only transportation; it is also a danger.

In this situation, her knowledge is not fully practical; it is virtually practical. Nevertheless, it has one more mark of practicality, pushing it beyond Kay's idle knowledge of how to build a house, namely, the will for the remote end is present. No longer can we say that the relation to the will is incidental. This virtually practical knowledge actually provides guidance to the agent. Kay's virtually practical knowledge only potentially provides guidance.

Ultimately, then, knowledge is practical through something extrinsic to it, namely, through an act of will. No knowledge is prescriptive by nature, apart from an act of will. No knowledge is categorically imperative by nature.

Some knowledge does have an act of will follow necessarily upon it, but not because of the nature of the knowledge, as if the knowledge had prescriptive force of itself; rather, it is on account of the nature of the will. Like any power, the will moves to act in the presence of its object; reason merely provides this object. It does so as it knows the world; it does not do so as if "trying" to engage the will. Rather, as reason happens to know what is good (among the other things that it observes about the world), the will is necessarily engaged.

No knowledge begins fully practical. The knowledge of the good, just discussed, is materially practical. Even after the will is engaged, such that it desires the known good, the knowledge does not become fully practical; it is not in the how-to mode of practical knowledge. It is not moving the person to act with a kind of efficient causality. It is drawing on the person's desires with a kind of final causality.

The first knowledge of the good, then, cannot depend upon the desire of the will, for the will presupposes the knowledge. Rather, the first knowledge depends upon nonconscious inclinations, the inclinations of the various powers and of the soul itself. Reason first perceives a reality beyond itself and only then perceives its own action; it then perceives itself tending toward knowledge. Finally, reason perceives the good. It grasps the good of knowledge but it grasps it as a good of the person, which is the object of the will.

Only now is the will engaged. With a full-fledged desire, the will moves to the good of the person. With an imperfect desire, it moves to

ACTION

the partial good of knowledge. Still, we have no fully practical knowledge. At this point, the only practical knowledge is incidentally so, even though this very knowledge has given rise to desire in the will.

Now reason perceives that the good of the person requires action; it requires actually doing what attains this good. Or, perceiving it differently, it recognizes that the person must act; the person must attain the good. Now we have virtually practical knowledge. When will follows upon this judgment, then we have fully practical knowledge.

The first how-to knowledge is not fully practical; rather, it is virtually practical. We must know what we ought to do before we can will it. When we do will it, then our knowledge becomes fully practical and is transformed into an imperative. First, however, must come the knowledge without the will. Of course, a willing for the end might be present, in the background, but the will for what ought to be done here and now can follow only upon the how-to judgment of what ought to be done in general.

10.6.2: The Grand Picture

God directs us to our end by giving us the power to understand the direction inherent in our nature, a direction that he himself has placed there. This direction, however, is not arbitrary, as if God could make us with some other natural inclinations than those we have. Indeed, there are not two acts, one by which God makes our nature and another by which he adds on our natural inclinations. To make our nature is simply to make us with an end and inclined thereto.

If God begins by seeking to share his goodness with others, then he must make these others with an intellectual nature, for only by this nature can a creature possess God and love him. If that intellectual nature is not created with concepts but must acquire its knowledge, then it must have some means of gaining knowledge; it must be able to abstract concepts. Then it must have something properly disposed from which the concepts may be abstracted, namely, ideas of the imagination. These in turn must be acquired, which implies the power of sensation. All of this requires that this potential intellectual nature must have a body. Since a body corrupts, this intellectual nature shares in the eternity of God through procreation within the species. Procreation requires the power to grow and take in nutrients.

ACTION

In short, if God wishes to share his good with a potential intellectual nature, like ours, then this nature must have the various powers that we find ourselves to have. God is not constrained to make such a nature, but if he wishes to share his good, then this is the nature he wishes to make.[40]

Part of what it means to have this nature is to have inclinations. A human nature is not some mathematical nature with inclinations patched onto it. A human nature in itself is ordered to an end. The making of the nature is the making of the order to the end. "The nature of anything is a certain inclination (implanted in it by the first mover) ordering it toward its proper end."[41] God does not give us inclinations so that we can figure out our end; rather, he gives us an end, which is to give us inclinations, and he gives us a mind by which we can grasp reality, including the reality of our own ends.

God need not jury-rig a special practical knowledge with preset goods. He need only create a power that can grasp the world around it. This power, with no special default settings, becomes aware of the ends in nature. It does not become aware of what is going to be in the future; rather, it becomes aware of what already is present within nature. God need not jury-rig the will to desire certain goods. He need only create the will as a power that seeks the good of the whole person as perceived by reason. When reason grasps the various particular goods, the will by nature desires.

In short, the natural law is not a special setting of our nature; it is the spontaneous outgrowth of our nature. There is nothing "hypothetical" (that is, optional) about the natural law and the ought-statements discovered by our reason. It is part of our nature, inseparable from what we are. Its categorical nature does not arise from any special moving force of reason; it arises from what we are. We can no more throw off the moral ought than we can throw off our natures.

I suppose, however, we can try. As Alasdair MacIntyre recounts it, the modern ethical project is one such enduring attempt.[42] Can we have ethics without nature? No, we cannot; furthermore, any attempt

---

40. See *Summa contra Gentiles,* II, cap. 28–30; *Q. de potentia Dei* 3, 15.

41. *In Metaphysicorum,* lib. 12, lect. 12, n. 2634. "Ipsa natura uniuscuiusque est quaedam inclinatio indita ei a primo movente, ordinans ipsam in debitum finem."

42. MacIntyre, *After Virtue,* 51–61.

ACTION

to do so inevitably drives a wedge between is and ought. Or rather, any attempt inevitably destroys any oughts beyond those created through our own whimsical wants. The real divide between Aquinas and modern ethical theory is not whether we can derive an ought-statement from an is-statement; it is whether we have a human nature with an impetus at its center, driving onward toward our completion. Barring such a nature, ethics is only a game people play.

Modern man can wish to throw off his nature; nevertheless, the nature remains. It continues to draw us on to a fulfillment beyond ourselves.

BIBLIOGRAPHY

Works of Aquinas

Aquinas, Thomas. *Scriptum super Sententiis magistri Petri Lombardi.* Edited by P. Mandonnet and M. F. Moos. Paris: P. Lethielleux, 1929–1947.
———. *In duodecim libros Metaphysicorum Aristotelis expositio.* Edited by M. R. Cathala and R. M. Spiazzi. Rome and Turin: Marietti, 1935.
———. *Quaestiones disputatae de potentia.* Vol. 2. Rome and Turin: Marietti, 1949.
———. *Quaestiones disputatae, t. 2: Quaestiones disputatae de virtutibus in communi.* 10th ed., edited by E. Odetto, 707–751. Rome and Turin: Marietti, 1965.
———. *Opera Omnia iussu Leonis XIII P. M.* Rome: Editori di San Tommaso, 1982–1996.

Other Works

Anscombe, G. E. M. "Modern Moral Philosophy." In *Ethics, Religion, and Politics,* 26–42. Minneapolis: University of Minnesota Press, 1981.
Ashmore, Robert B. "Aquinas and Ethical Naturalism." *New Scholasticism* 49 (1975): 76–86.
Boyle, Joseph M. "Practical Reasoning and Moral Judgment." *Proceedings of the American Catholic Philosophical Association* 58 (1984): 37–49.
Brock, Stephen L. "The Legal Character of Natural Law According to St Thomas Aquinas." Ph.D. diss., University of Toronto, 1988.
———. "Natural Inclination and the Intelligibility of the Good in Thomistic Natural Law." *Vera Lex* 6 (2005): 57–78.
———. "Natural Law, the Understanding of Principles, and Universal Good." *Nova et Vetera* (English edition) 9 (2011): 671–706.
Butera, Giuseppe. "The Moral Status of the First Principle of Practical Reason in Thomas's Natural-law Theory." *Thomist* 71 (2007): 609–31.
Chappell, Timothy. "Natural Law Revived: Natural Law Theory and Contemporary Moral Philosophy." In *The Revival of Natural Law: Philosophical, Theological and Ethical Responses to the Finnis-Grisez School,* edited by Nigel Biggar and Rufus Black, 29–52. Sydney: Ashgate, 2000.
Connell, Richard J. *Nature's Causes.* New York: Lang, 1995.
Davidson, Donald. "How Is Weakness of Will Possible." In *Essays on Actions and Events,* 21–42. Oxford: Clarendon Press, 1980.

BIBLIOGRAPHY

Dewan, Lawrence. "Jacques Maritain and the Philosophy of Cooperation." In *Altérité vivre ensemble différents: approches pluridisciplinaires,* edited by Michel Gourges and Gilles-D Mailhiot, 109–17. Montréal: Editions Bellarmin, 1986.

———. "St. Thomas, Our Natural Lights, and the Moral Order." *Angelicum* 67 (1990): 285–307.

———. "St. Thomas, John Finnis, and the Political Good." *Thomist* 64 (2000): 337–74.

———. "Natural Law in the First Act of Freedom: Maritain Revisited." In *Wisdom, Law, and Virtue,* 231–41. New York: Fordham University Press, 2008.

Di Blasi, Fulvio. *God and the Natural Law: A Rereading of Thomas Aquinas.* South Bend, Ind.: St. Augustine's Press, 2006.

Dolan, S. Edmund. "Resolution and Composition in Speculative and Practical Discourse." *Laval theologique et philosophique* 6 (1950): 9–62.

Feingold, Lawrence. *The Natural Desire to See God according to St. Thomas Aquinas and His Interpreters.* Ave Maria, Fla.: Sapientia Press of Ave Maria University, 2010.

Finnis, John. *Natural Law and Natural Rights.* Oxford: Clarendon Press, 1980.

———. "Natural Law and the 'Is'-'Ought' Question: An Invitation to Professor Veatch." *Catholic Lawyer* 26 (1981): 266–77.

———. "Natural Inclinations and Natural Rights: Deriving 'Ought' from 'Is' according to Aquinas." In *Lex et Libertas: Freedom and Law according to St. Thomas Aquinas,* v. 30, edited by Leo Elders and Klaus Hedwig, 43–55. Rome: Studi Tomistici, 1987.

———. *Aquinas: Moral, Political, and Legal Theory.* Oxford: Oxford University Press, 1998.

Finnis, John, and Germain Grisez. "The Basic Principles of Natural Law: A Reply to Ralph McInerny." *American Journal of Jurisprudence* 26 (1981): 21–31.

Flannery, Kevin L. "The Aristotelian First Principle of Practical Reason." *Thomist* 59 (1995): 441–64.

———. *Acts Amid Precepts: The Aristotelian Logical Structure of Thomas Aquinas's Moral Theory.* Washington, D.C.: The Catholic University of America Press, 2001.

Flippen, Douglas. "Natural Law and Natural Inclinations." *New Scholasticism* 60 (1986): 284–316.

Foot, Philippa. *Natural Goodness.* Oxford: Clarendon Press, 2001.

———. "Goodness and Choice." In *The Is-Ought Question: A Collection of Papers on the Central Problem in Moral Philosophy,* edited by W. D. Hudson, 214–27. London: Macmillan, 1969.

———. "Morality as a System of Hypothetical Imperatives." In *Virtues and Vices and Other Essays in Moral Philosophy,* 157–73. Berkeley and Los Angeles: University of California Press, 1978.

———. "Moral Beliefs." In *The Is-Ought Question: A Collection of Papers on the Cen-*

BIBLIOGRAPHY

tral Problem in Moral Philosophy, edited by W. D. Hudson, 196–213. London: Macmillan, 1969.
Fortin, Ernest L. "The New Rights Theory and the Natural Law: Natural Law and Natural Rights by John Finnis." *Review of Politics* 44 (1982): 590–612.
Garrigou-lagrange, Reginald. *Providence.* St. Louis, Mo.: Herder, 1937.
Geach, P. T. "Good and Evil." *Analysis* 17 (1956): 33–42.
George, Robert P. "Natural Law and Human Nature." In *Natural Law Theory: Contemporary Essays,* edited by Robert P. George, 31–41. Oxford: Clarendon Press, 1992.
Gomez-Lobo, Alfonso. "Natural Law and Naturalism." *Proceedings of the American Catholic Philosophical Association* 59 (1985): 232–49.
Grisez, Germain. *Contraception and the Natural Law.* Milwaukee: Bruce Publishing Company, 1964.
———. "The First Principle of Practical Reason: A Commentary on the Summa Theologiae, 1-2, Question 94, Article 2." *Natural Law Forum* 10 (1965): 168–201.
———. "The Structures of Practical Reason." *Thomist* 52 (1988): 269–91.
———. "Natural Law, God, Religion, and Human Fulfillment." *American Journal of Jurisprudence* 46 (2001): 3–36.
———. "The True Ultimate End of Human Beings: The Kingdom, Not God Alone." *Theological Studies* 69 (2008): 38–61.
Grisez, Germain, John Finnis, and Joseph M. Boyle. "Practical Principles, Moral Truth, and Ultimate Ends." *American Journal of Jurisprudence* 32 (1987): 99–151.
Harris, Errol. "Natural Law and Naturalism." *International Philosophical Quarterly* 23 (1983): 115–24.
Hart, H. L. A. "Positivism and the Separation of Law and Morals." *Harvard Law Review* 71 (1958): 593–629.
Hayden, R. Mary. "Natural Inclinations and Moral Absolutes: A Mediated Correspondence for Aquinas." *Proceedings of the American Catholic Philosophical Association* 64 (1990): 130–50.
Jacobs, James M. "The Precepts of the Decalogue and the Problem of Self-Evidence." *International Philosophical Quarterly* 47 (2007): 399–415.
Jensen, Steven J. "The Error of the Passions." *Thomist* 73 (2009): 349–79.
———. *Good and Evil Actions: A Journey through St. Thomas Aquinas.* Washington, D.C.: The Catholic University of America Press, 2010.
Lee, Patrick. "Is Thomas's Natural Law Theory Naturalist?" *American Catholic Philosophical Quarterly* 71 (1997): 567–87.
Lisska, Anthony J. *Aquinas's Theory of Natural Law: An Analytic Reconstruction.* Oxford: Clarendon Press, 1996.
Lombardo, Nicholas E. *The Logic of Desire: Aquinas on Emotion.* Washington, D.C.: The Catholic University of America Press, 2011.

BIBLIOGRAPHY

Long, Steven A. "St. Thomas Aquinas through the Analytic Looking-Glass." *Thomist* 65 (2001): 259–300.

———. "Natural Law or Autonomous Practical Reason: Problems for the New Natural Law Theory." In *St. Thomas Aquinas and the Natural Law Tradition: Contemporary Perspectives,* edited by John Goyette, Mark Latkovic, and Richard S Myers, 65–193. Washington, D.C.: The Catholic University of America Press, 2004.

———. *The Teleological Grammar of the Moral Act.* Naples, Fla.: Sapientia Press, 2007.

MacIntyre, Alasdair. *After Virtue: A Study in Moral Theory.* Notre Dame, Ind.: University of Notre Dame Press, 1984.

Martin, Christopher. "The Fact/Value Distinction." In *Human Values: New Essays on Ethics and Natural Law,* edited by David Oderberg and Timothy Chapell, 52–69. New York: Palgrave Macmillan, 2004.

Matava, Robert Joseph. "'Is', 'Ought' and Moral Realism: The Roles of Nature and Experience in Practical Understanding." *Studies in Christian Ethics* 24 (2011): 311–28.

McInery, Ralph. "Naturalism and Thomistic Ethics." *Thomist* 40 (1976): 222–42.

———. "The Principles of Natural Law." *American Journal of Jurisprudence* 25 (1980): 1–15.

———. *Aquinas on Human Action: A Theory of Practice.* Washington, D.C.: The Catholic University of America Press, 1992.

———. *Ethica Thomistica: The Moral Philosophy of Thomas Aquinas.* Washington, D.C.: The Catholic University of America Press, 1997.

———. "Grisez and Thomism." In *The Revival of Natural Law: Philosophical, Theological and Ethical Responses to the Finnis-Grisez School,* edited by Nigel Biggar and Rufus Black, 53–72. Sydney: Ashgate, 2000.

Moore, G. E. *Principia Ethica.* New York: Barnes and Noble Books, 2005.

Morrisset, Paul. "Prudence et fin selon St. Thomas." *Sciences ecclesiastiques* 15 (1963): 73–98, 439–458.

Murphy, Mark C. "Self-Evidence, Human Nature, and Natural Law." *American Catholic Philosophical Quarterly* 69 (1995): 471–84.

———. *Natural Law and Practical Rationality.* Cambridge: Cambridge University Press, 2001.

Nelson, Daniel Mark. *The Priority of Prudence: Virtue and Natural Law in Thomas Aquinas and the Implications for Modern Ethics.* University Park: Pennsylvania State University Press, 1992.

Nielsen, Kai. "An Examination of the Thomistic Theory of Natural Law." *Natural Law Forum* 4 (1959): 63–71.

———. "The Myth of Natural Law." In *Law and Philosophy: A Symposium,* edited by Sydney Hook, 122–43. New York: New York University Press, 1964.

O'Connor, D. J. *Aquinas and Natural Law.* London: Macmillan, 1968.

BIBLIOGRAPHY

Paterson, Craig. "Finnis, Non-Naturalism, and Aquinas." In *Analytical Thomism: Traditions in Dialogue,* edited by Craig Paterson and Matthew S. Pugh, 171–94. Aldershot, U.K.: Ashgate, 2006.

Prior, Arthur N. "The Ethical Copula." *Australasian Journal of Philosophy* 29 (1951): 137–54.

Rhonheimer, Martin. *Natural Law and Practical Reason: A Thomist View of Moral Autonomy.* New York: Fordham University Press, 2000.

———. "The Cognitive Structure of the Natural Law and the Truth of Subjectivity." In *The Perspective of the Acting Person: Essays in the Renewal of Thomistic Moral Philosophy,* 158–94. Washington, D.C.: The Catholic University of America Press, 2008.

———. "The Moral Significance of Pre-Rational Nature in Aquinas: A Reply to Jean Porter (and Stanley Hauerwas)." In *The Perspective of the Acting Person: Essays in the Renewal of Thomistic Moral Philosophy,* 129–57. Washington, D.C.: The Catholic University of America Press, 2008.

———. "Practical Reason and the 'Naturally Rational': On the Doctrine of the Natural Law as a Principle of Praxis in Thomas Aquinas." In *The Perspective of the Acting Person: Essays in the Renewal of Thomistic Moral Philosophy,* 95–128. Washington, D.C.: The Catholic University of America Press, 2008.

———. "Natural Law as a 'Work of Reason': Understanding the Metaphysics of Participated Theonomy." *American Journal of Jurisprudence* 55 (2010): 41–77.

———. *The Perspective of Morality: Philosophical Foundations of Thomistic Virtue Ethics.* Washington, D.C.: The Catholic University of America Press, 2011.

Schultz, Janice L. "'Ought'-Judgments: A Descriptivist Analysis from a Thomistic Perspective." *New Scholasticism* 61 (1987): 400–26.

Schultz-Aldrich, Janice L. "Revisiting Aquinas on 'Naturalism': A Response to Patrick Lee." *American Catholic Philosophical Quarterly* 77 (2003): 114–31.

Slade, Francis. "Ends and Purposes." In *Final Causality in Nature and Human Affairs,* edited by Richard F. Hassing, Studies in Philosophy and the History of Philosophy, vol. 30, 83–85. Washington, D.C.: The Catholic University of America Press, 1997.

Smith, Randall. "What the Old Law Reveals about the Natural Law according to Thomas Aquinas." *Thomist* 75 (2011): 95–139.

Sokolowski, Robert. "What Is Natural Law? Human Purposes and Natural Ends." *Thomist* 68 (2004): 507–29.

———. "Discovery and Obligation in Natural Law." In *Natural Moral Law in Contemporary Society,* edited by Holger Zaborowski, Studies in Philosophy and the History of Philosophy, vol. 53, 24–43. Washington, D.C.: The Catholic University of America Press, 2010.

Staley, Kevin. "Metaphysics and the Good Life: Some Reflections on the Further Point of Morality." *American Catholic Philosophical Quarterly* 65 (1991): 1–28.

BIBLIOGRAPHY

Stevens, Gregory. "The Relations of Law and Obligation." *Proceedings of the American Catholic Philosophical Association* 29 (1955): 195–205.

Sullivan, Robert P. "Natural Necessitation of the Human Will." *Thomist* 14 (1951): 351–99, 490–528.

Tollefsen, Christopher. "The New Natural Law Theory." *Lyceum* 10 (2009): 1–17.

Torre, Michael D. *Do Not Resist the Spirit's Call: Francisco Marín-Sola on Sufficient Grace.* Washington, D.C.: The Catholic University of America Press, 2013.

Tumulty, Peter. "A Contemporary Bridge from Facts to Values: But Will Natural Law Theorists Pay the Toll?" *International Philosophical Quarterly* 28 (1988): 53–63.

Veatch, Henry B. "Natural Law and the 'Is'-'Ought' Question: Queries to Finnis and Grisez." In *Swimming against the Current in Contemporary Philosophy: Occasional Essays and Papers,* 293–311. Washington, D.C.: The Catholic University of America Press, 1990.

Veatch, Henry, and Joseph Rautenberg. "Does the Grisez-Finnis-Boyle Moral Philosophy Rest on a Mistake?" *Review of Metaphysics* 44 (1991): 807–30.

Zimmerman, M. "The 'Is-Ought': An Unnecessary Dualism." In *The Is-Ought Question: A Collection of Papers on the Central Problem in Moral Philosophy,* edited by W. D. Hudson, 83–91. London: Macmillan, 1969.

INDEX

Anscombe, G. E. M., 1, 166
Aristotle, 7, 29, 31, 88, 123, 135–36, 160, 184–85, 192, 198, 201, 205, 214
authority, 157–58, 160–61, 163

Brock, Stephen, 36n19, 45n2, 54–56, 72n17, 121n13, 146n32, 151n3, 155n14, 157n20, 183n15, 184
Butera, Giuseppe, 182–83, 185, 189

coercive power, 159–61, 163
command, 53–54, 127, 144, 146–47, 152–58, 160, 163–66, 174, 177, 186, 208, 211, 216, 218, 225
common good, 114, 138n20, 158, 161–62, 172, 182–83
composition, 9, 11t, 27, 127, 134–38, 140–41, 145–46, 149, 197, 222

deliberation, 94, 103, 133–34, 137–38, 144–45, 187, 195, 205–6
descriptivism, 3, 6, 8, 22, 61–71, 85, 121, 126–27, 139–50, 191, 201, 204, 216, 218–219, 225
desire: imperfect, 208–15, 217–18, 221, 223, 225–26; perfect, 210, 218
Dewan, Lawrence, 13n25, 33n16, 45n2, 54–56, 78n28, 81n32, 113, 114n7, 116, 157n20, 219n30

emotions, 44–53, 55, 57. *See also* passions
epistemological dependence, 13–14, 18–21, 28, 33–35, 38–43, 60, 74, 100, 107, 136
eternal law, 55–56, 58–60, 155–57, 182, 191

final end. *See* ultimate end
Finnis, John, 3n6, 4n7, 5n9, 6n12, 8n15, 12n23, 14nn26–27, 16–21, 42nn28, 30, 31; 45n2, 46n4, 59n36, 71, 73, 77, 79, 81, 83, 86–87, 106, 123n17, 129n4, 138n20, 153, 161–64, 166, 188, 189nn30–31, 207, 208n15, 216n27, 223n38
first principles, 4–5, 7, 14n26, 25–26, 31–37, 41, 45, 91n18, 123, 150, 176–78, 181–85, 187n26, 188–89, 198, 207, 218, 220
Flannery, Kevin, 42n30, 135n14, 184–85, 189, 214n24
Foot, Phillipa, 3n5, 62n2, 71, 88n12, 122n15, 151–52, 166, 168–70, 174, 187, 209n17, 219n30, 221n35
future, 42, 59n36, 69–70, 107, 111–12, 128–30, 133, 139–42, 180, 216, 228

Geach, Peter, 3, 61–62, 66, 218–19
God, 3–5, 7, 36, 42, 58–60, 63, 94, 104–5, 111–16, 152–53, 155–58, 164, 166, 182, 227–28
Grisez, Germain, 3–7, 8n16, 12–15, 16n31, 17n34, 21, 24, 36n21, 46n4, 47n8, 77n25, 92, 142n24, 150–51, 153–55, 163–66, 177n3, 181n10, 182–83, 187n26, 188–90, 193n40, 204n7, 207, 208n15, 215–20

Hart, H. L. A., 148
Hume, David, 2, 74, 126, 201

inclination, 14, 16–17, 24–25, 36, 38–61, 64–65, 66n8, 67–68, 70–71, 72n17, 73–78, 80, 82–86, 92–94, 97, 102, 104–21, 124–25, 129, 139–40, 142, 156–58, 163, 171–73, 175, 177–79, 185–87, 191, 198, 200, 207–9, 212–15, 221, 223, 226–28
incommensurability, 5, 7–8, 42, 188, 214, 217
intellect, 9, 16n31, 27–28, 32, 45–48, 50–51, 53, 55, 57, 61, 78, 80–83, 99–101, 103, 108–20, 124–25, 144, 171–72, 195, 201–2, 211, 213, 215, 216n27, 219, 227–28
is-statement, 1–2, 4, 6–7, 12–14, 16, 20–21, 138n20, 148–50, 229

judgment, 1, 3, 22, 25, 42, 63, 78, 86, 117, 121, 137–48, 154–57, 202–6, 208, 211, 222–23, 225, 227

knowledge: fully practical, 9, 11–12, 23, 25, 144, 146–48, 154–56, 165, 190, 201–8, 211, 215–21, 223–27; materially practical, 11–12,

INDEX

knowledge *(cont.)*
23–24, 60–61, 68, 70, 82–83, 89, 106, 126, 137, 143–45, 165, 175, 201–2, 220–21, 223–24, 226; purely speculative, 9–12, 23–24, 59, 61, 70–71, 73, 106, 165, 201, 221–23; virtually practical, 11–12, 23–25, 60, 69, 89, 109, 121, 126, 137, 142–44, 146, 148, 154–56, 165, 175, 201–6, 208, 211, 218, 220, 222, 225–27

Le Verrier, 20–21, 135–36
Lee, Patrick, 12n23, 18n36, 21n41, 23n43, 47n8, 69, 77n26, 79n30, 87, 95, 129n4, 139, 166, 201, 202n3, 208n15, 223n38

MacIntyre, Alasdair, 6–7, 228
McInerny, Ralph, 6, 8n16, 14n28, 17n35, 31, 33n15, 37, 42n31, 63n3, 68, 72n18, 78n28, 79, 91n19, 120n12, 125n18, 145n31, 176–77, 183n14, 193, 194n41
metaphysics, 31, 42, 77–78, 192, 195
Moore, G. E., 1–2

nature, 1, 3–4, 6–7, 10, 14n26, 17–28, 34, 45, 47–53, 55, 57–58, 59n36, 63–65, 66n8, 71–73, 77–79, 81, 83–109, 115, 118, 121–23, 125, 131, 136, 151–53, 155n13, 156–57, 159, 164–74, 176, 178, 185–86, 189–95, 197–202, 205–7, 216, 218–20, 224–29
necessity, 45, 102, 104, 127–28, 130–35, 137, 139, 141, 146, 148–49, 151–53, 158–64, 166–75, 180, 197, 219, 225
new natural law theory, 7–8, 16–17, 21, 34, 42, 60, 68, 85, 87, 95, 121, 142, 164, 165n38, 166, 181n10, 182, 188, 201, 208, 217, 223n38
Nielsen, Kai, 3, 18

O'Connor, D. J., 150–51
obligation, 25, 104, 127, 132–34, 138n20, 150–74
order of knowing, 17–21, 71, 79
ought-statement; 1, 4–8, 10–14, 16, 20–21, 25, 70, 126–29, 131–33, 139–41, 143–44, 148–53, 156, 158, 166–70, 172–75, 180, 228; hypothetical, 127–28, 150–53, 166–69, 172–75, 228; moral, 1, 8, 127, 150–53, 158, 160, 163–64, 166–68, 172–74, 228

passions, 44–45, 50, 52–54, 56–57, 102. *See also* emotions
per se nota proposition, 4, 12–15, 26–33, 35, 38–41, 91, 109, 114n7, 121, 123–25, 175–76, 178–81, 207
perverted faculty argument, 22, 121

physicalism, 21–23, 83, 85, 89, 108–9, 153, 190
powers, 18–19, 44–57, 67, 71, 73, 75, 78, 81–82, 89, 94, 96–97, 99–104, 106–7, 110–12, 114–18, 120–21, 124–25, 147, 151–52, 162, 167, 171, 185–87, 208, 213, 215, 219–21, 226–28
precepts, 5, 7, 11–12, 13n24, 14, 16, 21, 26, 35–38, 40–42, 49, 91n18, 98–99, 104, 107, 111–12, 113n3, 114n7, 127, 132, 134, 150, 153–57, 164–65, 175–80, 181n10, 182–85, 187–88, 190, 198–99, 207–8, 211, 215, 217–18, 223
prescriptive reason, 163–67, 174
prescriptivism, 3, 8, 61, 139, 218
principle of noncontradiction, 26, 31–34, 121, 123, 125n18
punishment, 153, 160, 196–97

ratio, 28–29, 31–40, 67, 77, 80–81, 100–101, 122, 124, 125n18, 175, 202
reason. *See* knowledge
reproduction, power of, 18–19, 22, 36, 44, 48, 50–51, 53–54, 73, 78, 89–98, 101–2, 106, 112, 114, 119–20, 167, 171, 219
resolution, 9, 11t, 127, 133–38, 140–41, 145–46, 149, 162, 179, 197–98, 222
Rhonheimer, Martin, 18nn36–37, 20n40, 22, 23n43, 42n31, 46n4, 66n8, 77n25, 79n29, 85n1, 86–87, 88nn10,12; 95, 107, 156n19, 165n38, 186n21, 190–92, 199, 204n7, 207–8, 218

sexual activity, 21, 44, 47–48, 78, 86–87, 89–92, 94–99, 101–2, 106, 120, 157
society, 42, 65, 111–13, 115–16, 125n18, 161, 170, 172–74
syllogism, 13–16, 27–28, 30–31, 33–36, 41, 43, 74, 91, 109, 125n18, 136–38, 150, 175, 180n8, 181n10

ultimate end, 5, 8, 45, 100, 103, 105, 182–84, 186–88, 198–99, 205, 209–12, 214–15, 217–20, 223n38

Veatch, Henry, 6, 13, 77, 78n28, 122, 123n16
virtue, 5, 56, 101, 107, 160, 182, 186–88, 219n30

will, 5, 22–23, 25, 44–48, 50–57, 59, 81, 83–85, 97, 100–101, 103–4, 107–25, 134, 144, 146–48, 152–61, 163–66, 168–72, 174, 183, 188, 190–94, 198–200, 202, 204–205, 208–13, 215–28; as natural, 209–10, 212 ; reasoned, 209–11

www.ingramcontent.com/pod-product-compliance
Lightning Source LLC
Chambersburg PA
CBHW030528010526
44110CB00048B/777